the BIG PICTURE *of* BUSINESS BOOK 3

Endorsements

"Hank Moore is a thought leader. Cognizant of the past, he weaves the accomplishments of others into dynamic strategies. I've worked with him and admire his writings."

—**George P. Mitchell**, Chairman of Mitchell Energy & Development.
Developer of The Woodlands and downtown renovation in Galveston

"Whether I'm at the office, at home, or on the road, I always have a stack of books I'm looking forward to reading. We all need people who will give us feedback. That's how we improve. Success has really been based on partnerships from the very beginning."

—**Bill Gates**

"Hank Moore truly embodies the concept of the Renaissance Man, from his worldly connections and involvement to his almost eerie sense of business acumen, in forecasting trends and patterns of commerce. To those of us who deal in the often-delicate balance of customer and company, it is blessing to have, in Hank Moore, a resource we can depend on for fair, statesmanlike and balanced observation. I count him as a valued business friend."

—**Dan Parsons**, President, Better Business Bureau

"Every book that Hank Moore writes is a keeper. That's because of his thought leadership and ability to target what is paramount. Houston Legends is not only required reading; it is blessed reading for those of us who are Houstonians and those around the world who wish they were. Hank Moore brings out the grits and guts of these pioneers like nobody else could. You will be recommending this book to your friends."

—**Anthony Pizzitola** MBA, CFM, CBCP, MBCI,
Quality Assurance Manager, Jones Lang LaSalle

"You can have brilliant ideas, but if you can't get them across, your ideas won't get you anywhere. Management is nothing more than motivating other people. The speed of the boss is the speed of the team. Get all the education you can but do something and make it happen."

—**Lee Iacocca**, past-Chairman, Chrysler Corporation

"Hank Moore knows more people than a person who just got elected as President of the United States, and more importantly he knows how to bring out their traits. I don't know how he does it."

—**George W. Strake Jr.,** Chairman-President, Strake Energy, Inc.

"Hank Moore works miracles in changing stuck mindsets. He empowers knowledge from without by enthusing executives to reach within."

—**Dino Nicandros**, past-Chairman of the Board, Conoco

"Mr. Moore is one of the true authority figures for business and organization life. He is the only one with an Ethics Statement, which CEOs understand and appreciate."

—**Ben Love**, Vice Chairman, Chase Bank

"Hank Moore's Business Tree™ is the most original business model of the last 50 years."

—**Peter Drucker**, business visionary

"Always ahead of the trends, Hank Moore's insights are deep, applicable beyond the obvious."

—**Lady Bird Johnson**, former First Lady of the United States.

"Hank Moore provides fresh approaches to heavily complex issues. His step-by-step study of the business layers makes sense. It shows how much success one could miss by trying to take shortcuts. There cannot be a price put on that kind of expertise."

—**Roy Disney**

"How can one person with so much insight into cultural history and nostalgia be such a visionary of business and organizations? Hank Moore is one of the few who understands the connection."

—**Dick Clark**, TV icon

"Hank Moore is a million-dollar idea person. He is one of the few business experts whose work directly impacts a company's book value."

—**Peter Bijur**, Chairman of the Board, Texaco

"30 minutes with Hank Moore is like 30 months with almost any other brilliant business guru. He's exceptional, unlike any other, and with a testimonial list to prove it. As a speaker, he's utterly content rich, no fluff, no 'feely-touchy' nonsense, right to the point and unashamed to tell the truth. There is nobody better. Every CEO needs him."

—**Michael Hick**, Director, Global Business Initiatives

"I could not have wished for a better boss and mentor in my first professional job than Hank Moore. He leads by example, and taught me valuable lessons not only about business, but also professionalism and ethics that have stood me well throughout my career. Indeed, when I was in a position to mentor others, I've often repeated "Hank Moore stories" to my staff, and they've all heard of my first boss. Over time, I grew to understand more and more that Hank Moore treats others with respect, and thereby commands respect. I was privileged to be trained by this creative and brilliant thinker who gets more accomplished in a day than most do in a week."

—**Heather Covault**, Media Relations Manager, Writer, Web Editor at Kolo, Koloist.com.

"Hank Moore brings alive the tales of these important individuals in a rich and detailed way that affords us all the opportunity to appreciate their contributions to our world and way of life. Well researched and experienced, Legends reflects Hank's personal relationships with those legends shaping the past, present, and future. Legends is a must read."

—**Nathan Ives**, Strategy Driven.com.

"Hank Moore has a wealth of knowledge. Not only is he fascinating to talk with, he's a fabulous writer as well. I'm so glad that he put all of his extensive knowledge of pop culture and business history down in a book for generations to come. Now we can all have access to the amazing stories behind many of the histories, corporations and who's who. Thanks Hank for sharing these wonderful stories. You Rock."

—**Kathryn C. Wheat Wiggins**, Author of *Networking: Naked and Unafraid*

"Hank Moore is a real king of business strategy in a time when there are all too many pretenders to that throne—and he knows how to write. The Business Tree is not for those who like their information presented slowly and interlaced with fluff. Moore's ideas are clearly and concisely presented. The book is all meat; and therefore, needs to be read and pondered, then read again. Hank's books contain an enormous amount of useful information that will help any executive to function more effectively. Highly recommended."

—**Daniel Krohn**, attorney at law

"Hank Moore writes this book from a fascinating and unusual point-of-view. He is both an advisor to top-level managements of business and non-profit organizations, and an avid student of popular culture, especially of pop music. Combining these two perspectives, he offers valuable and entertaining insights about motivating excellence in organizational behavior. Hank's book is full of warmth and good humor, as well as keen insight. It is also stuffed with facts—my favorites are: a description of a sizeable list of young inventors and entrepreneurs (many under ten years of age, all under twenty), and a list of cities describing the origins of their names. This book is an enjoyable and thought-provoking read."

—**Thomas J. Perrone**

"Hank Moore is one of the legends of business, as well as pop culture. He connects the genres for ultimate wisdom. This is an adventurous book, his 10th. The next one will go out of the stratosphere. This book series is a major undertaking. Hank Moore has crafted it masterfully."

—**Nancy Lauterbach,** 5 out of 5 stars, must read

"Hank Moore is a prolific writer with an amazing knowledge of his subject. Everyone will love this book."

—**Douglas B. Gehrman**

the BIG PICTURE of
BUSINESS

BOOK 3

BUSINESS STRATEGIES
and LEGENDS
Encyclopedic Knowledge Bank

HANK MOORE

NEW YORK

LONDON • NASHVILLE • MELBOURNE • VANCOUVER

the BIG PICTURE *of* BUSINESS BOOK 3
BUSINESS STRATEGIES *and* LEGENDS
Encyclopedic Knowledge Bank

Published in New York, New York, by Morgan James Publishing. Morgan James is a trademark of Morgan James, LLC. www.MorganJamesPublishing.com

ISBN 978-1-64279-813-5 paperback
ISBN 978-1-64279-814-2 eBook
ISBN 978-1-64279-815-9 hardcover
Library of Congress Control Number:

Cover Design by:
Rachel Lopez
www.r2cdesign.com

Interior Design by:
Bonnie Bushman
The Whole Caboodle Graphic Design

Morgan James is a proud partner of Habitat for Humanity Peninsula and Greater Williamsburg. Partners in building since 2006.

Get involved today! Visit
www.MorganJamesBuilds.com

Dedicated to Joan Moore.

TABLE OF CONTENTS

ACKNOWLEDGEMENTS

Remembrances to some of the business legends whom I knew and worked with: Malcolm C. Baldridge, George R. Brown, George & Barbara Bush, Winston Churchill, Dick Clark, John & Nellie Connally, Stephen Covey, Philip B. Crosby, Michael Dell, W. Edwards Deming, Roy Disney, Peter Drucker, Michael Eisner, Bill & Melinda Gates, Max Gotchman, Dr. Norman Hackerman, Gerald Hines, Ima Hogg, Lee Iacocca, Lady Bird Johnson, Lyndon B. Johnson, Ben Love, Clare Boothe Luce, J. Willard Marriott, Glenn McCarthy, Marshall McLuhan, Harris & Carroll Masterson, George & Cynthia Mitchell, Bill Moyers, Dino Nicandros, Earl Nightingale, Cactus Pryor, Anthony Robbins, Eleanor Roosevelt, Colonel Harland Sanders, Vidal Sassoon, Peter Senge, Allan Shivers, Roger Staubach, Jack Valenti, Dottie Walters, Jack Welch, Gus & Lyndall Wortham.

Also, acknowledgements to Imad Abdullah, Sharon Connally Ammann, Tom Arbuckle, H.E. Madame Sabine Balve, Jim Bardwell, Robert Battle, Valerie Berube, Judy Blake, Tom Britton, Robert Brooks, Dr. Lee P. Brown, Margie Nash Buentello, Sarah Buffington, Neil Bush, Crissy Butts, Tony Castiglie, Glenn Chisman, Sandra Collins, George Connelly, Mike Contello, Rob Cook, John Cruise, Hector & Arleigh De Leon, Jenna & Michael Devers, R.J. Diamond, Sue Ditsch, Deborah Duncan, Tony Durso, Tom & Anna Dutta, Alan & Gay Erwin, Dr. Ron Evans, Margarita Farmer, Mike Flory, Felix Fraga, Dr. Yomi Garnett, Martin Gaston,

Douglas & Christine Gehrman, Andrea Gold, Diane Payton Gomez, Glen Gondo, Sonia Guimbellot, Brett Hatfield, Phillip Hatfield, Bubba & Glenna Hawkins, Royce Heslep, Michael Hick, Mary Higginbotham, Bruce Hillegeist, Larry Holgerson, Derrill Holly, Richard Huebner, Susan & Robert Hutsko, Hiett Ives, Chris Kelso, Dana Kervin, Soulat Khan, Jon King, Kirby Lammers, Nancy Lauterbach, Torre Lee, Wea Lee, Steve & Barbara Levine, Mike Linares, Craig & Vicki Loper, Jayce Love, Anya Albert Lucas, Stuart & Laura Lyda, Jackie Lyles, Carol & Michael Marcantel, Hon. Tammy Collins Markee RCC, Aymeric Martinola, Wayne Mausbach, Don McCoy, Bertrand McHenry, Kathleen McKeague, Bruce Merrin, Amber Mesorana, Julie Moore, Larry Moore, Phil Morabito, Jesse Mueller, Larry Mueller, Lizz Mueller, Bill Nash, Howard Partridge, Dan Parsons, Monte & Linda Pendleton, Carla Costa Pereira, Leila Perrin, Tom Perrone, Joe & Courtney Peterka, Sue Pistone, Anthony Pizzitola, Travis Posey, Dino Price, Doug Quinn, Sally Mathis Ramsay, Roy & Gail Randolph, Connie Rankin, David Regenbaum, Ronney Reynolds, Jimmy & Lindsey Rogers, Tamra Battle Rogers, Donna & Dennis Rooney, Mike Rosen, Melissa Rotholz, Tony Rubleski, Monica Ryan, Jordan Rzad, Candice Sanderson, Rita Santamaria, Rick Schissler, Jack Shabot, Lisa Trapani Shumate, Previn Sonthalia, Bill Spitz, Maggie Steber, Rod Steinbrook, Gail Stolzenburg, George Strake, Bill & Cindy Taylor, Deborah Taylor, Jon & Paige Taylor, Jane Moore Taylor, Charlie & Laura Thorp, Rich Tiller, James & Carolyn Todd, Linda Toyota, Terri Tripp, Candy Twyman, Mary & Paul Vandenberg, David Wadler, Cameron Waldner, Jack Warkenthien, Louie Werderich, Kathryn C. Wheat, Chris Wiggins, Jennifer Wilhelm, Sara Wilhelm, Robert Willeby, Chanel Williams, Melissa Williams, Ronald Earl Wilsher, Kyle Wilson, Beth Wolff, Dr. Martha Wong, R.D. Yoder, Tom Ziglar.

Special dedications to the Silver Fox Advisors and the Better Business Bureau.

Chapter 1

CONCEPTS, BUSINESS MODELS
AND STRATEGIES

20 Original Business Concepts Developed by Hank Moore

When one advises companies on best ways to do business, you develop observations, tested circumstances and strategies.

Times of crisis and economic downturn get people thinking differently about the conduct of business. Organizations say that they need to re-evaluate and get back to basics, that nothing is guaranteed. They realize that the old ways of doing business will no longer work. They seek to better themselves as professionals and to rethink the business models. Changing times require new perspectives.

For some, these are stark new approaches. This is the reality for small business and entrepreneurial worlds. Welcome to the paradigms that many of us have operated under for some time.

Accepting change as a positive guiding principle, one then seeks to find, analyze and apply fresh approaches toward addressing the old problems. For many, times

1

of crisis mandate that they think boldly and get used to doing business that way henceforth.

This chapter is a compilation of all those that I developed, by virtue of working with 5,000+ client companies. Many of these have been further developed into book chapters and titles. Several are my trademarked concepts.

This is an exploration into the creativity, the opportunities and the potential rewards of reflecting differently upon business. Our intention and the experiences of many companies who have followed the model presented here is that organizations must now learn how to paint their own "big pictures" of business, rather than focusing upon certain niches. They benefit from change, while the non-change stagnates become additional casualties.

The Big Picture of Business

This is the subject of my book series, "The Big Picture of Business," nominated for the Pulitzer Prize.

Management must develop critical thinking skills, through organizational processes, problem solving, challenges to take risks and daring to innovate.

You've got to have a unique product worthy of the marketplace. You've got to have something to trade in exchange for others supporting you.

The enlightened company must be structured, conduct planning and measure the accomplishments according to all seven categories on my trademarked Business Tree: core business, running the business, financial, people, business development, Body of Knowledge (interaction of each part to the other and to the whole) and The Big Picture (who the organization really is, where it is going and how it will successfully get there).

The Business Tree™

Over many years as a business consultant, I kept getting called in to fix pieces of problems for companies. Most often, cutting expenses or having a new marketing program were the most common forms of band aid surgery that they thought would solve temporary problems.

Companies thought that selling more of something was all they needed, rather than what they were selling, to whom and the strains that increased volume and production capacity would have place upon other sectors of the organization. I remember one where the marketing people and the sales people would not communicate with each other, let alone coordinate activities. The results were increased sales with a multi-month time delay to produce products for a marketplace that was changing faster than was the equipment deliverability.

Through the years, I saw the wrong niche consultants being called in to fix the wrong problems, or what management incorrectly believed the problems to be. Most often, management was indeed the problem, or at least the logjam in the growth curve. The results were misspent funds, wasted efforts and the subsequent scapegoat of the consultants for what the companies could not or would not do.

Years of observations and follow-up advisory work for companies taught me that the root causes of problems in companies must be addressed, rather than to continue performing rounds of band aid surgeries. I also saw great nuggets of gold in those same companies, a bevy of talent, resources and a willingness to make the changes, all of which could be positively brought to bear for the benefit of their business.

Rather than criticize management for short sightedness, bad policies and wrong actions, it occurred to me that getting their companies back to basics and planning for the next strata would offer the opportunities to right the wrongs. Pro-active examinations followed by positively framed planning, to me, seemed to generate more results, foster more buy-in and create new strategies than would by playing the blame game.

The High Cost of Doing Nothing™

Each year, one-third of the U.S. Gross National Product goes toward cleaning up problems, damages and otherwise high costs of doing either nothing or doing the wrong things.

On the average, it costs six times the investment of preventive strategies to correct business problems (compounded per annum and exponentially increasing each year). The old adage says: "An ounce of prevention is worth a pound of cure." One pound equals 16 ounces. In that scenario, one pound of cure is 16 times more mostly than an ounce of prevention.

Human beings as we are, none of us do everything perfectly on the front end. There always exists a learning curve. Research shows that we learn three times more from failures than from successes. The mark of a quality organization is how it corrects mistakes and prevents them from recurring.

Running a profitable and efficient organization means effectively remediating damage before it accrues. Processes and methodologies for researching, planning, executing and benchmarking activities will reduce that pile of costly coins from stacking up.

Doing nothing becomes a way of life. It's amazing how many individuals and companies live with their heads in the sand. This mindset, of course, invites and tends to multiply trouble.

There are seven costly categories of doing nothing, doing far too little or doing the wrong things in business:

1. Cleaning up problems.
2. Rework.
3. Missed marks.
4. Damage Control.
5. Recovery and restoration.
6. Retooling and restarting.
7. Opportunity costs.

These are the primary factors of The High Cost of Doing Nothing™:

1. Failure to value and optimize true company resources.
2. Poor policies, processes, procedures, precedents and planning.
3. Opportunities not heeded or capitalized.
4. The wrong people, in the wrong jobs. Under-trained employees.
5. The wrong consultants (miscast, untrained, improperly used).
6. Lack of articulated focus and vision.
7. Lack of movement really means falling behind the pack, losing ground.

This is what could reduce the high costs:

1. Effective policies and procedures.
2. Setting and respecting boundaries.
3. Realistic expectations and measurements.
4. Training and development of people.
5. Commitments to quality at all links in the chain.
6. Planning.
7. Organizational vision.

Three Rights Offset a Wrong

There is much more good in companies that might be recognized at first glance. Rather than focusing on the negative, we look at the strengths and how they can elevate companies further.

The Business They're Really In™

What organizations say they do in external promotions to potential customers actually ranks low on the actual priority list. That occurs due to the agendas of individuals who guide the organization departing from the core business for which founders experienced. Add to that the realities of doing business and staying competitive.

Here is an average priority ranking for the core business activity of companies:

1. Revenue volume and its rewards (bonuses for key management).
2. Growth, defined as increasing revenues each year (rather than improving the quality of company operations).
3. Doing the things necessary to assure revenue (billings, sales, add-on's, marketing). Keeping the cash register ringing, rather than focusing upon what is being sold, how it is made and the kind of company they need to be.
4. Running a bureaucracy.
5. Maintaining the status quo. Keeping things churning. Making adjustments, corrections or improvements only occurs when crises warrant (band aid surgery).
6. Glory, gratification and recognition for the company and for certain leaders.
7. Furthering stated corporate agendas.
8. Furthering unwritten corporate agendas.
9. Courting favor with opinion leaders.
10. Actually, delivering the core business. Making the widget itself. Doing what you started in business to do, what you tell the customers that you do.
11. Doing the things that a company should do to be a good company.
12. Customer service, consideration or follow-up beyond the sale.
13. Looking after the people, in terms of training, empowerment, resources and rewards.

14. Giving back to those who support the company.
15. Advancing conditions in which core business is delivered.
16. Walking the Talk: ethics, values, quality, vision.
17. Giving back to the community, industry, Body of Knowledge.

The Busy Work Tree™

These are the components of a person's job, profession and career, with their percentages per role, function and activity:

1. **Core business**. Doing what the organization is supposed to do. (13%) Adding your own professional abilities, specialties, skills and expertise (5%)
2. **Deliverability of the product or service.** Administrative practices, procedures, operations, structure, and review (4%) Office maintenance-support (3%) Working with technologies (1%) Research and preparation (2%) Production and distribution of the product-service to clients-customers (13%)
3. **Accountability.** Reporting, tabulating, interpreting (6%) Projections, forecasting, planning (3%) Fiduciary responsibilities (1%)
4. **People.** Working with supervisors and colleagues (4%) Working with customers (10%) Working with other constituencies (3%) Training, empowerment, team building to do your job better (6%)
5. **Company goals, needs and vision.** Meetings (4%) Document production (3%) Delivering the core product-service (7%) Representing the company outside your office (2%)
6. **Professional development** (5%)
7. Body of Work, your long-term goals and contributions (5%)

Been There, Done That…People Often Say They Have…But Really Haven't.

Matching consultants with actual and emerging company needs is the corporate leader's quest. With a wealth of expertise available via outsourcing, one can quickly become a "kid in a candy shop," wanting whatever is readily available or craftily packaged.

Many consultants overstate and misrepresent what they do, stemming from:

- Eagerness to get business.
- Short tenure in consulting, believing that recent corporate experience readily translates to the entrepreneurial marketplace.
- Unfamiliarity with the actual practice of consulting at the executive level.
- Lack of understanding about business needs, trends and challenges."
- Professional rivalry with other consultants, resulting in the "I can do that" syndrome.

Niche consultants place emphasis in the areas where they have training, expertise and staff support for implementation…and will market their services accordingly. An accounting firm may suggest that an economic forecast is a full-scope business plan (which it is not). A trainer may recommend courses for human behavior, believing that these constitute a Visioning process (of which they are a small part). Marketers might contend that the latest advertising campaign is equivalent to re-engineering the client company (though the two concepts are light years apart).

Niche consultants believe these things to be true, within their frames of reference. They sell what they need to sell, rather than what the client really needs. Let the buyer beware.

Pop Culture Wisdom

There are many pop culture influences affecting our society, cultural upbringing, business concepts and working style.

In my years of advising senior management of business organizations, I found it clear that executives and leaders are more products of pop culture than they are of formal business training. Business dilemmas, solutions and analyses are framed first in their field of reference (pop culture teachings) and then reframed in modern business context.

I realized that presenting organizational strategies as an extension of previously-held pop culture values gets more understanding, comprehension, attention and support.

I have conducted countless strategy meetings where leaders cannot articulate business philosophies, but they can accurately recite lyrics from "golden oldie" song hits or TV trivia and advertising jingles.

Being one of the rare senior business advisors who is equally versed in pop culture, I found that bridging known avenues with current realities resulted in fully articulated corporate visions. Many a Strategic Plan was written by piecing together song fragments, nostalgic remembrances and movie scenarios, then converted into contemporary corporate nomenclature.

When we recall the messages of the songs, movies, TV shows and books of the previous decades, we realize that today's adults were formerly taught in their youths to:

- Think Big Picture.
- Conceptualize your own personal goals.
- Understand conflicting societal goals.
- Fit your dreams into the necessities and realities of the real world.
- Find your own niche.
- Get satisfaction from doing something well and committing to excellence.
- Seek truths in unusual and unexpected sources.
- Share your knowledge and learn further by virtue of mentoring others.

How individuals and organizations start out and what they become are different concepts. Mistakes, niche orientation and lack of planning lead businesses to failure. Processes, trends, fads, perceived stresses and "the system" force adults to make compromises in order to proceed. Often, a fresh look at their previous knowledge gives renewed insight to today's problems, opportunities and solutions.

All business leaders agreed that no road map was provided. Executives amassed knowledge "in the streets," through non-traditional sources. Few lessons made sense at the time and, thus, did not sink in. When repackaged years later, executives vigorously enjoyed the rediscovery process. The previously overlooked became sage wisdom. Knowledge they were not ready to receive as youngsters before became crystal clear in later times.

Executives and companies, in these troubled times, seek reflection and redirection. The plethora of seminars, training and writings do not emphasize Big Picture thinking. The need exists for a comprehensive resource on pop culture's relevancies toward business which opens up the mind and heart, pinpoints what it takes to make it and offers wisdom that is abstracted from within the readers' cultural upbringings.

The Path from Pleasure to Success

Every business, company or organization goes through cycles in its life. At any point, each program or business unit is in a different phase from others. The astute organization assesses the status of each program and orients its team members to meet constant changes and fluctuations.

Strategic Planning facilitates disciplined thinking about the organization, its environment and its future. It identifies conflicts, reinforces team building and serves as a vehicle for monitoring organizational progress.

The planning process is then translated into a company Vision. With that Vision, the organization will evolve steadily toward success. Without any kind of Vision, management will continually apply corrective techniques ("band aid surgery"), while the company stumbles and falls. The price tag for false surgery is six times that of front-end Vision…a concept that I call The High Cost of Doing Nothing™.

I've talked with many entrepreneurs and founders of companies. Most admitted enjoying the founding phase but lost interest shortly after giving birth. Over and over, they said, "When it stops being fun, I move on. "

After the initial honeymoon, you speak with them and hear rumblings like, "It isn't supposed to be this hard. Whatever happened to the old days? I'm ready to move on. This seems too much like running a business. I'm an idea person, and all this administrative stuff is a waste of my time. I should move on to other new projects."

When they come to me, they want the business to transition smoothly. They ask, "Are you the one who comes in here and makes this into a real business?" I reply, "No. After the caretakers come in and apply the wrong approaches to making something of your business, I'm the one who cleans up after them and starts the business over again." The reality is that I'm even better on the front end, helping business owners avoid the costly pitfalls attached to their losing interest and abdicating to the wrong people.

Most companies enjoy early success and wish things would stay as in the beginning. When "the fun ends," the hard work begins.

To go the distance, the organization must complete all seven stages of evolution. There are no fast-forward buttons or skipping steps in developing an effective organization, just as there are no shortcuts in formulating a career and Body of Work.

Trees in the Forest™

The biggest source of growth and increased opportunities in today's business climate lie in the way that individuals and companies work together. It is becoming increasingly rare to find an individual or organization that has not yet been required to team with others.

Lone rangers and sole-source providers simply cannot succeed in competitive environments and global economies. Those who benefit by teaming, rather than become the victim of others, will log the biggest successes in business years ahead.

Just as empowerment, team building and other processes apply to employees in formal organizational structures, then the teaming of independents can likewise benefit from the concepts. There are rules of protocol that support and protect partnerships, having a direct relationship to those who profit most from teaming.

Lessons Learned…But Not Soon Forgotten

Fine-tuning one's career is an admirable and necessary process. It is not torture but, indeed, is quite illuminating. Reflect upon what you were taught. Along the way, you reapply old knowledge, find some new nuggets and create your own philosophies.

To help in re-treading old lessons and augmenting with new ones, these are some pieces of advice to mid-level and upper executives:

- Executive development is a finely tuned art. It is a tireless yet energizing process.
- People who rise in upper corporate ranks do so for reasons other than themselves. The art is to understand and work with those factors, rather than to become a pawn of them.
- The old ways of rising to the top have changed. The savvy executive masters the new ways.
- Don't become a "flavor of the month." Trends and fads in business and in people will subside. Posture yourself for the long-term.
- Develop and trust your gut instinct. It's right most of the time.
- Senior level consulting is not something that one retires or downsizes into. It is not a part-time profession or something that one does in between jobs. Few corporate executives have what it takes to be a consultant.

- One is not a full-fledged consultant until they have done this and only this for 10 years. One does not become "senior" until they have at least a 20-year consulting track record, not counting working at jobs for someone else.
- People don't know why they believe in something. They just believe.
- We mostly control our own destiny. Each time we abdicate, blame, relinquish or do nothing, opportunities pass you by. Missed opportunities compound and can never be fully regained.

The Fatal Flaws of Corporate Thinking

Every business, company or organization goes through cycles in its evolution. At any point, each program or business unit is in a different phase from the others. Every astute organization assesses the status of each branch on its Business Tree and orients its management and team members to meet constant changes and fluctuations.

It's not that some organizations "click", and others do not. Multiple factors cause momentum, or the lack thereof. As companies operate, all make honest and predictable mistakes. Those with a willingness to learn from the mistakes and pursue growth will be successful. Others will remain stuck in frames of mind that set themselves up for the next round of defeat or, at best, partial-success.

Businesses do not always know that they're doing anything wrong. They do not realize that a Big Picture must exist or what it could look like. They have not been taught or challenged on how to craft a Big Picture. Managers, by default, see "band aid surgery" as the only remedy for problems, only when problems are so evident as to require action.

Book of Acronyms: Re-defining Business Terms

Organizations are accustomed to looking at concepts and practices one way at a time. Clinging to obsolete definitions and viewpoints have a way of perpetuating companies into downward spirals.

By viewing from others' viewpoints on life, we find real nuggets of gold with which to redefine organizations. Companies that adopt new viewpoints and defy their conventional definitions will create new opportunities, organizational effectiveness, marketplaces and relationships.

As a Big Picture business strategist, I encourage clients toward adopting new ways of thinking about old processes, including those that brought past and enduring successes. Symbolic are these phrase definitions I created for familiar business words. I have created new acronyms for well-known business terms, in order to help us visualize opportunities differently.

My acronym for BUSINESS:

Big-picture
Understanding
Symbiosis
In
Nomenclature,
Economics,
Systems, and
Services

Future Watch, Growth Capitalizing Upon Change

Businesses cannot exist in a vacuum. They must interact with the outside world. They must predict the trends and master the issues affecting the climate and opportunities in which they function. This includes stimulating "outside-the-box" thinking, building customer coalitions and distinguishing your company from the pack.

The future is a series of journeys along a twisting and turning course, affected by what we choose to do and the priorities that we assign. Along the way are warning signs that we either recognize or pay the price later for overlooking. Company futures are determined by choices that we make.

Our present tense and, thus, our future is further influenced by time and resources we spend interacting with other people and the actions of other people, directly or indirectly affecting us. The perspective of future actions is based upon mistakes we make and what we learn from them.

There are several schools of thought on the subject of futurism, depending upon the niche focus of those consultants who embrace the process. Some are marketing focused and say that the marketplace decides and drives all changes. I say that the marketplace cannot guide itself and needs to be steered and educated in order to make reasonable demands and foster achievable results. It is important that we not classify futurism as a champion or a subset of marketing, technology, training or research.

Futurism is what you will do and become, rather than what it is to be. It is what you can and are committed to accomplishing, rather than what mysteriously lies ahead.

Futurism means leaders and organizations taking personal responsibility and accountability for what happens. Abdicating to someone or something else does not constitute business strategy and, in fact, sets the organization backward.

Yesterdayism™

People are interesting combinations of the old, the new, the tried and the true. Individuals and organizations are more resilient than they tend to believe. They've changed more than they wish to acknowledge. They embrace innovations, while keeping the best traditions.

When one reflects at changes, he-she sees directions for the future. Change is innovative. Customs come and go…some should pass, and others might well have stayed with us.

There's nothing more permanent than change. For everything that changes, many things stay the same. The quest of life is to interpret and adapt that mixture of the old and new. People who fight change have really changed more than they think.

The past is an excellent barometer for the future. I call that Yesterdayism. One can always learn from the past, dust it off and reapply it. I call that Lessons Learned but Not Soon Forgotten. Living in the past is not good, nor is living in the present without wisdom of the past.

Trends come and go…the latest is not necessarily the best. Some of the old ways really work better…and should not be dismissed just because they are old, or some fashionable trend of the moment looks better.

When we see how far we have come, it gives further direction for the future. Ideas make the future happen. Technology is a tool of the trade. Futurism is about people, ideas and societal evolution, not fads and gimmicks. The marketplace tells us what they want, if we listen carefully. We also have an obligation to give them what they need.

In olden times, people learned to improvise and "make do." In modern times of instantaneous disposability, we must remember the practicalities and flexibilities of the simple things and concepts.

Non-Profit Legends™

This was the subject of my ninth book, "Non-Profit Legends," nominated for the Pulitzer Prize. Good citizens want to get involved with worthwhile causes. Volunteers are the lifeblood of non-profit organizations and the causes they exemplify. The art of volunteering is in aligning with the community and investing one's time for maximum impact.

Volunteering has the power to improve the quality of life and health of those who donate their time. People must be performing the good deeds from a selfless nature. Volunteering improves not only the communities in which one serves, but also the life of the individuals providing help to the communities.

People volunteer because they believe in their communities and in specific causes. They want to give back, as time permits. They want to make a difference. Many volunteers get to utilize skills that their jobs do not allow, thus rounding them out professionally. There is a personal fulfillment that comes in unexpected ways. Plus, volunteering constitutes socialization, while doing good work on behalf of important causes.

During the course of each year, 26% of Americans regularly volunteer in their communities. So said the Current Population Survey of approximately 60,000 households that obtains information on the nation's civilian non-institutional population. Volunteers are defined as people who perform unpaid work (except for expenses) through or for an organization.

Volunteering is a core value of citizenship. By giving back, volunteers gain new skills, expand professional networks, stay connected to their community and enjoy physical and mental health benefits.

The Fine Art of Failure

Success and failure are matters of perspectives. Out of every 10 transactions in our lives, five will be unqualified successes. One will be a failure. Two will depend upon the circumstances. If approached responsibly, they will become successful. If approached irresponsibly, they will turn into failures. Two will either be successful or will fail, based strictly upon the person's attitude.

A 90% success rate for a person with a good attitude and responsible behavior is an unbeatable percentage. There is no such thing as perfection. Continuous quality improvement means that we benchmark accomplishments and set the next reach a little further.

Throughout our lives, we search for activities, people and meaning. We venture down roads where we find success. Other activities bring us failure, from which we learn even more what to do to achieve success the next time.

We learn three times more from failure than from success. The longer that success takes to attain has a direct relationship to how long we will hold onto it. Success is easily attainable.

Visioning Scope

These are the seven steps toward vision:

1. Information…What we know, Technologies and tasks.
2. Education…Teaching, Processing Information, Modeling.
3. Learning…Mission, Absorbing Information, Techniques.
4. Insights…Synthesizing Information, Values, Applicability to society.
5. Knowledge…Direction, Experience Bank, Inspired Thoughts.
6. Strategy…Actions, Goals and Objectives, Viabilities, Creativity.
7. Vision…Qualities, Strengths, Realizations, Big Picture Scope.

These are the seven levels of Organizational Visioning:

1. Internal…Planning, Controls, Reorganization.
2. Internal…Team Building, Empowerment, Mastering the processes.
3. Internal-External…Fiscal Management, Economic Development.
4. External…Community Input-Output.
5. External…Communications—Image, Services, Accountability.
6. Enhance the Organization's Book Value.
7. Successfully Move Forward.

The Seven Lists: 7 Stages-Progressions to Business Success

7 Stages of Business Growth Strategy:

1. The business you're in. Clear understanding of what the business really is and why you've got what the target marketplace needs and wants.
2. Running the business. Core industry people must learn how to be managers. Give the administrative team enough resources to do

their jobs. Insist upon a holistic relationship to the rest of the tree-organization.

3.   Financial. Financial managers-personnel-consultants must focus beyond their own niche. Profit cannot be the only driving force.

4.   People. The largest, most overlooked branch of the tree-organization. Employees must be empowered. Management must develop people skills. Job descriptions, evaluations and advancements are documented and communicated.

5.   Business Development. Do things necessary to capture and maintain market share. Maintain sales, marketing, advertising, public relations, research and product development programs, interacting with each other.

6.   Body of Knowledge. Understand the relationship of each branch to the other. Research-know what's going on outside your doors. Develop the tools to change.

7.   The Big Picture. Business cannot grow without a holistic relationship to all parts of the tree-organization.

Fine Wine, Aged Cheese and Valuable Antiques

A professional's career and their collected Body of Work encompass time, energy, resources, perseverance and lots of commitment in order to produce. This holds true for any company, institution and for any person.

There are three key ingredients in developing deep leadership roots. Long-term success for the company and a healthy career for the individual are attributable to:

1.   The manner in which an organization or professional lives and conducts business on a daily basis. I symbolize this with the analogy Fine Wine.

2.   The evolution, education, enrichment, professional development, training and life experiences that one amasses. This continuum is symbolized by the analogy Aged Cheese.

3.   What of value is really accomplished and left behind. This shows that the business or person actually existed and contributed meaningfully to society, rather than just filling time and space on this earth. This is symbolized by the analogy Valuable Antiques.

Doing Business in a Distracted World

Many people have lost the ability to focus. Every time that you hear a ring, a buzz or a ding, you jump and focus on those distractions. When people get in your space or prioritize their momentary need to control your time, it takes you away from important matters and priorities. Attention is scarcest commodity.

The average person is bombarded by 1,200 messages every day. More active people may encounter up to 3,000 messages per day. Messages come from other people, phone calls, e-mails, texts, billboards, publications, radio, television, the internet, phone apps, junk mail, website views, social media people you know and people who network. It has created a "too much information" environment.

The average attention span is 8 seconds. Most humans cannot stay focused on one thing for more than 20 minutes at a time. This is attributable to transient and selective attention. 11% of children have been diagnosed with Attention Deficit Hyperactivity Disorder. 4% of adults have ADHD.

Distractions can and will derail productivity and cause people to spend more time on tasks. Overload memory capacity will get in the way of multi-tasking, kill time and reduce quality of work.

Here are statistics on what happens when one is interrupted:

- Employees report 9% higher rates of exhaustion and 4% increase in physical ailments, headaches or back pain.
- One minute of interruption is enough to wipe out your short-term memory, effectively halting your work and mental progress.
- 95% of employees experience a drop in general work quality.
- Work interruptions can cost you six hours per day.
- Interruption leads to greater error rates. The longer the interruption, the greater the chance of errors: 2.8 seconds of interruption doubled the rate of errors, and 4.4 seconds of interruption tripled the rate of errors.

Subtle distractors change what we are doing more than obvious ones. They depend upon how well we know the distractor. Strangers can be more easily dismissed, such as at networking events. Media distractions can be turned off or muted. Needy friends can be limited. The way that the action system expresses itself is affected by perceptions of those who distract.

Chapter 2

ENCYCLOPEDIC KNOWLEDGE BANK

Key Components of the Big Picture of Business

T his chapter is a comprehensive glossary of key business terms. All of these are my own definitions and interpretations as to how they fit into the Big Picture of Business.

Accountability	responsibilities for business actions, activities and strategies.
Acquisitions	bringing new talent into the company and new units into a roll-up.
Acronyms	See Chapter 25 in Book 1.
Adaptability	being able to change course, as circumstances warrant.
Addictive organizations	Those who challenge, blow whistles or suggest that things might be better handled are neither wanted nor tolerated. Addictive managers project externally originated criticism back onto internal scapegoats.

Advice and counsel	Selecting the most appropriate consultant for your company and optimizing expertise is one of the greatest challenges facing a decision maker.
Agreements	contracts, treaties, collaborations and personal commitments.
Anniversaries	See Chapter 20 in Book 1.
Annual meeting	This is a session to review activities of the past year and provide guidance on activities for the coming year. Shareholders are invited. Company management puts its best foot forward, in order to gain support and understanding of next activities.
Annual report	Document which celebrates the year, as the basis for helping business people to prepare for the future.
Associations in business	See Chapter 14 in Book 1.
Audits	Regular review of the financing, accounting, processes and resources. Bigger is the Institutional Review, which looks at people, marketplace prominence, opportunities to grow and how business areas to enter.
Automobile as a key force in business	See Chapter 6.
Benchmarking	Effective benchmarks must be applied to all aspects of the business; Core Business, Running the Business, Financial, People and the relationship of five major business functions to each other.
Better Business Bureau	An organization that advocates for members and consumers.
Big Picture of business	Look at the whole of the organization, then at the parts as components of the whole and back to the bigger picture. See Chapters 2-3 in Book 1.
Boards of Directors	People who guide policy and advise on strategies. See Chapter 28.

Body of knowledge	Understanding the relationship of all components of the organization to each other and how events and activities outside your company affect your ability to do business.
Bottom line	Measurement of profit after all expenses have been covered.
Branding	putting your best foot forward and projecting a positive image. See Chapter 21 in Book 1.
Budgets	Include financial projections, outlining expenses and measuring returns on the investments. See Chapter 27.
Business	There is a difference between knowing a product-industry and growing a successful business.
Business development	Establishment of markets, promotional activity and delivering products to market in timely cycles. See Chapter 7 in Book 2.
Business Model	Business needs to strategize and plan first, with models for each sub-heading (core business, running the business, financial, people, business development, body of knowledge and Big Picture).
Business philosophy	Take what you don't want to believe. Add what you have to believe. You come up with amazing answers. Expect the best but prepare for the worst. There is no plan that is fool-proof. Fight for and with the truth.
Business plan	Defines the core business, staff requirements, production process, marketing and distribution. The Strategic Plan goes further, defining where the company is going, how it will get there and how it will measure its progress.
Business Tree	See Chapter 4 in Book 1.
Busy Work Tree	See Chapter 24.
Capital	Funding to cover operations, staffing and business expansion.
Cause related marketing	Where companies give back to communities in which they do business. Championing causes and effecting community betterment serve to optimally present companies to the public.

CEOs	Chief Executive Officers of organizations, top administrative position.
Chains of command	Levels of management within the company structure, overseeing roles, tasks, technologies, people and processes.
Clichés	Without thinking, people say canned comments, often inventing contexts in which to frame them. Creativity often gives way to the familiar and the trite. It is amazing how often business discussions are derailed by clichés.
Collaborations	Parties willingly cooperating together. Working jointly with others, especially in an intellectual pursuit. Cooperation with an instrumentality with which one is not immediately connected.
Community leadership	See Chapter 19 in Book 1.
Competitive focus	What makes companies and industries stand out from the pack.
Competitive intelligence	What you know and when you know it.
Compromise	Research tells us that all of us agree on 95% of things. It's that 5% where we disagree that gets us into unnecessary confrontations. Too many organizations choose the wrong causes to fight, thus defeating the shared goals, opportunities and marketplace advantages they may have had. Business must pursue negotiations before resorting to litigation.
Confidence	Knowing that correct steps are taken and that the company is doing the best that it can.
Consultants	Selecting the most appropriate consultant for your company and optimizing their expertise is the greatest challenge facing a decision maker. True expertise is a rare commodity, and the successful company utilizes it on the front end, rather than on the costly back end. Matching consultants with actual and emerging company needs is the corporate leader's quest.

Continuous quality improvement	Quality should be viewed as a journey, rather than a destination. It applies to service industries and manufacturing operations. Even non-profit and public sector organizations must utilize quality approaches for staff and volunteer councils/boards. Employees must buy into the process by offering constructive input.
Core business	What the company started out to be and what its business base is now. See Chapter 3.
Core values	How organizations start out and what they become are different concepts. Mistakes, niche orientation and lack of planning lead businesses to failure. Processes, trends, fads, perceived stresses and "the system" force managers to make compromises in order to proceed. Often, a fresh look at previous knowledge gives renewed insight. Becomes what the person or organization stands for. Has conviction, commitment and ownership. Able to change and adapt.
Corporate communications	See Chapter 16.
Corporate culture	See Chapter 4.
Corporate Responsibility	means operating a business in ways that meet or exceed the ethical, legal, commercial and public expectations. These strategies, methodologies, policies, practices and programs are integrated throughout business operations, supported and rewarded by top management. See Chapter 25 in Book 2.
Corporate scandals	See Chapter 7 in Book 1.
Courage	Triggering events or life changes cause one to consider new ideas, ways of thinking.
Creativity	Along with knowledge of the industry in which one works, there is a creative art to being effective at every aspect of running and sustaining each facet of a successful business.

Customers	are the lifeblood of every business. Employees depend upon customers for their paychecks. Every organization has customers, clients, stakeholders, financiers, volunteers, supporters and other constituencies.
Customer focused management	goes beyond smiling, answering queries and communicating with buyers. Every decision must have customer outcomes.
Customer service	Companies must embrace customer service tenets. Satisfied customers talk to others, encouraging them to buy based upon quality of the company. Dissatisfied customers will aggressively discourage prospects from buying. See Chapter 26 in Book 1.
Cyclical effects	There are cycles in business, including upturns, downturns, aggressive competition, recessions and marketplace shifts.
Departmental planning	See Chapter 9.
Details	One must look at the Big Picture of business first, then at the pieces as they relate to the whole. There is a difference between knowing a product-industry and growing a successful business. It is possible for a company and its managers to know much about certain arts and sciences without having the will to pursue them.
Diversity	See Chapter 12 in Book 2.
Downsizing	Cutting back on budget, staffing and product focus, exemplifying the process of lean management.
Economic trends, downturns and recovery	See Chapter 7 in Book 1.
Emerging marketplaces	Where business may be developed in the future.
Employees	Lifeblood of company operations and the public face of companies.
Empowerment	Being allowed to make decisions on behalf of the company.

Enron	See Chapter 10 in Book 1.
Entrepreneurship	See Chapter 24 in Book 1.
Equity	Financial value, worth of the company ownership held.
Ethics	is the science of morals, rightness and obligations in human affairs. Ethics relates to every stage in the evolution of a business, leadership development and creative ways of doing business. It is an understanding how and why any organization remains standing and growing, instead of continuing to look at micro-niche parts. See Chapter 25 in Book 2.
Executive development	See Chapter 18 in Book 1.
Executives	Company division leaders and managers.
Expectations	What we wish employees to do and perform, as communicated verbally and written.
Experience	Track record of companies in sustaining business and that of employees as providing value to the enterprise.
Fact gathering	To get the best answers, one must ask the best questions, think beyond the obvious and stretch the idea process. Facts must be plentiful and real, in order to facilitate meaningful decision-making.
Failure	We learn three times more from failure than success. The longer that success takes to attain has a relationship to how long we will hold onto it. See Chapter 24 in Book 2.
Fear	Fear is the biggest contributor to failure, and it can be a motivator for success. It is difficult to figure how people will behave when the chips are down. The definition of bravery is a person who is scared but still does what he-she has to.
Feedback	Business needs to hear from customers on how they are doing. Feedback on the internal processes makes the company much stronger.

Foreign language terms used in English	Many terms have inculcated into the English vocabulary. See Chapter 26.
Funding	Getting the funds that you need from tight fisted management is an ongoing process. Cash outlays are justifiable either by dollars they bring in or dollars they stand to save for the organization. Cash outlays are always risks. Justify your risks in proportion to riskier ones they have previously funded.
Futurism	is a series of strategies, methodologies and actions which poise any organization to weather the forces of change. It is an ongoing process of evaluation, planning, tactical actions and benchmarking accomplishments. Futurism is a continuum of thinking and reasoning skills, judicious activities, shared leadership and an accent upon ethics and quality. See Chapter 15.
Genius	Ideas and concepts come to organizations in a variety of ways. Most have great thinkers inside and need to recognize the nuggets of gold that exist within. It is equally important to utilize consultants who really have insights and contribute original thinking.
Global business and Globalization	See Chapter 17.
Goals	Statements of purpose in the Strategic Plan. See Chapter 8.
Goods and services	What a company produces and sells in the marketplace.
Government regulations	Standards in the ethical conduct of business.
Greatness	The mining of golden ideas is both an art and a painstaking process. These are the seven levels of thinking and reasoning skills that lead to "genius" ideas and breakthrough concepts for a business.
Growth strategies	See Chapter 7.
Heir Apparents	Those company executives being groomed for management and leadership roles.

High Cost of Doing Nothing	See Chapter 10 in Book 2.
Ideas and Beliefs	Formulated ideas emerge, as people-organizations learn to hold their own outside their shells. Two-way communication ensues…opinion inputs and outputs craft ideas and beliefs. As people become more aware of their own learning, they tally their inventory of knowledge. Patterns of beliefs emerge, based upon education, experiences and environment.
Image and reputation	Every organization must educate outside publics about what they do and how they do it. This premise also holds true for each corporate operating unit and department. The whole of the business and each sub-set must always educate corporate opinion makers on how it functions and the skill with which the company operates.
Information and data	There is more information available now than ever before. Most of it is biased and slanted by vendors with something to sell. There exists much data, without interpretation. Technology purveys information but cannot do the analytical thinking.
Inventions	See Chapter 20.
Inventory	Goods on hand, ready to sell to customers. Goods being produced in order to meet upcoming demand.
Investor relations	See Chapter 27 in Book 2.
International trade	See Chapter 17.
Joint venturing	Partners come together for specific purposes or projects that may be beyond the scope of individual members. Each retains individual identity. The joint-venture itself has its own identity…reflecting favorably upon work to be done and upon the partners.
Just-in-time delivery	Inventory is ordered and stocked in a systematic manner, so that sales can be made with most everything available.

Knowledge	Amassing a Body of Knowledge, which leads to Wisdom, is a long and enjoyable process. It is the first step toward a career-life Strategy, which evolves into a Vision. Using a corporate analogy, a Mission Statement accounts for less than 1% of a Strategic Plan, which constitutes only 20% of a Corporate Visioning Program.
Language	Words are fun and connect your business to tomorrow. Technology cannot take the place of human communication…only may add to it. Every opportunity should be taken to enhance literacy skills of employees and entire organization. The language of success is initially found in a dictionary.
Leadership tasks	include recruiting, hiring and supervision. Companies are successful by possessing an attained art to human resources management, empowerment, team building, training, incentives and professional executive development.
Leadership development	Money is rarely the primary motivation for people in careers. All people in the organization need lots of professional attention, mentoring, training and administrative support. Few ever get their needs satisfied, and thus, companies realize reduced work output and a less-than-zealous attitude.
Management	Research tells us that 92% of all problems in organizations stem from poor management decisions. Having studied, worked with and mentored many managers over the years, I've concluded that few had sufficient management training up to that point.
Management styles	See Chapter 16 in Book 1.
Medium is the Message	See Chapter 13 in Book 2.
Mentoring	See Chapter 12.
Mission statements	What the company is all about. It must be succinct and realistic. It is usually the last thing to be revised when a new Strategic Plan is developed.

Negotiations	It takes more courage to pursue a compromise than to pursue an extremist position. Conciliation and reason must be pursued. The skill with which they are approached often spells the difference between total success and political suicide.
Networking	See Chapter 27 in Book 1.
Non-Profit organizations	See Hank Moore's book "Non-Profit Legends."
Objectives	Statements of actions and activities in the Strategic Plan. See Chapter 8.
Outside the Box thinking	Creative approaches to problems, challenges and opportunities.
Oxymoron's in business	See Chapter 14 in Book 2.
Partnering	A formal relationship between two or more associates. Involves close cooperation among parties, with each having specified and joint rights and responsibilities.
Path from Pleasure to Success	See Chapter 4 in Book 2.
People, corporate culture	See Chapter 4.
People skills	See Chapter 5.
Performance Based Budgeting	See Chapter 29 in Book 2.
Philanthropy	Corporate contributions should be budgeted and may be thought of as a part of business development, public relations and marketing. It is advantageous to make donations according to a philanthropy plan that is conducive to the corporate culture, goals and core values.
Physical plant	Where products are made, manufactured and assembled.

Planning	These are characteristics of good corporate plans and, thus, company philosophies: Focus upon the customer. Honors the employees. Shows business life as a process, not a quick fix. Portrays their company as a contributor, not a savior. Clearly defines their niche. Says and does things that inspire you to think. Is compatible with other communications. Remains consistent with their products, services and track record.
Professional development	Today's workforce needs three times the amount of training that it now gets in order to stay in business, remain competitive and tackle the future successfully.
Professional services	See Chapter 10.
Professionalism	The mark of any professional is the manner in which he/she corrects mistakes. Most often, this means correcting misperceptions about company attitude, rather than the condition of goods. The faster the correction, the better the level of satisfaction.
Public service	See my book "Non-Profit Legends."
Quality management	Success is determined by conformity to requirements. It is achieved through prevention, not appraisal. Non-conformance is costly. Make-good efforts cost more on the back end than doing things right on the front end.
Reading, Learning and Retention	See Chapter 22.
Recessions	See Chapter 6 in Book 1.
Remediating damage	Running a profitable and efficient organization means effectively remediating damage before it accrues. Processes and methodologies for researching, planning, executing and benchmarking activities will reduce that pile of costly coins from stacking up.
Reputation management	What the marketplace thinks of you and how valuable they see you to be.
Request for Proposals	See Chapter 18 in Book 2.

Respect	The basics of good business are rooted in respect. Respect is a valuable commodity that caring professionals must nurture and show toward their colleagues, customers, industry, marketplace and stakeholders.
Results Based Management	See Chapter 27.
Rollups	Two or more companies are put together, resulting in a larger entity.
Small business	Companies with less than 200 employees.
Stakeholders	See Chapter 11.
Statistics	Indicators of the marketplace in which business must function. By interpreting and examining the research, we can make better informed decisions. Statistics by themselves do no good, unless they are applied to the process of planning an organization's destiny. See Chapter 2 in Book 2.
Stewardship	Nurturing communities in which you do business.
Strategic Planning	See Chapter 8.
Success	Finding knowledge in unique ways. Doing work that you're proud of. Developing a philosophy, individually and organizationally. Handling mistakes and crises. Dealing with change and fear.
Succession planning	How the company will transition to new management, especially when the founder retires.
Supply chain management	Each link in the chain is important, including employees within your company and those outside suppliers with whom you do business.
Systems of Thought and Ideologies	Insights start emerging at this plateau. Connect beliefs with available resources and personal expertise. Measure results and evaluate outcomes of activities, using existing opinion, ideas and beliefs. Actions are taken which benchmark success and accountability to stakeholders.

Tactics	What the company will do to achieves goals and objectives, in what order and who will be accountable. Statements of details in the Strategic Plan. See Chapter 8.
Teamwork	It is becoming increasingly rare to find an individual or organization that has not yet been required to team with others. Lone rangers and sole-source providers simply cannot succeed in competitive environments and global economies. Those who benefit from collaborations, rather than become the victim of them, will log the biggest successes in business years ahead.
Technology	See Chapter 21.
Third party endorsement	Third party support can move mountains when you need it the most…or it can wreak havoc on your bottom line and the future in which you do business. Be honest about your current status. Take stock of opportunities. Make decisive actions and reap future rewards. See Chapter 11.
Training	Emphasis must be placed upon properly diagnosing the organization as a whole and then prescribing treatments for the whole, as well as the parts. Training should address most organizational aspects.
Values	Organizations must periodically assess and review their value systems as part of Strategic Planning and corporate Visioning processes. Every business leader should likewise develop and commit to nurturing their own personal value statements.
Visioning process	See Chapter 31.
Workforce	Categories of the work force: People who do things necessary to get by. People managed by others to meet quotas, schedules, procedures. People who make things. Administrative, managerial support. System upholders. People who sell something. People in transition. Idealists out to do meaningful things.
Y2K Bug	See Chapter 9 in Book 1.
Yesterdayism	Learning from the past but not living in it.

Strategies That Move Your Business Forward

Some key points to take away from this chapter:

- Founders and managers are not always leaders and need to be groomed as such.
- Know your strengths and weaknesses.
- Nurture the appreciation of employees.
- You are not alone in this struggle.
- Gain a better understanding of the overall business climate.
- Balanced growth and management.
- Importance of planning.
- Importance of leadership.
- Really need to take the discipline to write a business plan and use it.
- Measuring your business, on a regular basis.
- Being aware of trends in markets that may affect the way one does business.
- Organizational development is necessary.
- Need for better strategic planning and measuring against the plan.
- Business growth, plus meeting and seeing new opportunities.
- Becoming a planner and a strategist.
- Much wider diversity of knowledge.
- Emphasizes the importance of planning, relationships, loyalty and vision.
- Planning for change.
- Planning for growth.
- Embracing more sophisticated management techniques.
- Encompassing more forecasting and planning.
- An incredible amount of information, insight and wisdom.

Chapter 3

THE BUSINESS THEY'RE REALLY IN

Understanding and Prioritizing Core Business

T his chapter focuses upon prioritizing and realigning the primary reason for being in business. It is an in-depth look at Branch 1 of the Business Tree, the core of the business: how it is perceived, how it is developed, how it changes based upon marketplace demands, and what must be done so that company growth can continue. The rest of the tree cannot grow without this branch. It is who you are. It is what the business is to become.

All too often, companies fail because they are not clear about what business their company truly is. Without that knowledge, planning to sustain and grow is impossible.

Branch 1 is the easiest to climb onto. People get into businesses because they have expertise in one area, and if they are good at turning it into a business, they succeed. At the beginning of their work in the business, they are exceedingly comfortable with what they are doing.

Just as organizations start out to be one thing, as they grow, they often evolve into something quite different. What the founder started, if successful, will change over time and over generations of management. Disney started out as an animated movie studio pure and simple. It has expanded far beyond that, and now its core business is licensing its name: to retail outlets, cruise lines, credit card companies, ice shows and more.

As businesses change, management must be astute enough to re-shuffle its priorities. For example, the retail grocery store chain that has acquired so much property as it opened up stores becomes a property management company. The local bistro that grew into a chain, found its core business the selling of franchises.

I have worked with many businesses that had moved on from their original business model to something different at they grew and evolved. Case in point: the analytical instruments and equipment industry. Most of the niche companies in this area evolved and grew up because of chemical plant industrialization of the 1950s and 1960s. The founders worked in production environments where plants and factories had on-staff engineers, analyzer specialists, operators, lead chemists and other technical department managers.

These professionals came along in the same generation. They founded their companies to meet scientific niches. Their entrepreneurial efforts led to the research and development of the technology. They began serving a broad range of industrial, institutional and governmental client organizations, providing specialized equipment and services to assure accurate analyses and process control.

Cutbacks at chemical plants, water treatment facilities and such have all but eliminated the staff positions that utilize the equipment designed by these companies. Many of those people developed technologies at their plants and subsequently went into business to manufacture and distribute.

The client side changed, while many of these niche companies stayed basically the same. Over the years, factories, laboratories and plants merged. Their numbers have shrunk. Cost efficiency became the overriding factor. In industry, the analytical equipment buying decisions are made by purchasing agents rather than technically trained supervisors. As a result, equipment is bought, and vendors are expected to install. There is not as much follow-through. Equipment and systems are less integrated as they used to be. Development of operating software is usually done in-house or with their own consultants.

To address needs, many of these technology companies have moved beyond the making of equipment and into training customers in the use of the equipment, consulting on chemical issues, environmental audits, monitoring and other professional services. I recommended that they expand their priorities toward selling consulting hours and contracting for projects, moving from being just a manufacturer to a consulting business. They were able to expand in such a way as to show customers the connectivity of all equipment to each other. The by-product of being inside the plants was the uncovering of other needs, which resulted in the development and modification of other equipment to serve necessary functions.

Big Picture of Business lesson: Rigidly adhering to the initial core business makes one impervious to the next generation of customer needs. No organization can remain unchanged and expect to succeed.

During my work with a chain of credit unions, which were attempting to move further into the banking business, several priorities had to be examined, in order to expand the notion of core business.

We asked some key questions. Would small customers still come first? How do we compete with established banking companies? What kinds of additional services must we provide? Where do we find customers in previously under-served markets?

Having advised various independent banks in developing their strategic plans, I saw some common themes emerging. Each of the independents had said they wanted to avoid falling into the pitfalls of the big bank holding companies, yet all of them wanted to grow very large. Achieving a healthy balance of strength, size of deposits and customer focus with the credit unions was the strategy. The planning process fostered a culture that was commensurate with their rich history and the assurance of plenty customer service, enough to draw customers away from banks that had gotten too big.

Big Picture of Business lesson: Putting customers in the forefront of all management decisions and planning portends to the future of the business expansion.

Ranking Core Business by Priorities

As companies evolve away from their core businesses as originally established by the founders, a profound dissonance can develop within the organization itself regarding what it is and what it's priorities should be.

As a company grows, top management will claim its #1 priority to be revenue volume and its rewards, including bonuses for key management. At the same time, actually delivering the core business as it is promoted to its customers slips to #10 in the priority ranking. Increasing company revenue is #2, while customer service, or follow-up beyond the sale becomes #12. No wonder that top management, company professionals and workers find themselves pursuing differing goals, with inevitable conflicts that need to be resolved through planning, prioritizing and realigning the core business.

This chapter identifies agendas and priorities in specific industries, showing that what they promote themselves as being to customers and the outside world is very low on the priority scale within the organization.

Take energy companies, for example. Their #1 priority is marketing their products, while #2 is profiting their investors and executive. Yet they promote themselves as being all about finding new sources of energy. Take school systems. The number one priority of management is to raise funds through taxes and grants. Yet they promote themselves as being there to help their students learn.

Frame of reference is everything in business. Different people within the same organization have contrasting views as to the business they are really in (core business).

Organizations found themselves to become one thing, but they evolve into something else. In their mind, they're one thing. Other people think they are something else. The truth actually lies somewhere in between.

A company starts out to create the best widgets possible. After the art of building the first widget has been resolved, then the harsh reality of running a widget factory appears. People need to be trained to make and process widgets through the production chain. Other people must find and develop the widget marketplace.

Then come the onslaught of widget competitors and clones. The widget regulators get involved, as do the special interest groups.

The widget company decides to go public. Selling stocks, raising capital and working with the financial community becomes the priority. Constituencies start complaining that the company has veered from its initial mission. They're no longer the mom-and-pop widget maker that they once were. They've become a corporation, or a bureaucracy, or a bunch of marketers, or a technocrat institution, whichever constituency the critic does not belong to.

The company is no longer in the business that the founder started. Each camp sees the business differently, and both sides do not always meet within their own company. Turfs continue to be protected. Each niche believes their notion of core business is the one and only core business.

Therein lie the inevitable conflicts. Rather than try to inter-mingle differing contexts, organizations continue to mean different things to different employees.

Sadly, however, most organizations do very little to resolve conflicts of context. Problems continue to fester, costing the organization several leaves, twigs and limbs on each branch of its Business Tree™.

This chapter on prioritizing and core business gives an average priority ranking for companies-organizations. In addition to generic organizational priorities, each business, market niche and type of goods-services has industry-specific characteristics. These add further agendas and priorities to the general list. What they promote themselves as being externally is usually near the bottom of actual priority rankings, or perhaps a category unto itself. Included are some samples of organizational priorities in 30 key industries.

Ranking the Business They're In

Priorities change. Dedicated providers of the service stated in the original company mission become frustrated when they do not understand the reasons for the shifting priorities.

Often, what organizations say they are in external promotions to potential customers actually ranks low on the actual priority list. That occurs due to the agendas of individuals who guide the organization, departing from the core business for which founders were presumably educated and experienced. Add to that the harsh realities of doing business and staying competitive.

Here is an average priority ranking for the core business activity of companies:

1. Revenue volume and its rewards, including bonuses for key management.
2. Growth, defined as increasing revenues each year, rather than improving the quality of company operations.
3. Doing the things necessary to assure the revenue stream, including billings, sales, add-on's and marketing. Keeping the cash register ringing, rather than focusing upon what is being sold, how it is made and the kind of company they need to be in order to sustain the growth.
4. Running an organizational bureaucracy.
5. Maintaining the status quo. Keeping things churning. Making adjustments, corrections or improvements only occurs when crises warrant.
6. Amassing prestige and recognition for the company and for certain leaders.

7. Furthering stated corporate agendas.
8. Furthering unwritten corporate agendas.
9. Courting favor with selected opinion leaders and stakeholders.
10. Actually, delivering the core business. Making the widget itself. Doing what you started in business to do, what you tell the customers that you do.
11. Doing the things that a company should do to be a good company. Following the processes, policies and procedures to make better widgets and foster a better organization.
12. Customer service, consideration for the marketplace and follow-up service beyond the sale.
13. Looking after people employed by the company, in terms of providing training, empowerment, recognition, resources and rewards.
14. Giving back to those who support the company, including customers, stakeholders and communities in which the company operates.
15. Advancing conditions in which core business is delivered.
16. Walking the talk via ethics, values, quality and vision.
17. Giving back to the industry and amassing a body of business knowledge.

People in the organization whose jobs fall under each priority have vastly different perceptions of the organization, its mission, their role and the parts to be played by others. Some jockey for position to make their priority seem to advance higher. Some keep people on the lower numbered rungs in check, assuring that their priorities remain low. Some become frustrated because others' priorities are not theirs.

Other people build fiefdoms within the organization in order to solidify their ranking. Some do their job as well as possible, hoping that others will recognize and reward their contributions. Some do not believe they are noticed and simply occupy space within the organizational structure. Some try to take unfair advantage of the system. Others are clueless as to the existence of a system, pecking order, corporate agendas, company vision or other business realities.

Until a concerted effort to establish commonalties of purpose is made (known as a shared company vision), then organizational chaos likely will perpetuate. This negatively impacts productivity, morale and the delivering of the product-service. Customers always suffer the side effects from companies in chaos.

Breakdowns Per Type of Industry

In addition to generic organizational priorities, each business, market niche and type of goods-services has industry-specific characteristics. These add further agendas and priorities to the general list. What they promote themselves as being externally is usually near the bottom of actual priority rankings or perhaps a category unto itself.

Based upon my years of research, advising these industries, creating strategic plans and conducting performance reviews, here are some examples of organizational priorities, per key industry sector.

Retailers:
1. Keeping the cash registers ringing.
2. Moving case lots of merchandise, to justify negotiated prices and bonuses.
3. Sales of products.
4. Marketing of the store.
5. Making it difficult for customers to return merchandise.
6. Providing customer service, as it relates to making sales.
7. Overall customer goodwill service.

In external promotions, they say they're: Giving customers all they want and need.

Energy companies:
1. Marketing products.
2. Profiting investors and executives.
3. Perpetuating a system, mindset, industry, bureaucracy.
4. Engineering.
5. Energy production.
6. Research and development.
7. Serving the marketplace.
8. Issues advocacy.

In external promotions, they say they're: Finding new sources of energy.

Health care:
1. Revenues, billings, fees.
2. Maintaining the industry's pecking order of respect, status and deference.
3. Running bureaucracies.
4. Interface with insurance companies.
5. Patient care.
6. Professional association activities, publishing and image enhancement.
7. Health and wellness public education.

In external promotions, they say they're: Offering affordable health care for all.

School systems:
1. Raising funds through taxes, grants.
2. Perpetuating a bureaucracy.
3. Gaining acclaim and recognition. Priorities are directly commensurate to those of constituencies which the districts court.
4. Educating students.
5. Serving communities (taxpayer base).
6. Education for education's sake.

In external promotions, they say they're: There to help students to learn.

Media:
1. Selling advertising.
2. Influence buying, selling, peddling, fostering myths-perceptions.
3. Entertaining audiences, in order to deliver numbers to advertisers.
4. Giving the appearance of serving the public, to create cause-related marketing revenue stream.
5. Informing and entertaining audiences.
6. Serving the public as a community or public service.

In external promotions, they say they're: Caring and committed to serving communities.

Elected public officials:
1. Power, prestige, influence.

2. Championing own pet causes-issues-agendas.
3. Serving pet issues of selected constituencies.
4. Fund raising and other details of winning elections.
5. Serving general issues of overall constituency.
6. Advocating for the rights of those in need.

In external promotions, they say they're: Championing the cause of freedom everywhere.

Municipal bureaucracies:
1. Real estate trade, expansion, taxation.
2. Serving special interests, overtly or covertly.
3. Maintaining a bureaucratic structure.
4. Furthering the agendas of bureaucrat managers.
5. Serving taxpayer needs.
6. Providing a forum for taxpayer issues.

In external promotions, they say they're: Running efficient government.

Insurance companies:
1. Revenues from policy sales.
2. Policy renewals with minimum of marketing effort.
3. Paying for their organization to operate.
4. Paying a network of third-party administrators.
5. Denying as many claims as possible.
6. Serving clients.
7. Paying claims.

In external promotions, they say they're: Protecting policyholders for all eventualities.

Consultants:
1. Generating billings.
2. Marketing to get work, making claims and promises. Telling clients, they require what consultant sells, rather than overview of client needs-realities.

3. Hiring support personnel after the work is obtained.
4. Client service.
5. Professional development, in order to be all that was claimed in the marketing.
6. Running the consultancy as a business.

In external promotions, they say they're: Improving businesses, per their niche definition.

Airlines:
1. Filling the maximum numbers of seats at highest negotiated rates.
2. Competing with travel agencies to get customers to book directly.
3. Influential forces in communities, government entities.
4. Well maintained fleets of equipment.
5. Well trained and managed employees.
6. Committed to continuing customer service.

In external promotions, they say they're: The best transportation bargain around.

Entertainment industry:
1. Selling tickets to events, copies of product and repeat business.
2. Image marketing, to attract customers, glamour and attention.
3. Revenue enhancement from sales.
4. Running companies to produce, package and market products.
5. Show business…often smoke, mirrors, egos and sizzle.
6. The entertainment product itself.
7. Customer enjoyment, catering to customer wants and trends.

In external promotions, they say they're: Assuring that a good time is had by all.

Computer and software companies:
1. Vendors of products and consulting time.
2. Developers of sellable products.
3. Teachers of how to use their products.
4. Offer backup support to continuing customers.

In external promotions, they say they're: Providing full-scope business solutions.

Telecommunications:
1. Selling equipment.
2. Selling additional features.
3. Marketing company image, to help sell additional features.
4. Billing customers for add-ons.
5. Government relations, lobbying with opinion leaders.
6. Company agendas and administration.
7. Technology production-distribution-maintenance.
8. Customer service as it relates to selling more products and features.
9. Customer service as it relates to taking care of what was sold.

In external promotions, they say they're: A public trust, a human motivator.

Restaurant (one location):
1. Creating and serving food recipes they have perfected.
2. Making a fair profit, though driving force is food quality.
3. Taking personal care of customers.
4. Overseeing details to maintain restaurant consistency.
5. Marketing the restaurant.
6. Administration of the business.

In external promotions, they say they're: A unique dining experience.

Restaurant chain:
1. Opening new locations.
2. Realizing profits on all units.
3. Attracting investors for the next deals.
4. Edging out the competition.
5. Policies of uniformity and consistency.
6. Marketing of products, locations and chain image.
7. Ambience and atmosphere.
8. The food product itself.
9. Customer service.

10. Vendor-supplier activities.
11. Staff training, employee relations.

In external promotions, they say they're: A dining experience that is standardized.

Public lotteries:
1. Raising funds to pay for their own salaries, overhead and bureaucracy.
2. Selling false hope to people wanting to get rich quick.
3. Preying upon people who want instant riches.
4. Selling an addiction (buying tickets) to those who can least afford it.
5. Administering the process.

In external promotions, they say they're: Raising funds to benefit education and other politically correct causes.

Questions to Ask for the Business They Could Be In

Marketplace changes:
When the forces of change and the resistors of progress clash, who usually prevails?
Who are the forces of change in your core business, company and industry?
Who are the resistors of progress?
How do you create value in the marketplace?
How much has your company changed within the last year? How? In what ways?
Do you study forces outside your organization that could affect your livelihood?

Challenges-trends for growth businesses:
How cyclical are business trends?
How far behind the trends can a company stay and yet still survive?
How does a company on the downslide patch its problems?
How many companies have you seen fail because they did all the wrong things?
How are you keeping it from happening to your organization?

Understanding your market niche:
How does one define its market niche?

How are market niches expanded and changed?

What is the Big Picture of your business? Who paints it? Who should also be included?

Shouldn't Strategic Planning be conducted to assure long-term business success?

Researching the competition:

To what do you ascribe the success of your competition? Who really is your competition?

How will your company establish its own Point of Difference?

Creating new products and services:

Where are the new markets and consumers of the future?

How could business best go about creating new products and services?

Within any industry and company, wide priorities exist. Board members and line workers have different rank orders. Therein lies the inevitable source of conflict within every organization.

Rather than wish for what we think "used to be" or "ought to be," the challenge is to reconcile differences of opinion and create a unified organization. Since priority rankings will rarely be identical among employees, the purpose of shared company vision is to build commonalties.

Core values of thriving organizations of all sizes should portray themselves as a place or turf, as shared ideals and expectations, as a network of social allegiances and stakeholder ties, as a collective framework, reflecting diversity and pursuing the common good.

Chapter 4

CORPORATE CULTURE

C ompanies that have strong, definitive cultures are able to meet the future, with the goal to improve program effectiveness, accountability and achieve results. This means that company leadership is committed to:

- Establishing clear organizational vision, mission and priorities, which are translated into a four-year framework of goals, outputs, indicators, strategies and resources.
- Encouraging an organizational and management culture that promotes innovation, learning, accountability, and transparency.
- Delegating authority, empowering managers and holding them accountable for results.
- Focusing on achieving results, through strategic planning, regular monitoring of progress, evaluation of performance, and reporting on performance.
- Creating supportive mechanisms, policies and procedures, building and improving on what is already in place.

- Sharing information, knowledge, learning lessons and feeding these back into improving decision-making and performance.
- Optimizing human resources and building capacity among staff to manage for results.
- Making the best use of financial resources in an efficient manner to achieve results.
- Strengthening and diversifying partnerships at all levels.
- Responding to external situations and needs within the organizational mandate.

We are the products of those who believe in us. Find role models and set out to be one yourself. To get, you must give. Career and life are not a short stint. Do what it takes to run the decathlon. Set personal and professional goals, standards and accountability.

Corporate cultures stand for something. Making money is not enough. You must do something worth leaving behind, mentoring to others and of recognizable substance. Your views of professionalism must be known and shown.

There are four types of corporate cultures:

- Friendly, where the leaders are team builders and mentors. There is a commitment to communication and development. Team first is the mantra.
- Dynamic and creative working environment. By anticipating needs and developing creative standards, the company exhibits agility in transforming itself. Leaders tend to be entrepreneurs and visionaries. Employees take risks, and leaders are seen as innovative.
- Market driven, where results and getting things done are essential. People are competitive, focus upon goals and emphasize success. The leaders are hard drivers and producers.
- Hierarchy. This is conventional, formalized and structured. The leaders are organizers and monitors. Process control and quality management are valued.

There are seven levels of building corporate culture in each category:

1. Information Gathering Process. This is a snapshot of the realities of situations, as well as facts and figures. Understand the organization's truths.
2. Studying How the Organization Operates. Conduct performance reviews of successful activities, while also looking for efficiencies.
3. Enhance Efficiencies, Economies, Profitability. Shareholder value.
4. Process for and About Teams. Empowering and involving the organization's most valuable resource, its people.
5. Adapting to Changing Marketplaces, Relationships. Connect beliefs with expertise. Actions are taken with measurements of success and accountability to stakeholders.
6. Strategic Planning. Study the organization's core values. Has commitment and ownership. Able to change and adapt.
7. Futurism, Vision and Change Focused. Everything is done based upon beliefs and systems of thought. Committed to and thriving upon change.

Many companies do not have definitive corporate cultures. Thus, they do not optimize the business opportunities. They have not strategized who they really are, where they are going, how they will get there and how effective they are at reaching goals.

When cultures are not designated, the organizations lapse into clusters of culture, little fiefdoms of power bases. People in the niches feel emboldened to protect their turfs. Cohesion in the company is ragged at best.

Worse still is when organizations have splintered from other companies. Principals bring corporate cultures from the organizations where they used to work, presumably the cultures that they chose to leave. These companies bring management styles that are obsolete and understandings of employees that may not be current. Hybrid cultures in organizations take time to congeal. In the meantime, there may be damage done because of what the founders brought over with them.

Values and Ideals

Individuals and organizations amass values based upon a series of experiences. Often, values depend upon the context and reflect the facets of professional achievement:

1. The core Business You're In.
2. Rendering the service, making the products.

3. Accountability.
4. Your relationships and contributions to other people.
5. Professional and leadership development.
6. Contributions to the organization's overall goals and Big Picture.
7. Body of Work: accomplishments and anticipated future output.

Organizations must periodically assess and review their value systems as part of corporate culture analysis and visioning processes. Every business leader should likewise develop and commit to nurturing his-her own personal value statement.

Here are some examples of core values that could be included:

1. To be the best that one can be.
2. To be the best in the chosen field.
3. To create new applications and set new standards for the chosen field.
4. To successfully mentor others.
5. To creatively approach projects in ways that others did not or could not do.
6. To achieve results that are realistically attained and honestly reached.
7. To continue building respect and the self-assuredness to stay focused.
8. To do the right things and taking the best possible courses of action.
9. To continue growing professionally and evolving to the next tiers.

There are seven levels of values:
1. No Values. Either too young to know better or do not choose to develop further value systems. This is the crossroads, and those who advance further will experience success in life.
2. When we do business with others, we observe their values (one of the tenets of total quality management). Includes values of people temporarily in positions of authority, caretakers of our activities (such as public officials), and those with whom we must presently associate for business reasons. We may not agree with their values but understand how to work within them.
3. Basic Teachings. Things we learned or think we have assimilated from parents, teachers, friends and community resources. Periodically, this needs to be re-examined, updated and reapplied to current life circumstances.

4. Learning by Example.
5. Community Standards. Etiquette is sophisticated and must be mastered over time. If it's not the right thing to do, then a person has some real ethical considerations. By this stage, one is committed only to doing the right thing, doing it with class and inspiring others by example.
6. Values Learned by Living, Learning, Earning. Take nothing for granted. Change is inevitable and brings opportunities for those who are adaptable, creative and innovative.
7. Lessons from Mentorship, Risk Taking and a Balanced Life. Career and life Bodies of Work sprout from many roots. Must be viewed as a whole, the sum of the parts and the lessons learned to make each branch, limb, twig and leaf remain healthy.

There are seven levels of standards:
1. Base Level. Basics of food, clothing and shelter. Knowing right from wrong. Trying to pursue a good life and aspire to something higher.
2. Society's Lowest Common Denominators. Although knowing better, subscribing to prevailing philosophies and behaviors of others. This leads some to take advantage of the system, want more than one's share and fail to be accountable. Sadly, the common denominators are below what they used to be, and society continues to lower them. The mission of a successful person or organization is not to succumb quite that low.
3. Lessons from the School of Hard Knocks. Learning by experiences and successes. Becoming more familiar with one's strengths, weaknesses, opportunities and threats. Understanding what an organization can and cannot accomplish, represent and become. Maximizing one's resources to the most practical advantage.
4. Launching a Quest. Striving to learn more and go further. Includes intellectual pursuits, professional realities, nurturing of people skills and executive abilities. At this point, people change careers, and organizations revisit their goals and crystalize new visions.
5. Standards. Set and respect boundaries. Many times, people and organizations will attempt to violate those standards or fail to acknowledge their existence. The test is how consistently one sets, modifies and observes one's own standards.

6. Values and Vision. No person or organization stands still. It is not enough to accept change but more importantly to benefit from it. It is not enough to see yourself on a higher plateau and quest for more. Success comes from charting a course, encompassing value systems and methodically reaching goals.

7. Code of Ethics. Fundamental canons, rules of practice, professional obligations, accountability-measurability, professional development, integrity, objectivity and independence. Commitment to uphold and enforce codes of ethics (yours and those of others) and the ethical responsibilities of members in business.

Organizations have seven levels of core values:

1. Being Your Best Self. It is not acceptable to be a clone of what you perceive someone else to be.

2. Being Consistently Excellent, Upholding Standards to Remain So. There is no such thing as perfection. Yet, excellence is a definitive process of achievement, dedication and expeditious use of resources. Exponential improvement each year is the objective.

3. The Ability to Change, Adapt and Lead.

4. Learning from Experiences, Successes and the Shortcomings of All.

5. Thinking, Planning, Reflecting and Benchmarking.

6. Committing to the Next Great Challenge.

7. The ability to communicate and share with others. Core values of thriving organizations of all sizes should portray themselves as a place or turf, as shared ideals and expectations, as a network of social allegiances and stakeholder ties, as a collective framework, reflecting diversity and pursuing the common good.

Questions to Ask in Refining Corporate Culture

Management styles and leadership:

What constitutes a leader?

What are the differences between an executive and a leader?

What leadership qualities were you taught? What weren't you taught?

What are the most important things that executives are not taught on their way up the ladder?

Why do executives fail to go the distance and fall from the ladder?
What lessons in leadership do you reflect upon? Who were your role models?
Aren't many lapses in corporate credibility due to lack of true leadership?

Customer service:
How can customer loyalty be built and nurtured?
How should customers factor into management styles and decisions?

Marketing and Business Development:
What constitutes a good marketplace presence?
What are the elements of an effective marketing program?
How can branding establish a company's point of difference?
What advice would you give in selecting, screening and utilizing consultants?

Motivating employees:
What are a company's biggest challenges in managing people?
How loyal are your present employees? How many employees are drains to the company assets?
How many employees take pride in their work and see themselves as part of the Big Picture?
What are the costs of replacing and training workers?
How many generations are presently in the workforce? How do they differ?
What are the costs of a non-empowered and under-educated workforce?

Building and sustaining quality:
What constitutes quality and excellence?
How might companies best showcase and benchmark their accomplishments?
If problems outweigh accomplishments, how will you turn that tide?
How can business become more ethical?
How might the ethical things that you do be communicated to your stakeholders?

Chapter 5

BEHAVIORS IN THE WORKPLACE,
PROTOCOLS ON THE JOB

C orporate cultures become uneven and ragged because they tolerate uneven and bad behaviors from employees. Often, companies put up with those who were not adequately screened and trained to be part of team cultures.

Most people take their behaviors to work. Some training refines behaviors, tempering them for a corporate culture.

When there is a problem, companies issue boiler-plate statements that they do not tolerate bad behaviors. However, they do not say what they are doing to fix the problems. Often, there is no repercussion for bad behaviors, which get tolerated again. With enough bad behaviors being repeated, they become institutionalized and reshape corporate cultures.

There are four types of behaviors: assertive, aggressive, passive and passive-aggressive.

Workplace problems come from the overall impact that their behaviors have on the team's mission and effectiveness. Dysfunctional behaviors harm the team's ability to deliver to its clients. They damage the cohesion of the team and result in an unnecessary adverse impact on one or more individuals within the team.

Chronic bad behaviors may include rudeness, bullying, passive aggressiveness, lack of awareness and emotional conflicts.

You see the widest differences in people skills at the retail level. Younger people may be shy and have not yet developed the gift of gab. They may appear distant or non-communicative but in fact have not developed communications techniques.

When retail workers make inappropriate comments or appear distracted, they cost businesses their customers. These people need to be trained and mentored, as relationships are the building blocks and life.

Tell them something positive, and they don't know how to respond. Some people give too much information, as if customers really care what kind of day they are having. Some inject opinions into the discussion.

Negative behaviors include aggression, lapses in judgment, negativity, disruptions, borderline personality disorder and anti-social skills.

They may exhibit themselves in the workplace by:

- Being chronically late.
- Playing games on one's phone.
- Interrupting.
- Gossiping about colleagues.
- Skipping meetings.
- Exhibiting poor body language toward others.
- Being critical.
- Hogging credit for other people's work.
- Leaving people out of processes.
- Jumping into something too soon.
- Being distracted during meetings.
- Not responding to emails or phone calls in a timely manner.

Roles Played by Parents

Helicopter parents pay close attention to children's experiences and problems, particularly at educational institutions. Helicopter parents hover and oversee their children constantly.

Lawnmower parents go to whatever lengths necessary to prevent their child from having to face adversity, struggle or failure.

Snowplow parents constantly forces obstacles out of their kids' paths. They have an eye on the success of their child, and anyone or anything that stands in the way has to be removed.

The bulldozer style of parenting ultimately results in a psychologically fragile child, fearful of failure, without learning coping strategies and poor resilience.

These are the results of a New York Times poll regarding behaviors of parents:

- 76% reminded their adult children of deadlines they need to meet, including for schoolwork
- 74% made appointments for them, including doctor's appointments
- 15% of parents with children in college had texted or called them to wake them up, so they didn't sleep through a class or test.
- 8% of parents said they had contacted a college professor or administrator about their child's grades or a problem they were having.
- 11% helped write an essay or school assignment.
- 22% helped them study for a college test.
- 16% helped write all or part of a job or internship application.
- 14% told them which career to pursue.
- 14% helped them get jobs or internships through professional networks.
- 11% of parents with adult children call their child's employer if he or she had an issue at work.
- 12% gave $500+ per month for rent or daily expenses.

The High Cost of Bad Behaviors

Poor communication can result in delayed or failed projects, low morale, missed performance goals and lost sales. The cumulative cost per year due to productivity losses resulting from communication barriers is more than $26,000 per employee. 40% of business productivity is lost to these communications inefficiencies and that the majority of respondents are in customer-facing and decision-making roles. The negative impact on critical business processes, new revenue and customer satisfaction is huge.

Poor listening leads to errors, ineffective decisions, costly mistakes, hurt feelings and a loss of team cohesion. This undercuts trust, weakens communication and reduces profits.

These are the reasons why people don't listen:

- They take a position that they are right, and the other person is wrong.
- They don't take ownership of the problem, and it is your fault.
- They have emotional filters and feel like a victim.
- They are insensitive and selfish.
- They are unaware of how their attitude affects others.
- They are fearful of criticism.
- They are uncomfortable with being given task-oriented instructions and supervision.
- They are frustrated when others do not treat them in as way, they are entitled.
- They set barriers to what other people are thinking.
- They do not want to give you what you want immediately.
- They do not want your help, ideas or supervision.

These are some reasons for poor listening skills:

- Not concentrating.
- Listening too hard.
- Missing the main points and details.
- Jumping to conclusions.
- Getting over-stimulated.
- Tolerating or creating distractions to communication.
- Not caring about what is said.
- Faking attention.
- Interrupting with canned answers.
- Criticizing the speaker.
- Focusing on the speaker's delivery.
- Personal appearance of the speaker.
- Generational and cultural biases.

63% of research survey respondents say they have witnessed behavior at work that was disruptive to culture, productivity and the business itself but didn't report it to management.

The business as usual processes being used to develop and improve interpersonal skills in the workplace isn't working. More time is to be spent on helping employees gain awareness of the impact of poor skills, with the right support to replace those skills with more business enhancing skills.

It is estimated that organizations lose billions of dollars annually in errors, customer dissatisfaction, damaged goods and accidents due to poor decision-making skills, communication, accountability and the use of common-sense skills.

The current success rate for organizational hires is 14%. If further research is put into looking at the total person and truly fitting the person to the job, then the success rate soars to 75%. That involves testing and more sophisticated hiring practices.

Retaining good employees, involving training, motivation and incentives, is yet another matter. According to research conducted by the Ethics Resource Center:

- Employees of organizations steal 10 times more than do shoplifters.
- Employee theft and shoplifting accounting for 15% of the retail cost of merchandise.
- 35% of employees steal from the company.
- 71% of employees are currently looking for another job.
- 28% of those who steal think that they deserve what they take.
- 21% of those who steal think that the boss can afford the losses.
- 56% of employees lie to supervisors.
- 41% of employees falsify records and reports.
- 31% of the workforce abuses substances.

The worst phrases and jargon used in society that should be discouraged in the workplace include:

- Small talk.
- Tired, trite expressions.
- Telling customers what they would do if they did not have to work now.
- Telling customers what they don't like and whom they don't like.
- Wishing that needy customers would go away.
- Running down the competition.
- Telling war stories about past customers.
- Saying inappropriate things to customers and to outside stakeholders.

These communications do NOT belong in the workplace, including on the telephone, in meetings, in interface with customers and in memos, texts and e-mails:

- Internet abbreviations such as OMG, BTW, LOL, etc.
- Street talk that is only recognizable by certain groups.
- Expressions drawn from "flavor of the month" movies or TV shows.
- Ethnic expressions.
- Out-of-date historical terms.
- Off-color jokes.
- Sexist expressions or gestures.
- Talking in multiple languages, designed to exclude others from the conversations.
- Unnecessary texting.
- Poor etiquette.
- Age discrimination.
- Bullying behaviors.
- Emotional, psychological or physical abuse.
- Laughing at other people in the meetings.
- Talking politics in the workplace.
- Talking negatively about others who are not in the room.
- People talking too much in code or slang.
- People talking too technical or micro-niche oriented.
- Knowingly telling lies.
- Generational jargon talk.
- Generational quirks that get institutionalized into employee behavior.

These lessons should be learned from bad behaviors:

- Speaking with brashness has repercussions.
- Some words and expressions cannot be taken back.
- Carefully choose your words, verbal and written.
- People will model behaviors, good and bad.
- Frames of reference matter.
- Policies and procedures should deal with bad behaviors.

Human Communications in the Workplace

Language shapes thoughts. Language is adapted from other influences. Thought patterns grow, often in wrong directions.

These are the seven biggest communication obstacles:

1. Lack of people skills and manners.
2. Use of the wrong facts.
3. Denial or avoidance of the real issues.
4. Non-communication.
5. Saying the wrong things at the wrong times, for the wrong reasons.
6. Failure to pick up subtle clues.
7. Failure to master communication as an art.

These are the seven levels of communicating:

- Sending out messages we wish-need to communicate.
- Sending messages which are intended for the listener.
- Communicating with many people at the same time.
- Eliciting feedback from audiences.
- Two-way communication process.
- Adapting and improving communications with experience.
- Developing communications as a vital tool of business and life.

Here are some current statistics about the magnitude of telephone technology and social media in the workforce:

- 75% of companies have people using their own mobile devices for work. 24% of companies have policies that allow it.
- 49% of companies require network compliance. 85% of employees are not familiar with that fact.
- 93% of employees admit to violating compliance policies. 10,000 new federal and industry regulations associated with compliance have been created in the last five years.
- There has been a 40% growth in global data generated each year.
- In infrastructure, there is a fear of upgrading because some piece of equipment is broken.

- Being a better business than just, a huge technology footprint hopes that the same procedures are not just repeated again.
- The average person spends 24 hours per week on-line, 43% of it on office time.

I offer these pointers for effectively communicating:

- Speak with authority.
- Make the most of face-to-face meetings, rather than through artificial barriers.
- Remember that voice inflection, eye contact and body language are more important than the words you use.
- Charts, graphs and illustrative materials make more impact for your points.
- Don't assume anything. If in doubt about their understanding, ask qualifying questions. Become a better listener.
- Sound the best on the phone that you can.
- Get feedback. Validate that audiences have heard your intended messages.
- Attitude is everything in effective communications.

Chapter 6

HOW THE AUTOMOBILE TRANSFORMED
BUSINESS AND SOCIETY

T
he 20th Century was typified by the automobile and its support industries (notably energy, highways, retail and parts) as the most significant factors in commerce growth and development. In 1921, President Warren G. Harding proclaimed in that "the motor car has become an indispensable instrument in our political, social and industrial life."

Carl Benz invented the first motorcar in 1879. Henry Ford built his first car in 1896 and founded Ford Motor Company in 1901. Ford epitomized the American myth. He was born into a farming family in Michigan, was mechanically proficient as a child and became a machinist. In 1891, he moved to Detroit, as an engineer with the Edison company. Experiments with engines led in 1896 to his first automobile. In 1899, he founded Detroit Automobile Company. In 1903, he founded the Ford Motor Company, introducing the Model N. In 1908, he introduced the popularly priced Model T.

Ford introduced assembly-line production and techniques in 1913, using standardized, interchangeable parts. He trained employees so that each could work as quickly and efficiently as possible. This large-scale manufacturing production model has been adopted in countless other industries, allowing for mass production. In 1915, Ford doubled his workers' pay. In 1941, Ford became the last automaker to unionize. Ford revolutionized production to the assembly line, making cars affordable to enough people outside of the upper class.

Ransom Olds introduced the marketing of cars in 1901, produced to be affordable and convenient to operate. General Motors was founded in 1908 by William Durant, fostering mergers of companies in order to offer cars in all price ranges. GM set the pattern of introducing new models each year. Walter Chrysler was president of American Locomotive Works and then joined GM in 1911, followed by founding his own corporation to make cars in all price ranges.

John Studebaker taught his five sons to make wagons in Ohio. His sons Clement and Henry became blacksmiths in South Bend, IN, in 1852, making metal parts and complete wagons. They built wagons for settlers going westward, the military and fancy carriages. In 1875, brother Jacob started running the carriage factory. Studebaker designed the carriages pulled by the Budweiser Clydesdales in 1900. Next generations of Studebakers joined the company, which began making automobiles in 1902. An assembly line plant was built in Hamilton, Ontario, Canada, in 1941. Studebaker merged with Packard in 1950. In the 1960s, Studebaker diversified by manufacturing appliances, auto parts and missile components.

By 1914, the production of automobiles exceeded that of wagons and carriages for the first time. In 1929, the peak year of the auto boom, more than five million were sold. The industry produced trucks during World War I, and afterward the commercialization of truck production resulted. Bus production followed in the 1920's. Unionization came to the industry in the 1930's.

During World War II, the industry retooled its production processes to include vehicles and machinery for military uses. Turmoil produced opportunities and change, which inspired systems of managing change. At each stage were bursts of innovation.

Affordable energy was essential to the operation of automobiles and later aircraft. Over 40 percent of all energy consumption is by industry. In 1870, coal replaced wood as the primary energy for industrialization. In 1910, petroleum replaced coal as the primary energy source. Leadership in the field of energy meant people of determination and vision, who saw in "black gold" the way of life that we now enjoy. In 1861, the first gusher came in Pennsylvania.

In 1862, John D. Rockefeller went to Ohio to investigate oil as an investment. He bought a refinery. In 1870, he formed Standard Oil of Ohio.

By 1875, he operated large refineries in New York and Pennsylvania. In 1876, 90 percent of the oil business was under his control. At the end of his life, he donated generously to charity, at one time handing out dimes on the street to the less fortunate.

In 1901, Joseph Stephen Cullina went into court in Beaumont and got the right in advance to kill any marauder who might oppose his charge to clean up and quiet down in the skyrocketing boomtown. In 1901, oil was discovered at Spindletop, near Beaumont.

In 1903, William Stamps Farish and Robert E. Blaffer met at a boarding house in Beaumont. They joined forces to form a drilling partnership. The next year, they moved to Houston to concentrate on the nearby Humble field where oil was discovered in 1904. In the early years, they were so short of operating money that they lived in a shack in the fields. By 1908, they had become comfortably established. Harry Wiess knew the vast benefits of energy from the constant addition of knowledge through chemistry, physics and other sciences that are now applied to every product.

In 1911, Farish, Blaffer and Wiess joined forces with Ross Sterling and Walter Fondren in founding the Humble Oil & Refining Company. Humble became one of the giants in the industry through association with Standard Oil Company of New Jersey. Humble Oil became Enco-Esso, later Exxon and now ExxonMobil Corporation.

In 1902, Texaco was founded. In 1916, Gulf Oil was founded. In 1917, Phillips Petroleum was founded. In 1918, Sinclair Oil was founded.

Automobiles changed the economy. Today, 4.25 million people work directly within the automotive industry. Car manufacturing became one of the largest industries in the world and has been the driving force behind growth in the oil and gas industry.

Cars gave people a way to get around quickly, travel for work and visit more places. Until the early 1900s, few people lived more than a few miles from where they grew up. Before cars were invented, moving just a short distance away meant hours of buggy travel on rough roads. Suddenly, people had a new mode of transportation that could get them more places, which meant leisure travel became something folks could afford.

There were population shifts, typified by moves from farms to cities. Demographic changes led to the influx of women in the workforce. Cities experienced economic supremacy. With rapidly increasing affluence, wages were up, and consumer choices were up. All of these factors inspired business innovations and successes.

Development of Retailers and Shopping Centers

Markets were built where people settled into communities. The Galleria Vittorio Emanuel was built in 1878 in Milan, Italy, becoming the prototype for shopping centers. The term "mall" comes from pall-mall, a game with a wooden ball and mallet that was played on a grassy fairway known as a mall.

The railroads cut across the countryside. Suburban developments sprung up and required concentrations of retail marketplaces. With the popularity and economy of auto travel, the shopping centers became destinations. Dusty roads to reach marketplaces were replaced by highways and later freeways, toll roads and connected arteries.

In 1930, there was one automobile for every 4.9 Americans. The first supermarket was founded, an expansion of the corner grocery store. The Great Atlantic and Pacific Tea Company was founded in 1859 to trade in tea, coffee and spices, later evolving into the A&P supermarket chain.

Shopping malls began expanding in the 1920s, moving into the suburbs in the 1950s. In 1950, there were 100 shopping centers in the U.S. The prototype of modern shopping centers was introduced in 1956. Indoor shopping malls started in 1929, and they became climate-controlled by 1960.

Improving the nation's highway system became a government priority in the 1950s. Highway systems led families to newly-built suburbs, followed by retail clusters, specialty shops, local merchants and service providers. Industry groups adopted common practices, standards and service models. The International Council of Shopping Centers was founded in 1957. Construction firms, suppliers and vendors catering to retail facilities grew. Other specialties that accompanied this growth included parking, security, lighting and marketing service companies.

The catalogs of stores like Sears and Montgomery Ward spawned large retail stores, thus anchoring shopping centers and malls.

Richard W. Sears and Alvah C. Roebuck started in 1888 by reselling watches purchased in lots, renamed Sears, Roebuck and Company and began diversifying into non-watch lines. By 1894, their mail-order catalog had grown to 322 pages, including sewing machines, bicycles, sporting goods, automobiles and more. By 1895, the company had $800,000 in sales and a 532-page catalog. In 1906, Sears opened its catalog plant and Sears Merchandise Building Tower in Chicago. In

1933, Sears released its first Christmas catalog. The first retail store opened in 1925, which spawned a national chain. Sears began diversifying, adding Allstate Insurance in 1931 and Homart Development Company in 1959 for the building and leasing of malls. Sears established such major brands as Kenmore, Silvertone, Craftsman, DieHard, Toughskins and Supertone.

Montgomery Ward worked for various dry goods stores. While working for a St. Louis wholesale house, he became acquainted with the situations of farmers who found it difficult to find goods at fair prices. He figured a strategy to acquire goods wholesale and offer by mail at small markups, thus eliminating the expense of running a retail operation. In 1872, he opened a mail-order dry goods business in Chicago, the first one-page catalog offering 30 items. The business and the catalog continued to grow. In 1900, the company relocated to the Ward Tower in Chicago. His fortune was distributed to various charities, notably Northwestern University.

Marshall Field moved to Chicago in 1856 and worked as a traveling salesman and clerk for a wholesale house. He then partnered in and managed other stores, the result being Marshall Field and Company in 1881. It manufactured items and sold them under the company name. By 1895, the store was grossing $40 million per year. He donated to the University of Chicago and the 1893 Chicago Exposition. His descendants continued running the retail chain and owned three Chicago newspapers.

James Cash Penney began working for the Golden Rule chain of stores in the Midwest in 1898. The owners offered Penny a partnership in a store in Wyoming in 1902. He opened two more stores and bought out the owners in 1907. By 1913, there were 34 stores, he incorporated as J.C. Penny Company and moved the headquarters to Salt Lake City, UT. The number of stores reached 1,400 by 1929. Penney was involved in founding the University of Miami and created the James C. Penney Foundation in 1954.

Roland Hussey Macy worked on a whaling ship and in 1843 opened the first dry goods store. The first Macy's was established in Haverhill, MA, in 1851 to serve mill industry workers. In 1858, Macy moved the store to New York City, north of where the other dry goods stores were located. The store expanded into neighboring storefronts, offering more departments. After R.H. Macy died in 1877, ownership passed to family and other partners. In 1902, the flagship store moved to the corner of 34th Street and Broadway, a department store expanded to a full block. The building and the Macy character were in the 1947 movie classic "Miracle on 34th Street." In 1978, the building was added to the roster of National Historic

Landmarks. In 1983, Macy's expanded beyond the New York area, merging in 1994 with Federated Stores and in 2006 acquiring the May Stores.

Adam Gimbel founded a general store in Vincennes, IN, in 1887, moving to Milwaukee, WI. He acquired a second store in Philadelphia, PA, then a third in New York City in 1910. Gimbel's became the leading rival to Macy's. Gimbel's went public in 1922 and bought an upscale chain from Horace Saks, known as Saks Fifth Avenue. The Slinky toy made its debut at Gimbel's, rolling down the escalator. The Gimbel's chain closed in 1986.

In 1960, there were 3,680 shopping centers in the U.S. The golden era of growth was the 1960s and 1970s. The number of shopping centers and malls increased to 22,100 by 1980.

Then came the specialty chains. The first Gap store opened in 1969 in San Francisco, CA. By 2002, Gap Inc. operated 4,100 stores worldwide, including The Gap, Banana Republic and Old Navy.

Debbi Fields opened her first cookie store in 1977 in Palo Alto, CA. By 2002, 715 Mrs. Fields Cookies operated in 12 countries.

Eddie Bauer founded his first shop in Seattle, WA, in 1920 (when he was 21 years old), opening in the back of a hunting and fishing store. He expanded the line and renamed it "Eddie Bauer's Sport Shop." He developed heavy wool garments for outdoorsmen. He received more than 20 patents for clothing and outdoor equipment. In 1945, Bauer offered his first mail-order catalog. His principal business became manufacturing of clothing and catalog sales. In 1971, the company was sold to General Mills, who shifted the focus to casual clothing and expanded to 61 stores. Cross-branding with Ford Motor Company ensued. The Spiegel catalog company purchased Eddie Bauer from General Mills in 1988. Eddie Bauer Home was launched in 1991, selling furniture, décor, linens and tableware.

Sebastian S. Kresge was a salesman whose territory included several of the Woolworth stores. He decided to open his own 5-cent and 10-cent store, in 1897 in Memphis, TN, with a second added in Detroit. In 1912, the S.S. Kresge Corporation was chartered, with 85 stores. In 1962, the chain opened the first Kmart store in Garden City, MI, expanded to department store status. In 1977, S.S. Kresge Corporation changed its name to Kmart Corporation.

Herbert Marcus, his sister Carrie and her husband A.L. Neiman founded a department store with women's clothing in Dallas, TX, Neiman-Marcus, in 1907. The store premiered the first annual fashion show in the U.S. in 1927. Men's clothing was added in 1929. Stanley Marcus joined the store in 1927 and became the CEO in 1950. He was responsible for massive expansion and innovations such as the Distinguished Service in Fashion Award, the first haute couture boutique to introduce weekly fashion shows, the first to host concurrent art exhibitions, the International Fortnight celebrations, his and hers gifts, holiday catalog and more. Stanley Marcus stood as a beacon for women's fashions globally.

Sam Walton became the youngest Eagle Scout in Missouri's history. He worked for J.C. Penny Co. as a management trainee, did military service in World War II and then took over management of a variety store. He established a chain of Ben Franklin stores, having 15 of them by 1962 and the Walton's store in Bentonville, AR. The first Wal-Mart superstore was opened in 1962 in Rogers, AR. When he died in 1992, the chain included 1,960 Wal-Mart and Sam's stores. In 1998, Walton was named by Time Magazine as one of the 100 most influential people of the 20th Century.

John Wanamaker started working as a delivery boy at age 14 and entered the men's clothing business at 18. In 1861, with Nathan Brown, he founded Brown and Wanamaker, which became the leading men's clothier in the U.S. within 10 years. In 1875, he opened a dry goods and clothing business, inviting other merchants to sublet from him. In 1896, he purchased A.T. Stewart in New York and broadened the department store chain. In 1918, Wanamaker's stores piped music to each other, this innovation giving birth to commercial radio.

The food court concept came to malls in 1971. These clusters have provided home for local and chain restaurants, offering a variety of tastes and menus. The food court concept was popularized in malls and then expanded into airports, office buildings, hospitals, core business centers, amusements parks, sports arenas and festival marketplaces.

Shopping centers became community destinations in the 1970s. Promotions included walking events, tutoring programs, school field trips, branch banking, holiday shopping extravaganzas, art shows and fitness facilities. Many centers offer space for non-profit programs to have presence where large numbers of people will visit.

Shopping centers have grown and diversified over several decades. They offer price-point merchandise for all budgets and attract families, youths and all ethnicities. Shopping centers and malls reflect dreams, opportunities and commercial answers for growing populations.

Other retailing concepts spawned by shopping centers include outlet malls, antique stores, dollar stores, retailers located in historical buildings, upscale shopping destinations, branded shops, village concept outdoor malls, technology storefronts, interactive experiences, connecting walkways to retailers and on-line stores.

Drive-in Movie Theatres

The original cinemas were machines in arcades. By 1920, the movies were projected in theatres with auditorium seating, many with the trappings of fine performing arts houses. Most movie theatres were in downtown areas. By the 1930s, movie palaces were built in neighborhood locations.

With the spread of automobiles, people living in outlying areas, in new suburbs and in countryside locales wished venues at which to see films. The first outdoor theatres had rows of chairs, where people could watch the movies on plain white screens.

On June 6, 1933, Richard Hollingshead set up screens and projectors outside his New Jersey home. He developed a ramp system where people could sit in their cars and watch the screen at upward angles. The next drive-in theatres were built in fields, where rows of automobiles could park. Grounds were often not paved.

At auto theatre parks, each car could get a sound box. The concession stands were gathering places. As the drive-ins grew, they added playgrounds for children. Theatres constructed signs, electric-lit displays and added promotional events to draw crowds.

Jack Corgan became an architect of drive-in theatres in the 1940s. Corgan built towers, over-sized screens, landscaping, carousels, art modern, high-definition speakers, fencing, high-quality restaurant facilities and indoor attractions. Attendants helped drivers to jump-start cars, provide gasoline refills, merry-go-rounds and an atmosphere of family fun entertainment.

Elements of weather affected the experience, including heat, rain, wind, ozone, snowfall, ice and sleet. Weather affected maintenance of properties by the owners.

In 1949, Harvey Elliott, drive-in manager said: "The drive-in theatre is no fad. This is a country on wheels. We like to eat on wheels, telephone on wheels and listen to the radio on wheels. Why not see a movie on wheels?"

Profits from the theatres did not come from movie ticket sales, which covered film rental fees. Concession stands grew into restaurants. Car-hop service to cars was initiated at many theatres. One of the expectations of movies was that the intercom would cut into movie sound, with that familiar line: "The snack bar will close in five minutes." For the next 30 minutes or more, further closing announcements would be made.

The serving of pizza at drive-ins in the 1950s began popularizing a food that was heretofore found only at Italian restaurants. It created a demand for pizza that was subsequently served by pizza restaurants and chains.

After World War II, drive-in theatres flourished. In addition to populations of families and children, drive-ins became places for romantic dates. Some were dubbed "passion pits." Scenes in some movies took place in drive-ins, notably *The Blob, Christine, Spies Like Us, Pee Wee's Big Adventure, Polyester, Twister* and *Grease*. At the peak, there were 5,000 drive-ins in 1958.

Movies targeted at drive-in audiences were made. There were the horror and science fiction genres. American International Pictures, Allied Artists, Monogram Pictures and other studios served drive-in audiences. Many of the films achieved cult status, including *Night of the Living Dead, I Was a Teenage Werewolf, The Amazing Colossal Man, High School Confidential, Motorcycle Gang, Monsters From the Ocean Floor, Sorority Girl, Little Shop of Horrors, Poor White Trash, It Conquered the World, Texas Chainsaw Massacre, Attack of the Killer Tomatoes* and the Vincent Price horror movies.

There were the teen beach films starring Annette Funicello and Frankie Avalon. Disc jockey, Alan Freed, produced a string of rock n' roll musicals starring 1950s recording stars. Many 1960s rock and pop stars had films, including *Catch Us If You Can, Because They're Young, Ferry Cross the Mersey, Gidget, The Love-Ins, Get Yourself a College Girl, Ski Party, How to Stuff a Wild Bikini, Sing, Boy, Sing, Fastest Guitar Alive, Surf Party, Hold On, Love in a Goldfish Bowl* and the Elvis Presley musical movies.

The biggest competition to drive-in movies came from suburban second-run houses and television, which aired old movies. Hollywood studios began making flashier and exotic movies to give audiences what they could not get on TV. These films made their way to drive-ins in the 1960s and 1970s.

The next challenge to market share by the drive-ins came in 1978 with the advent of home videotape machines. The video industry was served by stores that rented and sold tapes of films for home viewing.

By the 1970s and 1980s, drive-ins were sitting on valuable real estate. They closed, and home VCR entertainment replaced them. Theatre owners evolved into real estate business people, selling the land and serving as landlords to the shopping malls that occupied the spaces. Drive-in movie theatres are important pieces in American nostalgia.

Drive-in Restaurants

The automobile took people to experience dining in new and unique settings. As streets and highways moved out from city and town centers, new business meccas emerged. As Americans became acclimated to traveling for work and recreation, the roadsides began accommodating the needs of mobile travelers.

Along the roadsides, retail centers began to grow. Restaurants sprung up, affording menu items that not readily available at home. People wanted to drive and explore new sights.

Remote restaurants and retail looked different from downtown storefronts. Many looked like curbside attractions and others like country restaurant destinations. Curb service had begun at a Memphis drugstore in 1905.

In 1920, there were eight million automobiles on American roads, a 300% increase from 1915. In 1921, J.G. Kirby and R.W. Jackson created the Pig Stands Company, with their first drive-in restaurant on the Dallas-Fort Worth highway.

In 1921, three Californians opened Montgomery's Country Inn in Los Angeles. The location was inviting, and servers appeared throughout the property, dressed in snappy uniforms. The structure looked like a Hollywood fantasy, and there was an aura of showmanship to serving food and entertaining the customers. By 1930, the name changed to Tam O'Shanter Inn, with the roadhouse concept growing along highways. This was one of Walt Disney's favorite lunch spots. Other Hollywood figures dined there, including Mary Pickford, Tom Mix and Gloria Swanson.

In 1923, Roy Allan and Frank Wright founded A&W Root Beer in California, expanding to the east coast. In 1927, J. Willard Marriott opened a competing root beer stand in Washington, D.C., with the chain evolving into hotels, institutional catering and food services.

In the 1930s, drive-in restaurants were circular, with high neon signs and grandiose architecture. One such drive-in was dramatized in the 1973 movie *American Graffiti*, with scenes filmed at Mel's Restaurant in San Francisco, CA. That name alone inspired the moniker Mel's Diner in *Happy Days*, the TV series inspired by *American Graffiti*. In the 1940s, the diners expanded into roadhouses, as dramatized in the 1945 film *Mildred Pierce*, with scenes filmed at Henry's Restaurant in Glendale, CA.

The car hops were costumed, had standards of behavior and offered showmanship. Carhops had their own slang jargon: "stretch" for coke, "draw" for coffee, "mammy" for malted milk, "Hollywood Bowl" for fruit salad, "airedale" for hot dog, "jaw breaker" for steak sandwich, "hug one" for orange juice, "bowl of red" for chili and beans, "treat" for grilled ham and cheese sandwich, "D.P." to cut something in half, "Sally Rand" for chicken salad sandwich, "mean egg" for deviled egg sandwich, "churn" for buttermilk, "school boy" for peanut butter and jelly sandwich and "creep" for draught beer.

Harland Sanders began selling fried chicken in 1930 at his roadside restaurant in Corbin, KY, the location being a former Shell filling station. In 1936, he was bestowed the title of Kentucky Colonel by Governor Ruby Laffoon. The original recipe was finalized in 1940. Sanders was re-commissioned a colonel in 1950 and began to dress the part.

Sanders opened his first franchise in 1952 in South Salt Lake, Utah. Franchisee Pete Harman commissioned the renaming of the company to Kentucky Fried Chicken and introduced the bucket in 1957. This author met Sanders when he opened his fourth franchise in 1959 in Austin, Texas. The KFC chain grew, challenging the dominance of hamburgers in the fast-food industry. Sanders sold the company in 1964 but remained a spokesperson for the company until his death in 1979. The company was acquired in 1988 by PepsiCo.

In 1934, Doug Prince opened Prince's Hamburgers in Houston, TX, a series of drive-in restaurants, replete with colorfully costumed carhops. For 45 years, Prince's was a popular hangout for the youth clientele. One by one, the restaurants closed, as fast-food chains began dominating the burger market. Prince's sons shifted their focus to running corporate dining rooms. In the 1990s, due to popular demand, Prince's Hamburgers returned to business in the format of 1950s nostalgic diners.

Part of the reason for the demise of drive-in restaurants in the 1950s and 60s is attributed to emerging fast food chains. Teenagers discovered cars and sought out venues for themselves apart from the family dining restaurants. Diners in the suburbs began looking differently and broadening their menu items. The emergence of theme restaurants concentrating on Mexican food, pizza, Asian food and more tended to splinter the market that full-service diners used to dominate.

Fast Food Chains and Restaurant Legends

The fast food industry developed after World War II. Soldiers came home, and the Baby Boom resulted. Low-cost loans enabled many to buy homes in the suburbs. This stimulated the building of highway systems and freeways. On those roadways were shopping centers, the first retail outstretch since the strongholds of downtown business districts. This became a boon to the automobile and energy industries, with more cars on the roads, driving longer distances. To cater to all those cars and families, the roads became dotted with restaurants, featuring take-out items.

Restaurants spread to the roadways. Then followed the fast food chains. McDonald's began as a barbecue shop in 1940 in San Bernardino, California. In 1948, it was reorganized by brothers Richard and Maurice McDonald as a hamburger restaurant, featuring the "Speedee Service System." In 1955, Ray Kroc opened the ninth McDonald's franchise in Des Plaines, Illinois, and purchased the McDonald brothers' equity, growing the chain worldwide.

Whataburger was founded in Corpus Christi, Texas, in 1950 by Harmon Dobson and Paul Burton. Burger King began in 1953 in Jacksonville, Florida, as Insta-Burger King. The next year, it was taken over by Miami Franchisees David Edgerton and James McLamore, renaming it Burger King. White Castle was founded in 1921 in Wichita, Kansas, by Billy Ingram and Walter Anderson, known for small square burgers, also known as sliders. Jack in the Box was founded in 1951 in San Diego, California, by Robert O. Peterson.

Sonic Drive-In was founded in 1953 in Shawnee, Oklahoma by Troy Smith. Burger Chef was founded in 1954 in Indianapolis, Indiana, by Frank and Donald Thomas. Burger Chef was purchased in 1982 by the company that operates Hardee's, converting all store names to Hardee's. Steak 'N Shake was founded in 1934 in Normal, Illinois, by Gus Belt. Carl's Jr. was founded in 1941 in Delray Beach, Florida, by Carl Karcher. Wendy's was founded in 1969 in Columbus, Ohio, by Dave Thomas and named after his daughter.

The kids' meal debuted in 1973 at Burger Chef, known as the Funmeal. McDonald's added the Happy Meal to its menu in 1978. Other fast-food restaurant chains followed suit. Toys were added to the combo, in order to market children's meals. The chains today are using children's meals to influence healthier eating choices.

Regional restaurants began copying the fast food chains. The 1960s and 1970s saw massive new entries into franchising. The 1980s and 1990s brought still more food concepts, as people were now consuming most of the meals on the go.

Music in Automobiles

The first music in automobiles came from songs people could sing along to, glancing at sheet music. Hit tunes about cars in the 1905-1925 era included: *In My Merry Oldsmobile, I'm Going to Park Myself in Your Arms, Take Me Out in Your Buick, The Long Way Home* and *I'm Wild About Horns.*

The first car radio was introduced in 1904. By 1920, the vacuum tube was perfected to the point that radio receivers could be viably placed in automobiles. The first car radios were expensive (up to $500). By the late 1930s, push button radios were a standard feature. By the late 1940s, there were millions of AM car radios in use, allowing drivers to hear music, news, sports and dramatic radio programming along their commutes.

The first FM radio receiver was introduced to automobiles in 1953. Chrysler Corporation sought to discontinue car radios as being too expensive and in 1956 introduced an alternative, a 45RPM record player that was housed in the glove compartment. In 1957, lower-cost radios were installed, with power being a hybrid of transistors and low-voltage vacuum tubes. In 1963, a tubeless solid-state radio was introduced. Stereo speakers were introduced for cars in 1960.

Philips introduced the audio cassette in 1964, and a dashboard player with radio and cassette player was introduced in 1968. In 1966, Ford and Motorola jointly introduced the 8-track tape, affording a better-quality sound and noise reduction.

In 1984, Pioneer introduced the first compact disc, which compressed music onto thin discs, with incredible sound. CDs began appearing in cars in 1987, and multi-disc changers for home use revolutionized the consumption of music. As CDs appeared in cars, so too did DVDs, where movies and cartoons could be shown to family members in the back of vans and SUVs.

From 2010 forward, musical media adapted for automobile use included satellite radio, Bluetooth, internet radio, USB, iPod and entertainment centers in vehicles.

The recording industry adapted its products to reflect improving technology and nodding to the importance of automobiles as growing consumption of music. By the late 1950s, heavier base lines and stronger instrumentation gave the records a fuller sound on car radios. Berry Gordy's Motown sound was optimized when heard on car radios. So was Phil Spector's Wall of Sound, and he referred to his thunderous production as "little symphonies for the kids." Same for 1970s rock, which sounded ideal via 8-track tapes and boom boxes.

The Automobile Has Made Possible So Much More

Other automobile compatible industries include auto parts, repair shops, oil and lubrication, service stations, auto clubs and insurance.

The car spawned the food take-out and delivery phenomena. Car phones had their impact by allowing the mobile phone industry to grow. Car related inventions have inspired industries to produce cruise-control, cup holders, tinted windshields, catalytic converters, heated seats, climate control systems, safety features, sunroofs, convertible seats, emissions controls and electric vehicles.

The customization of cars and trucks created industries producing designer interiors, stretch limousines, recreational vehicles, mobile homes and children's cars.

Industries affected by population shifts have included motor transport services, accessories for moving, storage units and transportation networks.

Warren Avis founded a rental car company in Ypsilanti, MI, in 1948. Avis became the second largest rental car company in the U.S. by 1956, inspiring the advertising slogan, "When you're number two, you try harder." It also operates Budget Car Rental, Zipcar and other companies.

John D. Hertz began his career as a reporter for a newspaper in Chicago. In 1904, he took a job selling cars, although he could not drive. He saw a solution for the inventory of trade-in cars, as a taxicab company. He founded the Yellow Cab Company in Chicago in 1915, followed by a cab manufacturing company in 1920. He acquired a rental car business in 1924, renaming it the Hertz Drive-Ur-Self Corporation. In 1933, Hertz bought an interest in the Lehman Brothers investment bank. The Hertz Corporation went public in 1953.

Perry Brink founded an armored transportation service in Chicago, IL, in 1859, to guard money and valuables while in transit. Security services were added, for offices and homes, as well as logistics services. Brink's is headquartered in Richmond, VA, and has 650 branch offices in 150 countries.

Charles Goodyear ran a retail store, selling hardware and farm implements. In 1830, the India rubber industry came into being. Goodyear sought to manufacture rubber products of superior quality. About 1838, he acquired a patent for a process where sulfur could eliminate the stickiness of rubber. By 1844, he perfected the vulcanization process. Goodyear exhibited rubber goods at expositions in London and Paris in the 1850's. After Goodyear's death, the rubber industry grew and prospered.

Entertainment venues made possible by cars, urban sprawl and populations on the move included miniature golf courses, bowling alleys, game parlors, art workshops, workout facilities, sporting venues, water attractions and theme parks.

Other phenomena created and affected by the automobile include hotel chains, toll roads, luggage, logistics and delivery services, greater access to healthcare, interstate highway system, public transportation, riding lawnmowers, water vehicles, farm and ranch equipment and the transportation of goods. The automobile sector accounts for 10% of the jobs in America.

The automobile's first era of growth had one car per family. It evolved to one per person. Cars are a symbol of personal growth, independence and attitude.

Popularization of automobiles opened up new possibilities, industries, challenges and opportunities. They influence each part of the economy and the lives of consumers.

Assembly line production techniques created for cars have been adapted to other industries. Cars brought flexible work schedules, relaxation time, family fun and business travel.

Cars represent individual freedom, mobility and independence. Pursuing quality of life is more pleasurable, and we see lots of sights, locales and people. Automobiles are inspirational forces.

Operated by Funtime Drive-In Theatres, Incorporated

Chapter 7

PLANTING AND NURTURING
GROWTH STRATEGIES

Moving Forward, Addressing Changes

Every organization and community in America is presently at a crossroads. Two current options exist. Business can be seen and known as a dynamic community that addresses its problems and moves forward in a heroic fashion as a role model to the rest of the world. Or, the organization can bury its head in the sand and hope media attention dies down, becoming a generic tagline for troubled communities.

Preparing for growth is an ongoing process accomplished through a connected series of strategies and actions that will position any organization to weather the forces of change and thrive in new market environments. The process of evaluation, planning, tactical actions and benchmarking takes striving for growth out of the esoteric and into routine practice.

Rolling plans allow for revisions and adjustments. The creation of its components becomes a continuous exercise. The effect of changed circumstances, heightened demands and supply conditions can be incorporated into the plan.

In fixed plans, annual reviews are made, but they are getting information regarding the progress of the economy. In rolling plans, the yearly reviews serve as the basis for the revised new plan every year. The uncertainty will evaporate because of the long-term investment decision of the company and its commitment of resources toward the plan.

First comes a re-thinking of the overall business, its growth strategies, its purpose, its plans for the future, its mission and its evolving corporate culture. This parallels the whole look of The Business Tree and how the strategies will be nurtured through its branches, limbs, trunk and roots.

Most trees (analogous to organizations) limp along because of their own unhealthy approach to life. They may not have been properly nurtured from the inception. Some were not meant to live long. Some were conceived for the wrong reasons. As a result, pruning and watering rarely ever occur. Preventive maintenance is seen either as a luxury or a threat to the status quo. They try to live and breathe just as other trees do.

Some trees are damaged by incidents not of their own making but from which their health will be tested as to their ability to rebound. These include hurricanes, tornadoes, flooding or drought (analogous to economic downturns). Normally recurring damages include heavy rainfall and snowfall. Other forces causing damage can include activity disruption on the lot (analogous to business forces outside their perimeters).

Some business trees are the result of overgrown root systems from other trees (spin-offs from other companies). There may be poison or disease in the soil (conditions such as lack of appropriate regulations and sanctions). Their livelihood could be threatened by the lack of deed restrictions or other neighborhood protection (failure to groom stakeholders and friends who could support the company).

Trees suffer neglect by professionals whom the owners contracted to nourish. They may be damaged because of treatments with the wrong equipment or supplies.

Harmful environmental factors include fads in site maintenance that favor sparseness as a means of cost containment and a failure by the property owner to take ownership for any of these eventualities. This is analogous to consultants and staff members charged with upkeep of the company.

Planning on the front end is the answer to the question of organizational survival. Refusing to do so, companies instead apply surgery only when they have to. Damages are compounded when surgery is applied at the wrong time, too little too late, applied to the wrong branches or by the wrong experts-consultants.

To benefit from change and to grow, each organization must take actions to move forward. Understand where you've been and where you might go. Research the trends. Spot some opportunities. Predict and benefit from cycles in business.

Planting seeds in your Business Tree means heeding messages from the marketplace, revealing the changing conditions, new global business imperatives and partnering concepts. With pruning and nurturing come the recognition of new stakeholders and other changes outside of the organization's influence that may profoundly affect them. Growth trees come from putting more focus upon running a successful organization.

Developing Business Growth Strategies

A growth plan or strategic plan is a must for any organization that intends to survive and thrive in today's rapidly changing business environment. Look at the whole, then at the parts as they relate to the whole, then at the whole again. Plan to grow and grow by the plan.

Next is a profile of the core business, the ancillary business and the outcomes possible by expanding business unit potential. It includes the management structure, operational facets, facilities, staff resources, timelines, organizational chart and more.

If one believes the other books and consultants selling growth strategies, the key to growth lies within their specialty niche, whether it be human resources organization, training, technology, sales, marketing, coaching, or financial planning. This is simply not true. Instead, I contend that business owners and principals must analyze all aspects of the operation and use them together to promote a coherent vision for the organization.

I have conducted numerous audits of companies that followed expensive branding programs sold by marketing consultants with the failure to deliver promised benefits. One involved a rollup of home service provider companies. They launched an expensive branding campaign to define their teams as appearing in a timely manner to get the gigs, selling immediacy as the benefit to calling them.

Focus groups showed that disgruntled customers felt that the rollups lacked the localized integrity of the predecessor companies. Yes, the new teams were on time to get the engagements but failed to do the follow-through in a timely manner. Thus, the marketing messages did not reflect the realities of company service.

I visited with commercial contractors in their quest to enter the home services market. We studied the pros and cons of small localized "mom and pop" contractors, as well as the services rendered by high-volume sales-oriented rollup companies.

The strategy emerged as a recommitment by commercial contractors that, in order to get the big contracts, they had to be "best in class." Because they were regulated and documentation oriented, they would bring those same high standards to the work they did for homes and families as was expected of them in the commercial arena.

This recommitment to quality drove their work product, their customer service and their business philosophies. As a result, their marketing messages, and the levels of customer satisfaction, retention and referrals underscored their strategy. Many commercial contractors were then able to parlay their success rates in residential work as further assurance to corporate jobs of their attentiveness to service and quality.

One of the biggest growth areas is the rollup into extended service companies. Garden centers and home improvement chains are nurturing preferred provider lists for landscapers, installers, etc. I am advocating more companies that aggressively seek the best providers and market their services as a holistic company with a high profile.

Another of the biggest growth industries, I predict, will be marketplace websites who become online marketers of products, services and processes not readily available to mass customer bases. With the success of eBay and Amazon.com, a host of niche-oriented websites emerged. In most cases, a programmer started a company, picked a cause and got experts in that niche to provide the resources for a successful web-based company. Etsy, a website to sell handmade clothing goods, does more than $100 million in annual sales.

I think there are still other marketplace type websites yet to be created. The ultimate clearinghouse for business professional services has yet to be created. In 1998, I came up with a concept, and it has yet to be initiated by some enterprising entrepreneur.

Distinguishing your company from the pack always involves developing strategy first, with marketing as a sub-set that reflects the company's abilities to deliver the goods, put customers first and reap referrals. Branding is a sub-set of marketing, which is driven and overseen by business strategy.

Planned, orderly growth for companies means generating constant, reliable ideas and creative approaches for management. It means understanding and adapting to external influences that profoundly affect the climate in which companies do business.

A farmer's cooperative in the Midwest dairy industry noticed an erosion of their market share. Concerned over successful advertising campaigns by California and other states to carve market sectors for their dairy industry, this cooperative wrongly thought it was the job of government to get their business back. My observation was that such an impractical position would not serve to create a re-emerging business climate. Instead, the cooperative was advised to research other areas of the world where their products could find fame. They wisely decided to enter previously under-served markets, utilizing e-commerce. The resulting marketing of services by this pro-active strategy was very successful.

Sadly, some executives and their companies eschew planned, orderly growth and choose to take other paths. In 1984, I was asked by a major corporate CEO to meet with and analyze the capabilities of a young emerging business executive named Ken Lay. During the session, Mr. Lay asked me, "How can I buy instant credibility?" I replied, "You earn it the old-fashioned way. If one persists in taking short cuts and cutting ethical corners, it will catch up with you. I strongly advise you not to go down that road and take it slow and steady." Mr. Lay said that he understood and respected my position but did not take my advice.

With chagrin, I watched Enron's antics and predicted the company's downfall as far back as 1990, though its scandals and fall from grace did not surface until the fall of 2001. Thereafter, I wrote a dossier on the danger signs that Enron had displayed along the way. It included entering businesses beyond the core, taking unfair advantage of the supply chain and incorrect community posturing.

After each round of corporate scandals, business and public officials always proclaimed, "There will be a time to go back and review what happened. That time is not now." I kept retorting, "If not now, when?" In my speeches and corporate retreats, I always reviewed the lessons that business should have learned from each wave of scandal and economic decline.

The fact that business persists in burying its head in the sand, denying the ethical lessons to be learned and continuing to seek easy buttons explains why new waves of business crises keep occurring.

I have steered full-scope planning processes for hundreds of companies and have conducted independent audits of previous plans and why they failed. Generally, I found them mired in trite phrases lifted out of pop culture or created as rationales for slanted, limited points of view.

It is time to reflect and widen the focus upon where businesses live, how they operate and where they are headed.

Imperatives for the New Order of Business

It is crucial for those who wish to survive to know and comprehend the business they are really in. Prioritize the actual reasons why you provide services, customers you seek and the external influences affecting your ability to do business. Where all three intersect constitutes the growth strategy.

Broaden the scope of your products and services by redefining the core business. Find new and creative ways to work with companies other than your own. Collaborations, partnering and joint venturing enable the major business emphasis for economic survival and future growth.

Focus as much as you can upon customer service. Dispel the widely held expectations of poor customer service. Building relationships is paramount to adding, holding and getting referrals for further business. Research shows that retaining 2% of customers from deflecting has a larger impact on your company's bottom line than cutting 10% out of operating expenses.

Plans do not work unless they consider input and practicalities from those who will carry them out. Know the people involved and develop their leadership abilities. Plans must have commitment and ownership.

Markets will always seek new and more profitable customer bases. Planning must prepare for crises, profit from change and benchmark the progress. "More of the same" is not a growth strategy. A company cannot solely focus inward. Understand forces outside your company that can drastically alter plans and adapt strategies accordingly.

Evaluate the things that your company really can accomplish. Overcome the "nothing works" cynicism via partnerships and long-range problem solving. It requires more than traditional or short-term measures. He who upsets something should know how to rearrange it. Anyone can poke holes at organizations. The valuable ones know the processes of pro-active change, implementation and benchmarking the achievements.

Take a holistic approach toward individual and corporate development. Band aid surgery only perpetuates problems. Focus upon substance, rather than "flash and sizzle." Success is incrementally attained, and then the yardstick is pushed progressively higher.

Vision is an organization's way. Corporate culture is the methodology by which each organization can successfully accomplish its vision.

For companies to succeed long-term, the visioning process begins with forethought, continues with research and culminates in a strategic plan, including mission, core values, goals, objectives (per each key results area), tactics to address and accomplish, timelines and benchmarking criteria.

Corporate visioning goes beyond the strategic plan. It sculpts how the organization will progress, its character and spirit, participation of its people and steps that will carry the organization to the next tiers of desired achievement, involvement and quality. Companies spend six times more each year in performing band aid surgery on ailing structures. The investment in planning and visioning will reduce the opportunity costs and preclude the need for so much unnecessary fixing of pieces of the problems.

The level of achievement by a company is commensurate to the level and quality of its vision, goals and tactics. The higher is the company's integrity and character, the higher its people must aspire.

Any company or organization must look forward in order to survive and succeed. The skill with which one analyzes plans and crafts their future makes the difference between the company merely surviving and moving forward in a growth mode.

Growth strategies are only successful when they come out of the development stage and into the weekly practice of business. There are no shortcuts.

Chapter 8

STRATEGIC PLANNING

Nurturing Growth Oriented Organizations

Businesses do not start each day by focusing upon all of their dynamics in equal percentages. They usually do not get that far. It is much too easy to get bogged down with minutia. This book and my advising activities are predicated upon educating organizations on the pitfalls of narrow focus and enlightening them on the rewards of widening the view.

Will every business ever operate completely wide-scope focused? No, because vested interests and human nature want to keep attention upon the small pieces. Those organizations with the wider horizons and the most creative mosaic of the small pieces tend to stand out as the biggest successes.

People and companies make decisions based upon partial business models and the wrong information all the time. There is no reason why they cannot make new decisions based upon a widened scope of business, a fresh set of eyes and the desire to acquire new information.

The successful organization develops and champions the tools for change. The quest is to manage change, rather than to fall victim of it. This chapter includes organizational cycles and what full-scope planning could encompass, per each branch on The Business Tree. These guidelines are offered for the process of growth-oriented planning.

A content outline for a strategic plan, with major headings, is included. This chapter discusses levels of planning that may be utilized by organizations and the basics of company growth realities that must be reflected in the planning process.

Every business, corporation, entrepreneurship, professional association and non-profit organization goes through cycles in its lifetime. To assume that definitive cycles do not occur is to bury one's head in the sand. To predict and predate the cycles means greater success, earlier than fate would have it.

At any point, each organization is in a different phase from others in their industry. The astute organization assesses the status of each program and orients its team members to meet constant change and fluctuation. Phases in the life cycle of every organization include:

1. **Conception.** A great idea is born, and everyone is off and running.
2. **Birth.** The decision is made to form a company to take that idea to fruition.
3. **Childhood.** The organization starts to swell, and its people learn the ropes.
4. **Youth.** Through trial and error, a slow, steady growth occurs.
5. **Maturity.** The organization reaches its stride.
6. **Stagnation.** The bureaucratic mindset has taken over. Running an entity is more important than remaining consistent to the company vision which may have never existed or been developed.
7. **Decline.** Losses abound in terms of people, processes, market share and enthusiasm. This is a signal to take actions to rejuvenate the enthusiasm and, hopefully, to launch a new growth curve in the company's next era.
8. **Death.** There simply is no use for the dead organization any longer. It has played out, outlived its usefulness and cannot come back in some other business capacity.

In business, position number eight is not an option, and strategic planning should not wait until position seven (decline) before embarking upon the process. The best time to regularly implement strategic planning programs is at every stage, numbers one through five. If your company develops strategies continually, then stagnation will rarely ever occur, and the organization will avoid going into a decline.

Guidelines for Planning the Company's Future

Strategic planning is not something that happens once and for all. Leadership should examine their organization's strategy and initiate and periodically re-initiate the process when any of the following conditions exist:

1. There seems to be a need to change the direction of the organization.
2. There is a need to step up growth and improve profitability.
3. There is a need to develop better information to help management make better decisions.
4. Management is concerned that resources are not concentrated on important things.
5. Management expresses a need for better internal coordination of company activities.
6. The environment in which the organization competes is rapidly changing.
7. There is a sense that company operations are out of control.
8. Management of the organization seems tired or complacent.
9. Management is cautious and uncertain about the company's future.
10. Individual managers are more concerned about their own areas than for the overall health of the organization.

Strategic planning fulfills a variety of practical and useful purposes. It constitutes disciplined thinking about the organization, its environment and its future. It facilitates the identification of conflicts in perspective. It provides the reinforcement of team building and cohesion. It is a vehicle for monitoring organizational progress.

Strategic planning is a road map for company growth and progress. In order to be an effective process, the plan must be measurable, motivating, realistic, holistic and consistent with the culture of the organization. Since most organizations do not have corporate cultures, this process tends to evolve one or change a culture that has evolved by default.

Every strategic plan should draw upon the organization's history. Depending upon the nature of the company, it should be 2-5 years in duration, with revisions annually. Realistic plans must contain attainable goals that can be measured for success. The writing of the plan should involve as many people in the organization as possible, representing each branch of the tree.

Many events and circumstances cause an organization to realize that a comprehensive look at its future is essential to avoid past pitfalls. At this crossroads, seven strategic questions must be asked of the organization:

1. Do you have financial projections for the next year in writing?
2. Do you have goals for the next year in writing?
3. Are the long-range strategic planning and budgeting processes integrated?
4. Are planning activities consolidated into a written organizational plan?
5. Do you have a written analysis of organizational strengths and weaknesses?
6. Do detailed action plans support each major strategy?
7. Do you have a detailed, written analysis of your market area?

Differentiation should be made of the different kinds of planning processes that businesses utilize. Many refer to one when they are thinking of or actually needing another. Though none of these can substitute for a strategic plan, each is a component of the larger, more holistic future projection process.

A business plan is a front-end document, enough to get initial financing. An operational plan addresses facilities, policies and procedures. Sales and marketing plans address business development.

If one believes vendors and niche consultants, the definition of growth strategies are what their specialty is. It may be human resources organization, training, technology, health and wellness, sales, marketing, advertising, public relations, core business or life coaching. Few of those consultants have written full-scope strategic plans and do not really comprehend what the visioning process actually is.

Steps in the Strategic Planning Process

An effective strategic plan may be developed in a couple of months for small organizations. For mid-size companies, it takes three or four months because performance reviews of programs must be accomplished, and further time is necessary for studies of trends and marketplaces.

Large corporations devote nine months to the process because it entails holding many meetings. The planning process becomes a "campaign" in the organization, with status updates, receptions to call attention to progress and celebrations of accomplishments. It is a long process but seeks to build cohesion in oversized organizations, attempting to amass buy-in at each step along the way.

In each case, assemble a team of thought leaders. Ask each to write down their ideas and set an agenda to keep the process on-track and on-time.

Although every strategic planning process is uniquely designed to fit the specific needs of a particular organization, every successful model includes most of these steps.

Vision: A clear and realistic identification of the organization's vision and mission is the first step of any strategic planning process. The vision sets out the reasons for organization's existence and the ideal state that it aims to achieve.

Most companies need to review their original vision. By recalling the wider scope thinking that created the company, then this new strategic planning process is consistent with original intentions, with newer processes and further benchmarks added.

Mission: The mission identifies major goals and performance objectives. Both are defined within the framework of the organizations philosophy and are used as a context for development and evaluation of intended and emergent strategies.

I cannot overemphasize the importance of a clear vision and mission. None of the subsequent steps will matter if the organization is not certain where it is headed.

The mission statement is usually the last element to be updated, after other aspects of the plan unfold. It can be grand, but it cannot be pompous. It must be pertinent and achievable.

Goals: Effectiveness is defined as the increase in value of people and their activities as resources. Because standards are spelled out, one knows what is expected. The main reason why people do not perform is that they do not know what is expected of them. Through goal setting and achievement, one becomes actualized. With goals, one can be a winner. Without goals, one merely averts-survives the latest crisis.

Objectives: Use indicators and indices wherever they can be used. Use common indicators where categories are similar and use special indicators for special jobs. Let your people participate in devising the indicators. Make all indicators meaningful and retest them periodically. Use past results as only one indicator for the future. Have a reason for setting all indicators in place. Indicators are not ends in themselves, only a means of getting where the organization needs to go. Indicators must promote actions.

Objectives under one's own responsibility helps one to identify with the objectives of the larger organization of which he-she is a part. A sense of belonging is enhanced.

Achieving goals which one set and to which one commits enhances a person's sense of adequacy. People who set and are striving to achieve goals together have a sense of belonging, a major motivator for humanity.

Tactics: This is the section of the strategic plan where the action really is. Having broad vision and lofty goals is the wider-scope perspective. Then, each objective must be measured to each goal. Objectives must then be delineated by tactics. Put simply, tactics spell out who is responsible for what activities, on what timelines and according to which prerequisites. Thereafter, all benchmarks of success will be judged against specific tactics and how they fit into goals and objectives.

Environmental Scan: Once the vision and mission are clearly identified, the organization must analyze its external and internal environment. The environmental scan analyzes information about the organization's external environment (economic, social, demographic, political, legal, technological, and international factors), the industry and internal organizational factors.

SWOT Analysis: SWOT is Strengths, Weaknesses, Opportunities and Threats. This is a comprehensive look at the organization's own situation. It candidly addresses the real and perceived issues. Usually, as the process moves forward, companies are relieved to see that concepts they may have felt were problematic are actually opportunities in disguise. They see that the strengths and opportunities far outweigh the weaknesses. Armed with these insights, the strategic plan becomes more specific in addressing circumstances. It also addresses problems of marketplaces in which the company must participate.

Gap Analysis: Organizations evaluate the difference between their current position and desired future through gap analysis. As a result, an organization can develop specific strategies and allocate resources to close the gap and achieve desired new objectives.

Benchmarking: Measuring and comparing the organization's operations, practices and performance against others is useful for identifying the "best" practices. Through an ongoing systematic benchmarking process, organizations find a reference point for setting their own goals and targets.

These are realities of a healthy benchmarking mentality:

- Some facets of the company will be proven to be working well. Others inevitably will have exhibited room for improvement.
- Successfully benchmarked companies cannot become defensive.
- The goal is to help the organization improve overall.
- If one's benchmarking partners are chosen carefully, they will out-perform the overall organization.
- It is a sign of strength to admit shortcomings and be the hero in bolstering certain units. The best benchmarked departments are eager to learn from others.
- Benchmarked companies take pride in adapting the processes so that they will work better. Thus, they don't have to reinvent what somebody did elsewhere. They adapt, rather than adopt.

The most common benchmarking mistakes are that internal processes are unexamined, that site visits "feel good" but do not elicit substantive data or ideas and that questions and goals are vague. The effort is too broad or has too many parameters. The focus is general and not upon actual processes. The team is not fully committed to the effort. Homework and/or advanced research is not assigned and conducted, and the wrong subjects for benchmarking are selected. Other mistakes include failing to look outside its own organization and industry and where no follow-up action is taken.

Strategic Issues. The organization determines its strategic issues based upon and consistent with its vision and mission, within the framework of environmental and other analyses. Strategic issues are the fundamental issues the organization has to address to achieve its mission and move towards its desired future.

Strategic Programming. It is necessary to address strategic issues and develop deliberate strategies for achieving their mission. Organizations set strategic goals, action plans and tactics during the strategic programming stage. Strategic goals are the milestones the organization aims to achieve which evolve from the strategic issues. The goals are specific, measurable, agreed upon, realistic and time/cost bound. Action plans define how the organization gets to where it needs to go, and the steps required to reach strategic goals. Tactics are specific actions used to achieve strategic goals and implement strategic plans.

Emergent Strategies. Unpredicted and unintended events frequently occur which differ from the organization's intended strategies, and it must respond.

Done in a vacuum, without top-down support:

One person writes it for the unit-company and presents.	18%
CEO creates it and pressures executives and staff to support.	23%
Internal team devises the plan and presents for approval.	27%
Non-qualified advisor writes (perhaps as part of an audit).	29%
Qualified external advisor writes the plan, and executives later adopt.	53%
Combination of team with advisor develop the plan.	64%

Done with full top-down support and management encouragement:

One person writes it for the unit-company and presents for action to be taken.	31%
CEO creates it and pressures executives and staff to support.	39%
Non-qualified advisor writes (perhaps as part of an audit).	47%
Internal team devises the plan and presents for approval.	58%
Qualified external advisor writes the plan, and executives later adopt.	53%
Combination of the planning team with qualified advisor develop the plan.	85%
Combined with Corporate Visioning and departmental plans.	94%

Dynamics and Benefits of Strategic Planning

In strategic planning for emerging industries, the company must define itself as either a first-mover or late-comer. First-mover advantages include industry leadership, brand name, entrance barrier and the position of being a standard setter. Late-comer strategies take a wait and then invest attitude, embracing cost leadership and imitation. Expect to see new entrants with the advent of new or improved technologies.

In growing industries, such as healthcare, the technologies are being standardized. There is already a large established market, with customer acceptance of products. Industry winners emerge, and well-financed new entrants seek pieces of the marketplace.

Strategic planning for growth industries means expanding the domestic and international markets aggressively. There are increased economies of scope. Planning helps establish industry standards, fending off new comers by managing value-chains and globalization strategy.

Maturing industries have saturated markets and slow growth. There are many competitors. Competition drives down price, which translates to low profit margins. Long-time customers tend to be sophisticated and demanding. The competition drives production costs. There is much industrial consolidation, with opportunities for mergers and acquisitions.

Strategic planning for maturing industries focuses upon cost leadership, process-driven competition and scale economy. The plan looks to streamline product lines, acquire or eliminate rival firms, look for new technologies or products and look toward new markets.

There are seven levels of planning that may be utilized by organizations, paralleling Business Tree branches:

1. Information Gathering Process. Also known as pre-planning research, this is a snapshot of the realities, situations, facts, figures and truths.
2. Studying How the Organization Operates. These insights occur during the conducting of performance reviews of activities, while also looking for efficiencies.
3. Financial. Strategic companies must enhance efficiencies, economies and profitability, focusing upon the company's impact upon shareholder value.
4. Process for and About Teams. In large organization, the planning and visioning processes become big events. Subsequent meetings and activities are orchestrated in such a way as to empowering and involve the organization's most valuable resource, its people.
5. Business Development. In adapting to changing marketplaces and business relationships, the organization connects beliefs with expertise. Actions are taken with measurements of success and accountability toward the company's stakeholders.
6. Strategic Planning. This important process enables the organization to study and refine its core values. The company that possesses commitment, ownership and the ability to change and adapt will survive the tough times and stay successful longer.
7. Focus Upon Change and Growth. At this level, the organization is highly sophisticated in conducting the strategic planning process. Everything is done based upon beliefs and systems of thought. The company's leaders and employees are all committed to and thrive upon change.

Chapter 9

DEPARTMENTAL PLANNING

Two kinds of planning take place throughout the sophisticated organization: top-level strategic direction and departmental planning.

Divisions, business units, departments, functional areas and individuals with assigned authorities must implement key plans. This planning will articulate the objectives, activities and tasks for which they are responsible. These plans must be in concert with the strategic objectives, the corporate culture and the institution's overall Vision.

Those who must ultimately execute know the infinite number of detailed activities and the exact resources needed to generate and follow through workable programs. These departments and individuals must conduct unit planning, estimate financial and strategic gain, and calculate human and other resource requirements.

Each business unit is responsible for developing its own plan, lined up against corporate guidelines and reflecting corporate Vision.

The top-level team cannot implement the entire plan. 95% of all implementation actions take place beneath the top-level team at the departmental, functional, business unit or individual level.

Questions to ask each department:

1. Do you have financial projections for the next year in writing?
2. Do you have goals for the next year in writing?
3. Are your strategic planning and budgeting processes integrated?
4. Are planning activities consolidated into a written organizational plan?
5. Do you have a written analysis of organizational strengths and weaknesses?
6. Do detailed action plans support each major strategy?
7. Do you have a detailed, written analysis of your market area?

Leadership should examine their unit's strategy and initiate and periodically re-initiate the strategic planning process when any of the following conditions exist:

1. There seems to be a need to change the direction of the department-unit-division.
2. There is a need to step up growth and improve profitability.
3. Better information needs to be developed so management makes better decisions.
4. Management is concerned that resources are not concentrated on important things.
5. Management expresses a need for better internal coordination of department-unit-division activities.
6. The environment in which the department-unit-division competes is rapidly changing.
7. There is a sense that department-unit-division operations are out of control.
8. Management of the department-unit-division seems tired or complacent.
9. Management is cautious and uncertain about the department-unit-division's future.
10. Individual managers are more concerned about their own areas than for the overall well-being of the department-unit-division.

Functional areas and departments are different. Functional departments must factor these dynamics into their unit plans:

Priority issues and key challenges facing the overall institution, which this department addresses.

2. Description of the functional business areas.
3. Our values and how they fit into the overall organization's values.
4. Personnel responsible for implementing the department's plan.
5. Objectives and priority actions.
6. Strategies include targets, steps and anticipated outputs.
7. Employees: staffing, policies and procedures, roles and responsibilities.
8. Programs include rules, standard operating procedures, control measures and guidelines.
9. Accountability and record keeping.
10. Major Milestones: List early successes and accomplishments. Benchmark accountability. Measure successes under a changed environment.
11. Benchmarking Progress: Inputs to Outcomes. Anticipated Next Steps.
12. Institutional benefits: Ties activities back to the overall organization.
13. Appendices.

Defining Performance Standards for Production Work:

Planning: schedule, expedite

Inventory: control, measure, purchase

Transportation: ship, receive

Maintenance: equipment, facilities

Defining Performance Standards for Technical Work:

Design of the product or service

Research and Development of new products

Writing: procedures, manuals, systems, testing

Customer Relations: complaints, contracts, inspection, start-up, debug, install

Feasibility: studies, materials, processes

Quality: measure, rework, scrap, recapture, sustain, heighten

Defining Performance Standards for Financial Work:

Budgeting: develop, approve, control, report

Expenses: approve, control, remit, report

Accounts Receivable: bill, control, follow-up, report

Payroll: calculate, approve, submit, report

Defining Performance Standards for Management, Administrative Work:

Meetings: set up, run, attend, plan

Reports: generate, read, write, review

Correspondence: read, write, approve

Literature: read, write, business-to-business, consumer materials

Legal: information, analyze, synthesize, testify, develop strategy

Security: set up, monitor, control, advocate

Planning: goals, objectives, strategy, vision, implementation, review, advocate

Organizing: structure, growth

The 10 Most Common Benchmarking Mistakes:

1. Internal processes are unexamined.
2. Site visits "feel good" but do not elicit substantive data or ideas.
3. Questions and goals are vague.
4. The effort is too broad or has too many parameters.
5. The focus is general and not upon actual processes.
6. The team is not fully committed to the effort.
7. Research is not assigned and conducted.
8. The wrong subjects for benchmarking are selected.
9. The effort fails to look outside its own organization and industry.
10. No follow-up action is taken.

Benefits of Departmental Planning:

1. Enhance problem prevention capabilities of the organization.
2. Group based strategic decisions reflect the best available alternatives.
3. Team motivation should be enhanced.
4. Gaps and overlaps in activities should reduce.
5. Resistance to change should be reduced.

Internal Criteria for Successful Departmental Plans:

1. Performance Management.
2. Career Development.
3. Training and Development.
4. Promotion and Succession Planning.
5. Change Management.
6. Adjustment to New Policies and Procedures.

7. Staff Culture.
8. Recognition of Performance.
9. Staff Development and Retention.
10. Management of Information.

Chapter 10

PROFESSIONAL SERVICES GUIDEBOOK

Utilizing and Maximizing Professional Services for Business

P rofessional services firms exist around and in support of many industries. They include lawyers, advertising professionals, architects, accountants, financial advisers, engineers, and consultants. They include solo practitioners, consulting organizations or professional collaborations, providing customized, knowledge-based services to clients.

Services are often misunderstood and under-valued. Professional services are occupations in the tertiary sector of the economy requiring special training and track record. Some professional services require holding professional licenses such as architects, accountants, engineers, doctors and lawyers.

Professional services firms sell knowledge and expertise, rather than physical products. Manufacturing plants spend efforts maintaining their machinery and warehouses. Services firms must coach their teams. Without expert professionals and a strong reputation, the firm will not last. The real business of professional services is the expertise of their people and track record of service.

Every engagement is different. Customize services to each client, industry, circumstance and situation. Draw knowledge from past engagements. Cite precedents and case studies often.

Clearly understand the contexts of the professional engagements. One consultant cannot be all things to all clients. Conversely, one cannot take a niche engagement and turn it into something else, though many startup consultants try to do so.

There is a five-level pyramid of service engagement. The first and most crowded level of participants includes vendors. The next level is handful of key vendors who will always be asked to bid on project services. The next level is the preferred vendor who gets all the assignments, per his-her area of expertise. Toward the top of the pyramid is the fourth level, the niche professional who advises on any and all things relative to their niche. At the top of the pyramid are those of us who advise the client on any and all things, seen as a top-tier wisdom source, rather than a vendor peddling their wares.

Internal professional service providers have one set of operating protocols. External advisors have others. External professionals should not think of themselves as hourly workers. View these services as adding value in ways that internal projects cannot cover. They bend on the small things but do not compromise standards. They accommodate budgets, timelines and team operations while focusing toward big picture outcomes.

There has been a proliferation of the marketplace by wanna-be consultants. The internet has blurred service delivery. Many sites exist to market consultants. Adapting to technology is important, but marketing cannot substitute for the thoughtful and ethical rendering of professional services.

Top professionals believe in teaming with other professionals, rendering best value for clients. Establishing a synergy with other consultants is important. Some engagements may require other participation, team structuring and changing criteria. Top professionals are aware of turns, changes and prioritization.

Differentiating Various Service Providers

Prospective clients should inquire about the consultant's respect among current and recent clients and reputation among affected constituencies within the business community. Look at their activity in professional development and business education. If they do not pursue a program of ongoing knowledge progression, they are obsolete and not valuable to clients.

Examine potential consultants regarding their own track record at mentoring other business professionals. Check to see that they give beyond the scope of billable hours. Pro-bono community involvement is a factor because it indicates character, ethics and integrity. If they have done little or none, they are not worth hiring. Top professionals know the value of giving back to the community that supports them, becoming better consultants as a result.

The highest levels of professional advisers provide the following professional services: Develop strategy. Mentor leaders. Conduct performance reviews. Manage other consultants. Inspire culture and change. Conduct Visioning, planning and future-focused activities.

There are very few that perform all those services for clients. I see many niche service providers claim that they do those things. Many fool the clients into thinking that their niche expertise is the umbrella over senior services. Sadly, client organizations get hurt by false promises. I often get called in to fix the damage done by unskilled, partially focused and off-track consultants.

The second tier of business advisors provide solid niche professional services. These sub-sectors include:

- Accounting.
- Architecture.
- Engineering.
- Financial management.
- Healthcare consulting.
- Human resources management.
- Legal services.
- Management consulting, defined as computer oriented.
- Marketing.
- Process improvement and quality.
- Public relations.
- Sales planning, training and strategy.
- Technology.
- Training and organizational development.

The third tier include service providers and vendors. These include:

- Banking.
- Branding.

- Computers, hardware and software.
- Equipment for plant and office operations.
- Environmental consultation, cleanup and improvements.
- Industry specific services required.
- Installation and repairs.
- Insurance.
- Logistics.
- Outsourced services, such as call centers.
- Supplies.
- Transportation.
- Workforce development.

The most successful professional service advisors provide clear goals, give prompt feedback and treat clients and colleagues like winners. They get involved in the clients' decision-making processes, seek informed opinions often and keep them updated on challenging goals.

In dealing with people in crisis, it is important to speed up the process, assuring early wins and benchmarking the progress of the project. Emphasize what works and with what additional resources are needed.

Leading professional advisors are more encouraging than critical. They stretch goals, are generous in spreading credit around, are prompt in dealing with underperformers and are effective in communicating with partners.

The consulting work varies from high-diagnosis to high-execution. It may start as highly customized and then evolve into programs. Listen to clients to where their industry and customers are with the issues. Talk to opinion leaders in their industry. Professionals give diagnoses and recommendations based upon many factors, offering creative approaches to problems.

Entrants into the Consulting Arena

As the fallout from corporate downsizing and recession occurred, many people were thrown into the workforce. Many fell into jobs for which they were not really suited. Many downsized and out-of-work people were forced to reinvent themselves.

Many became "consultants" of one sort or another. Many fell victim to frauds and scams. Services and websites sprung up to capitalize upon the avalanche of new entrepreneurs. Some sites offered the platforms to become a "consultant" with a national firm by paying them subscription fees. The already inflated world of "reputation management" websites lured people into buying advertising in order to create the facade of being a "consultant."

Distinctions must be drawn into three consulting categories (and percentages of their occurrence in the marketplace):

1. Vendors selling products which were produced by others. Those who sell their own produced works are designated as subcontractors. (82.99%)
2. Consultants conduct programs designed by their companies, in repetitive motion. Their work is off-the-shelf, conforms to an established mode of operation, contains original thought and draws precedents from experience. (17%)
3. High level strategists create all knowledge in their consulting. It is original, customized to the client and contains creativity and insight not available elsewhere. (.01%)

As one distinguishes past vendors and subcontractors, there are six types within the 18% which constitute consultants (with their percentages in the marketplace):

1. Those who still lead in an industry and have specific niche expertise. (13.5%)
2. Those who were downsized, out-placed or decided not to stay in the corporate fold and evolved into consulting. (28%)
3. Out of work people who hang out consulting shingles in between jobs. (32%)
4. Freelancers and moonlighters, whose consultancy may or may not relate to their day jobs. (16%)
5. Veteran consultants who were trained for and have a track record in actual consulting. That's what they have done for most of their careers. (2%)
6. Sadly, there is another category: opportunists who masquerade as consultants, entrepreneurs who disguise their selling as consulting, people who routinely change niches as the dollars go. (8.5%)

Clients are confused and under-educated, not able to discern the "real deal" consultants from the hype. That is why those of us who are veterans write books and articles, speak and advise on best practices. Enlightened clients hire real consultants and get great value, as opposed to companies who fall prey to under-prepared resources.

The biggest source of growth and increased opportunities in today's business climate lie in the way that individuals and companies work together. t is becoming increasingly rare to find an individual or organization that has not yet been required to team with others. Lone rangers and sole-source providers simply cannot succeed in competitive environments and global economies. Those who benefit from collaborations, rather than become the victim of them, will log the biggest successes in business years ahead.

Just as empowerment, team building and other processes apply to formal organizational structures, teaming of independents can likewise benefit from the concepts. There are rules of protocol that support and protect partnerships, having a direct relationship to those who profit most.

Professionals who succeed the most are the products of mentoring. The mentor is a resource for business trends, societal issues and opportunities. The mentor becomes a role model, offering insights about their own life-career. This reflection shows the mentee levels of thinking and perception which were not previously available. The mentor is an advocate for progress and change. Such work empowers the mentee to hear, accept, believe and get results. The sharing of trust and ideas leads to developing business philosophies.

7 Levels-Tiers of Qualifying Professional Services Providers

1. Wanna-be consultants. Vendors selling services. Subcontractors. Out-of-work people who hang out "consulting" shingles in between jobs. Freelancers and moonlighters, whose consultancy may or may not relate to their day jobs. (26%)
2. Entry-level consultants. Those who were downsized, out-placed, retired or changed careers, launching a consulting practice. Prior experience in company environment. (19.5%)
3. Grinders. Those who do the bulk of project work. Conduct programs designed by others. 1-10 years' consulting experience. (35.49%)
4. Minders. Mid-level consultants. Those with specific niche or industry expertise, starting to build a track record. 10-20 years' consulting experience. (13.5%)

5. Finders. Firms which package and market services. Most claim they have all expertise in-house. The more sophisticated ones are skilled at building and utilizing collaborations of outside experts and joint ventures. (3.5%)

6. Senior level. Veteran consultants (20 years+) who were trained for and have a track record in consulting. That's what they have done for most of their careers. (2%)

7. Beyond the strata of consultant. Senior advisor, routinely producing original knowledge. Strategic overview, vision expeditor. Creativity-insight not available elsewhere.

7 Plateaus of Professional Service Collaborators

1. Want to Get Business. Seeking rub-off effect, success by association. Sounds good to the marketplace. Nothing ventured, nothing gained. Why not try!

2. Want to Garner Ideas. Learn how others work. Intend to package what the other does as your capabilities later. Each is scared of the other stealing business or scooping a client.

3. First Attempts. Conduct programs that get results, praise, requests for more.

4. Mistakes, Successes & Lessons. Crisis or urgent need led the consortium to be formed. Project required a cohesive team approach and multiple talents.

5. Continued Collaborations. Consortium members are tops in their fields, truly understand teamwork and had prior successful experiences in joint-venturing. The sophisticated ones are skilled at building-utilizing collaborations of experts.

6. Want and advocate teamwork. Members want to learn from each other. All are prepared to share risks equally. Early successes spurred future collaborations. Joint-venturing is considered an ongoing process, not a "once in awhile" action.

7. Commitment to the concept and each other. Each team member realized something of value. The client recommended the consortium to others. Members freely refer business to team members, without jealousies or the fear

7 Tiers of Professional Services

Within every corporate and organizational structure, there is a stair-step ladder. One enters the ladder at some level and is considered valuable for the category of services for which they have expertise. This ladder holds true for managers and employees within the organization, as well as outside consultants brought in.

Each rung on the ladder is important. At whatever level one enters the ladder, he-she is trained, measured for performance and fits into the organization's overall Big Picture. One rarely advances more than one rung on the ladder during the course of service to the organization in question.

1. Resource. Equipment, tools, materials, schedules.
2. Skills and Tasks. Duties, activities, tasks, behaviors, attitudes, contracting, project fulfillment.
3. Role and Job. Assignments, responsibilities, functions, accountability.
4. Systems and Processes. Structure, hiring, control, work design, supervision.
5. Strategy. Planning, tactics, organizational development.
6. Culture and Mission. Values, customs, beliefs, goals, objectives, benchmarking.
7. Philosophy. Organizational purpose, ethics, long-term growth.

Evolution of Top Professionals

1. Education and Growth. Acquiring a profession, knowledge base and perspective. Values and work ethics instilled by family, environment and workplace.
2. Evolution. Pursuing a career. Paying substantial dues. Acting as though they will one day be management. Thinking as a manager, not as a worker. Learning and doing the things it will take to assume management responsibility. Doesn't expect status overnight.
3. Experience Gathering. Understands that careers evolve. Learning from successes and failures, experiences, training and assimilation. Was a good "will be," taking time in early career to steadily blossom. Being mentored by others. Measure own output and expect to be measured as a profit center to the company.
4. Grooming. Learning to seize-create opportunities. Thinking like the boss. Accelerated commitment to training and professional development.

Developing people skills. Has grown as a person and as a professional… and quests for more enlightenment. Learn to pace…and be in the chosen career for the long-run. Don't expect that someone else will be the rescuer or cut corners in the path to artificial success. Contribute to the bottom line…directly and indirectly.

5. Seasoning. Has paid dues and knows that, as the years go by, one's dues paying accelerates, rather than decreases. Realizes there are no quick fixes. Maintains standards, marketplace sensitivity-predictability, making decisions, delegating. Acts as a mentor to still others. Sees this continuum as "continuous quality improvement."

6. Meaningful Contributions to Business. Sense of perspective: the more you know, the more you realize what you don't know. Learns to manage change, rather than falling victim to it. Learns from failures, reframing them as opportunities. Learns to expect, predict, understand and relish success. Champions planning, leadership for progress.

7. Body of Work. Acquiring visionary perception, Big Picture durability for the long-run. Study and comprehend the subtleties of life. Top professionals never stop learning, growing, doing and achieving.

Priorities of Professional Practice
1. Client relationships
2. Service, value and excellence.
3. Maintaining costs and keeping profitability.
4. Referral generation.
5. High productivity.
6. Practice management.
7. Clients who are empowered to be their best.
8. Balance of personal and professional.
9. Sustaining the practice.
10. Contributing to the community.
11. Providing things that are not available elsewhere.
12. Achieving the next higher plateaus.

7 Plateaus of Professionalism
1. Learning and Growing. Develop resources, skills and talents.
2. Early Accomplishments. Learn what works and why. Incorporate your own successes into the organization's portfolio of achievements.

3. Observe Lack of Professionalism in Others. Commit to sets of standards at role, job, responsibilities and relationships. Take stands against mediocrity, sloppiness, poor work and low quality. Learn about the culture and mission of organizations.

4. Commitment to Career. Learn what constitutes excellence and pursue it for the long-term. Enjoy well-earned successes, sharing techniques with others.

5. Refining career with several levels of achievement, honors, recognition. Learn about planning, tactics, organizational development, systems improvement. Active decision maker, able to take risks.

6. Mentor-Leader-Advocate-Motivator. Finely develop skills in every aspect of the organization, beyond the scope of professional training. Amplify upon philosophies of others. Mentoring, creating and leading have become the primary emphasis for your career.

Beyond the Level of Professional. Never stop paying dues, learning and growing professionally. Develop and share own philosophies. Has earned a track record, unlike anything accomplished by any other individual, all contributing toward organizational philosophy, purpose, vision, quality of life, ethics, long-term growth.

Chapter 11

FRIENDS AND LOYALTY PROGRAMS

Customers and Corporate Rewards Programs

F riends are special. They inspire us, support us and ask us to be more and go further. Friends get close during certain periods of their lives because they are willing to share common experiences together.

Friendships develop out of need or utility, out of pleasure and for the greater good. Some friendships last many years in our lives. However, most are transitory and depend upon changing circumstances. Some friendships last for seasons.

Here are the kinds of friendships:

- People who work together.
- People came from somewhere else and now find themselves together.
- Befriended out of personal respect.
- Each has a connection to others and may be assigned together for now.
- People engaged in community service.
- Friends from other cultures.
- Teams put together by others, including mentors and advisors.

- New friends.
- Old friends.
- Neighbors.
- Friends reconnected and staying in touch for the long-term.
- People achieving good together.

Fate brings friend to friend, then leaves the rest to human nature. Here are recommendations to get the best in friendships:

- Associate higher.
- Choose friends with similar values.
- Choose friends who can stretch, motivate and encourage you.
- Choose friends that have a thirst for knowledge.
- Choose friends who are doers and achievers.
- Give what you expect to get.

Loyalty Rewards Programs

Loyalty programs engage customers, predict behaviors and increase sales. They are an important part of high-impact marketing, affect customer service, heighten customer retention and create business referral generation.

Loyalty is not just about cards and points. It means connecting shoppers to what they need now and in the future.

Loyalty programs allow retailers and hospitality companies to:

- Target and understand who their customers are.
- Track customer purchases.
- See how regularly customers visit.
- Track their return rate.
- Pull together touch points through a streamlined system.
- Track your business data from a dashboard.
- Learn insights into customers' preferences and buying habits.
- Provide special offers to regulars.
- Show customers benefits that they get with "bricks and mortar" stores that they cannot get from online resources.
- Some loyalty programs live in customers' smart phones as applications. Digital loyalty programs are becoming the trend.

Rewards programs can offer birthday and anniversary gifts, discounts and invitations to exclusive events. They may provide information, classes, hotlines, blogs and access to insider communities. Some such programs offer special shipping on mail orders and charity tie-ins.

Loyalty reward programs are ideally utilized for restaurants, retail stores, salons, automotive services, florists, beauty suppliers, large retail chains, clothing stores, pet shops, travel programs, hotels, department stores and specialty retailers.

Rewards programs are predicated upon points, spending, levels of loyalty and VIP memberships. Some are value-based programs where customers become brand ambassadors. There are partnered programs, gaming programs and hybrid rewards programs. Gift card programs widen the appeal to friends of existing customers.

Airline loyalty programs offer points on future flights. Hotel loyalty programs offer bonus stays and access to a wider selection of hotels than customers might find through their own research. Loyalty programs for rental cars get free upgrades for cardholders. Punch cards for free food in restaurants have been a staple of the hospitality industry for 70 years.

Banks charge a fee for rewards card programs. This accrues points for use on a variety of purchases. The gold card gets holders a printout of purchases by category, which is useful in tracking business expenses and in preparation of taxes.

Grocery store rewards program include points toward discounted gasoline, special discounts (such as four times fuel points on credit card sales), quantity discounts on sale merchandise and specials that were not on the weekly sale circular.

Reward programs for internet purchases include Amazon Prime, where the upfront annual fee gets VIP services such as free shipping, special offers and access to specialized services. This is instead of transactions first and rewards later.

Many loyalty programs include applications for faster checkout, bonus points and special offers. Retailers offer private sales, information on products and brand gifts for purchases past set goals.

The Panera Bread loyalty card program generates $2 billion per year in digital, mobile, web and kiosk sales. Coffee chains offer free points, mobile payment, advance orders, access to Wi-Fi and special events.

Loyal customers mean more business, increased repeat sales and destination purchases. This saves marketing to wider nets, many who will not turn into customers.

It requires 5-25% more to acquire new customers than to sell to existing ones. Regulars spend 67% more than new customers. Engaged customers are five times more likely to buy from their favorite store. They return often and refer new customers. 82% of adults say they are loyal to brands. 63% of customers will modify their spending in order to maximize loyalty benefits.

A 5% increase in customer retention will increase company profit from 25-96%, depending upon the product, seasonality and coordination with other marketing.

Stores with loyalty programs can send emails to users, including newsletters, new product introductions, recommendations for bundling and cooperative offers with other retailers.

With loyalty programs come the opportunity to conduct customer research. Surveys can test new product offerings, learn differences of the company from its competitors and glean insights into how to do things differently. Think of the loyalty program as an online focus group.

79% of customers prefer businesses who show that they care. Customers will support cause related marketing and charity tie-in promotions that appeal to them.

Loyalty programs have created many companies who operate the software for tracking purchases, research on consumer buying habits and specialty marketing firms in the digital age.

When rewards programs are done wrong and without adequate coordination, they may be a waste of time and resources, becoming a burden for customers with little interest in getting into the program.

Companies need to create the best rewards program for their business. Rewarding customers has the advantage of immediately motivating incremental spending. Customers will happily identify themselves with succeeding visits, giving the data the company needs to create deeper customer connections and motivate targeted behaviors.

It is About So Much More Than Sales

Loyalty should be across the board, company-wide and in communities of stakeholders. Getting more customers is marketing. Handling greater volumes involves every branch of your Business Tree: core business, running the business, financial, people and business development, plus the trunk (Body of Knowledge) and roots (the Big Picture).

Ways in which your loyalty program goes further and is more successful:

- Looks at how you provide service beyond the sale.
- Covers ways in which you solve problems and recover from glitches.
- Keeps your employees seen by customers as authority figures with the ability to make decisions and get action.
- Gives reasons why customers should refer your company to their friends.
- Inspires customers to write positive reviews.
- Enlightens your constituency about new things happening in the company.
- Facilitates long-term loyalty, further than just punch-card bonus goodies.

Loyalty to employees is important. Loyal workers stay longer and give you their best effort. The best workers serve as role models for new hires.

Loyalty should be reflected in onboarding and training. It can be discovered and rewarded in performance reviews. It shows well in staff interactions, projects, teamwork, feedback and interactions with customers.

Loyalty to customers, each other and the company is a continuum of a service culture.

Loyalty Building Affects the Business Climate

These recommendations are offered in a loyalty program for gaining and maintaining third party support of business initiatives:

- List your company's current friends and update regularly.
- Determine why friends support you and what would happen if their backing was lost.
- Understand why some people and groups oppose you. Ascertain what would have prevented their objections and what it would take to turn them around.
- List whom you want to win as friends and with whom you are most afraid of becoming enemies.
- Analyze what your competitors are doing to win friends and build coalitions.
- Foresee what would happen if you sat still and did nothing.
- Project the financial and other benefits of pro-active building of credible third-party endorsements.

- Make this loyalty initiative a primary responsibility for top management.
- Retain an outside adviser with demonstrated expertise in issues management, business forecasting, community relations, cause-related marketing, minority relations, government relations and grassroots constituency building.

Third party support can move mountains when you need it the most, or it can wreak havoc on your bottom line and the future in which you do business. Be honest about your current status. Take stock of opportunities. Make decisive actions and reap future rewards.

Anticipated Results of Loyalty Toward Customers

- Your company's product-service is efficient and excellent, by your standards and by the public's.
- The organization is sensitive to the public's needs and behaves flexibly and humane in meeting them.
- Company management and staff are professional and competent. They demonstrate initiative and utilize their best judgment, with the authority to make the decisions they should make.
- Your company has a good reputation and is awake to community obligations. It contributes much to the economy and provides leadership for progress, rather than following along.
- The company always gives customers their money's worth.
- Charges are fair and reasonable.
- The organization employs state-of-the-art technology and is in the vanguard of its industry and marketplace.
- Management is quality oriented and provides a good place to work. Your company offers a promising career and future for people with ideas and initiative. Your people render quality work, are highly creative and are results-oriented.
- The size of your organization is necessary to do the job. Your integrity and dependability make the public confident that the company will use its size and influence rightly.

Chapter 12

INFLUENCES, ROLE MODELS AND MENTORS

How influences stick with us, for recall.
The kinds of influences that we shape for others.

Professionals who succeed the most are the products of mentoring. The mentor is a resource for business trends, societal issues and opportunities. The mentor becomes a role model, offering insights about their own life-career.

This reflection shows the mentee levels of thinking and perception not previously available. The mentor is an advocate for progress and change. Such work empowers the mentee to hear, accept, believe and get results. The sharing of trust and ideas leads to developing business philosophies.

The mentor endorses the mentee, messages ways to approach issues, helps draw distinctions and paints pictures of success. The mentor opens doors for the mentee. The mentor requests pro-active changes of mentee evaluates realism of goals and offers truths about path to success and shortcomings of mentee's approaches.

This is a bonded collaboration toward each other's success. The mentor stands for mentees throughout their careers and celebrates their successes. This is a lifelong dedication toward mentorship in all aspects of one's life.

Take a mentorship survey. Record the most important lessons you have learned in your career:

1. Ideas that you learned.
2. From whom you learned the ideas.
3. What was their relationship to you?
4. What was your age at the time?
5. What was the mentor's age at the time?
6. What the ideas and wisdom meant then.
7. What is the applicability of those teachings to your career now?

These are the seven levels where mentors are utilized:

1. Resource. Equipment, tools, materials, schedules.
2. Skills and Tasks. Duties, activities, tasks, behaviors, attitudes, fulfillment.
3. Role and Job. Responsibilities, functions, relationships, accountability.
4. Systems, Processes, Structure. Control, work design, supervision, decisions.
5. Strategy. Planning, tactics, organizational development.
6. Culture and Mission. Values, customs, beliefs, goals, benchmarking.
7. Philosophy. Organizational purpose, vision, ethics, long-term growth.

These are the seven levels of mentoring:

1. Conveying Information. The mentor is a resource for business trends, opportunities, an active listener and adviser on values, actions.
2. Imparting Experiences. The mentor is a role model. Insight offered about own life-career. Reflection strengthens the mentor and shows levels of thinking and perception which were not previously available to the mentee.
3. Encouraging Actions. The mentor advocates for progress, empowering the mentee to hear, accept, believe and get results. Sharing of feelings, trust, ideas, philosophies.

4. Paving the Way. The mentor endorses the mentee, wanting his-her success. The mentor messages ways to approach issues, drawing distinctions and painting pictures of success.

5. Wanting the Best. Continuing relationship between the mentor and mentee. Progress is envisioned, contextualized, seeded, benchmarked.

6. Advocating, Facilitating. The mentor opens doors for the mentee. The mentor requests pro-active changes of mentee, evaluates realism of goals, offers truths about path to success and shortcomings of mentee's approaches. This is a bonded collaboration toward each other's success.

7. Sharing Profound Wisdom. The mentor stands for mentees throughout careers, celebrates successes. Energy coaching and respect for each other throughout the relationship.

These are the seven levels of mentors:

1. Sets a Good Example. Individuals and organizations prove themselves by their characters, not just words, promises or personalities. Flash-and-sizzle wears thin and shows itself relatively soon.

2. Was a Good Team Player. The mentor took instruction from others and served as a good organization member has the makings of an effective leader. Poor team players, however, will remain so.

3. Abilities to Lead. Some people want to lead others. Some have limited opportunities to take charge. Of those, very few are "natural leaders." It takes experience, finesse and human dynamics to excel as a leader. Credit must be paid to second-line and third-line influencers…they inform, affect and steer the leaders.

4. Track Record. Has past accomplishments, especially abilities to encounter adversity and group discord, are indicative of his-her style. Leads by example.

5. Abilities to Inspire. The inspiring leader empowers followers to want and advocate good teamwork. It's more than an inspirational message…the team cares to be involved, rather than just following along.

6. Still a Team Player. A true leader serves on other people's teams, supports their objectives and flexibly functions in a variety of settings. One does not always lead in front but proves his-her measure through mentoring and complimenting other leaders.

7. Further Advance the Concept of Leadership. The proof is in the body of causes, relationships, projects, people, collaborations, objectives and accomplishments. Leaders don't just lead…they develop expertise in subjects, group dynamics, community alliances and other outlets for guided teams to be effective.

Mentors, Great Lessons from the Legends

My first mentor was Lady Bird Johnson, who served as First Lady of the U.S. from 1963-69. She was Claudia Alta Taylor, friend of my parents, when they were students at the University of Texas in the 1930s. I started visiting with Mrs. Johnson when I was 10, discussing societal issues around her family kitchen table in Austin, TX. She mentored me: "You are a visionary and a humanitarian. Now grow into the roles."

Over the ensuing years, she introduced me to some phenomenal people, all of whom were generous with their wisdom and advice. She introduced me to Winston Churchill, Eleanor Roosevelt, Mamie Eisenhower, Ima Hogg, Walt Disney, George R. Brown, Bob Hope, Lucille Ball, Jackie Kennedy, Oveta Culp Hobby, George Mitchell, Sam Rayburn, Thurgood Marshall and dozens of other humanitarians. She endorsed my work. Her endorsement appears on the back of this very book.

On July 11, 1960, in Los Angeles, CA, Lady Bird Johnson introduced me to Winston Churchill and Eleanor Roosevelt. We discussed lifelong humanitarianism. Sir Winston Churchill was 85 at the time. Mrs. Roosevelt was 75. I was 12. Churchill advised: "Remain an intellectual, but don't act like it." Mrs. Roosevelt said: "We teach other people the things we've most recently learned and applied."

President Lyndon B. Johnson taught me: "You always start out at the top. Come let us reason together. Books and ideas are the most effective weapons against intolerance and ignorance. Yesterday is not ours to recover, but tomorrow is ours to win or lose. We draw lessons from the past, but we cannot live in it."

One never forgets being in the presence of greatness and their shared wisdom. Another Churchill quote: "All great things are simple, and many can be expressed in single words: freedom, justice, honor, duty, mercy, hope."

I started my career in 1958, working as a radio disc jockey. Dick Clark was my role model. Mr. Clark's endorsement is on the back of this book.

At that radio station, I learned much from mentors. Cactus Pryor taught me: "They only care about you when you're behind the microphone. Fame is fleeting.

The public is fickle and quick to jump on the newest flavor, without showing loyalty to the old ones, especially those who are truly original."

From Bill Moyers, I learned these lessons:

- You cannot go through life as a carbon copy of someone else.
- You must establish your own identity, which is a long, exacting process.
- As you establish a unique identity, others will criticize. Being different, you become a moving target.
- If you cannot take the dirtiest job in any company and do it yourself, then you will never become "management."

From Bob Gooding and Neal Spelce, I learned: "Think like a world-class visionary. Grow into the role and not just remain a radio DJ."

In 1959, radio stations used to do live remotes from advertisers' locations. The first that I did was at the Armstrong-Johnson Ford dealership. The second was at what was at the fourth KFC franchise to open in the United States. It occupied one counter at 2-J's Hamburgers, an established Austin restaurant, owned and operated by Ralph Moreland.

There I was on live radio, interviewing Colonel Sanders about his new business enterprise. Rather than discussing the taste of the food, I asked about his desired legacy and the Big Picture goals of the organization. Already thinking like a visionary then, I asked the bigger questions. I was 11 at the time, and Colonel Sanders was 65.

KFC grew, and a burgeoning fast food industry engulfed it. There became too many competitors, too much franchising, too much hype and just as many who exited the industry as quickly as they entered it.

Fast forward 20 years to 1979. I was retained to come in and analyze the strategy and structure of KFC Corporation, asked to recommend changes and improvements. That's what I do for businesses of all sizes, coming in after the wrong consultants have given bad advice, after knee-jerk reactions to changing business climates had taken tolls on existing market players.

By 1979, there were other players dominating the fried chicken niche. Nationally, there were Popeye's and Church's. Locally, we had Frenchy's and Hartz. And then there were the players in the burger wars, who were adding chicken items to their menus.

Over at KFC, the Colonel had long ago sold his interest to a corporation and remained on the payroll as a commercial spokesman. Colonel Sanders died in 1979. Meetings commenced at headquarters about the future direction of the company and the product. The corporate owner was a liquor company. Its CEO asked me to envision the overall future of the fried chicken industry, not just the KFC "brand."

I commissioned focus groups. They verified what I already knew that KFC had too much of a white suburban image. By downplaying the Colonel on the packaging and amplifying the taste of the food, we had opportunities to broaden the KFC appeal.

I opined that we needed to go after minority consumers and aggressively build stores in inner-city neighborhoods. To test the premise, I staged a focus group dinner meeting at a prominent inner-city church, eliciting ideas and insights. One resulting project was "KFC Kalendar," an advertising campaign that showcased community events and public service announcements to diverse communities. I wrote editions of the Kalendar for radio and newspapers. Its recognition and success evolved into the national ad campaign: "We Do Chicken Right."

KFC was a watershed in my career (at that point 21 years long). It influenced what I've preached for the last 30+ years: determine who your stakeholders are. Learn all that you can about your customers, their customers and those affected by them. Extend your business model beyond what it once was and into new sectors. The branding does not drive the strategy but instead is a sub-sub-sub set of Big Picture strategy, which must drive all business disciplines.

Summit with the Great Mentors

You meet the greatest people through community service. I advised George H.W. Bush, on Thousand Points of Light. Advised Barbara Bush on the Houston READ Commission. LBJ on civil rights programs. Volunteering is worthwhile and enriches lives. Through community leadership roles, I worked with Ben Love, Lyndall Wortham, Audrey Hepburn, Ima Hogg, Oveta Culp Hobby, John Connally and many others who were mentors to me.

When I was 17 years old, I attended a reception and sat in the meeting room with Walt Disney and Howard Hughes. Disney said to me: "Don't forget this, kid. Good ideas have six ways in which to extend them. If it does not have that many arms and legs, it is not a good idea." At the other end of the couch was Howard

Hughes, who said: "I have some advice for you, kid. Keep a pocketful of note cards, so you can write down things that people like us say. You'll wind up with a series of books." True, as this is book #12.

John Connally was one of my favorites. He served as Secretary of the Navy under President John F. Kennedy. He then served three terms as Governor of Texas. During his first campaign, he came into my office and said: "Always affix the stamps on the envelope correctly. Everything that we do symbolizes the care and attention that we pay to the big matters." Four years later, I was given the first prestigious award of my career, at age 19. Bestowing the award, Governor Connally whispered to me, "Get used to wearing tuxedos," meaning that high-profile leadership positions would ensue. First Lady Nellie Connally was one of the great humanitarians, leaving her mark on communities and quality of life.

I met Bill Gates in Seattle, at a conference where I was the opening keynote speaker. Gates and I talked about charitable activities and community stewardship. I asked Gates: "Bill, was it ever about the money?" He replied no, that his career led to commitments to the better good. These words and related volunteering experiences led to my ninth book, "Non-Profit Legends."

This is further great wisdom that I learned from friends and colleagues:

"You perform your best work for free. How you fulfill commitments and pro-bono work speaks to the kind of professional that you are."
–Seymour Cohen

"Nobody is Number One forever. Life goes in rich cycles."
–Frank Sinatra

"Think of life as mathematical progressions.
The opportunities multiply when you take perspective."
–Paul Simon

"If someone drags you into the mud, you both get dirty.
The person who drags you in likes it."
–Allan Shivers

*"People worry so much about what other people think of them.
If they knew how little people think, they would not worry so much."*
–Adie Marks

*"People criticize you because of what you represent, not who you are. It is
rarely personal against you. Your success may bring out insecurities within
others. You might be what they cannot or are not willing to become."*
–Lee Iacocca

*"Houston, we've had a problem. Be thankful for problems. If they were less
difficult, someone with less ability might have your job. I was only a hero
by default. The flights were few and far between. There weren't that many
astronauts. The moon flights were so interesting and exciting."*
–James A. Lovell, astronaut

*"Don't taunt the alligator until after you've crossed the creek. A
tough lesson in life that one has to learn is that not everybody wishes
you well. If all difficulties were known at the outset of a long journey,
most of us would never start out at all. Only votes talk, everything
else walks. Americans will put up with anything provided it doesn't
block traffic. I'd much rather wear out than rust out."*
–Dan Rather

"I have this theory about performers who last for a long time, and that is, if
you break it down, music is not as big a part of it as personality and who you are.
I think that we are all 3 people. I am who I think I am, I am who you think I am,
and I am who I really am. The closer those 3 people are together, the longer your
career is going to last. People don't like to be fooled. Don't be afraid to give up the
good for the great."
–Kenny Rogers

The Mentor's Mentor

One of my most respected friends and colleagues is Bill Spitz. He embodies the
concept of business mentoring. He created mentoring programs and set standards
for many others who have guided successful businesses.

Bill Spitz founded and for more than 40 years ran Big State Pest Control, the largest independent pest control business in the Southwest. He merged this business with Waste Management Inc., largest firm of its kind in the world. He served as President of the National Pest Management Association and was elected into its Hall of Fame, recognized for contributions to professionalism of the industry.

Bill served as the first Adjunct Professor at the Hilton School for Hotel and Restaurant Management at the University of Houston. He served as president of Silver Fox Advisors; a business think tank (a position that I later held proudly).

He has a long track record of speaking, mentoring and business consultation throughout the U.S. under the umbrella Peak Performance. Bill Spitz helps business executives reach their full potential, maximize profitability and return on their investment as an advisor, coach, mentor and sounding board.

Bill himself was the product of mentorship. He knew full well the value of getting the best advice, applying the mentorship teachings to his own business and then sharing the valuable ideas with others. Mr. Spitz discussed customer loyalty, the costs of building repeat business and strategies to keep customers who are happy and who refer others. He successfully practiced and championed customer focused management.

In 1990, he began coordinating a CEO roundtable for the Greater Houston Partnership, bringing in Silver Fox members and other mentors to strengthen this valuable program. In later years, the Silver Foxes expanded the roundtable program.

In training and energizing other mentors, Mr. Spitz addressed the critical elements for constructing mentoring program that produce high-performing results. The practical use of stories and real-world examples illustrate key concepts, keeping members engaged and participating.

These are some of the key things that I learned through Bill Spitz:

1. **Planning**. List everything you need to do. Not only will this save time and improve efficiency, it's probably the most important driver of productivity and success. Every minute spent in planning—both short- and long-term—saves as many as 10 minutes in implementation. Planning helps managers and business owners define their goals and create an action plan for optimal performance and results.

2. **Organizing.** As your business expands, tasks become more complex and more people get involved. To ensure that everyone performs efficiently

and effectively, list and analyze your processes with an objective eye, organize your team's efforts, and eliminate clutter and redundancies.

3. **Staffing.** Recruitment is an essential initiative for any growing business. Any business owner or manager must approach the hiring process seriously and strategically. What do I mean by that? Don't focus only on identifying great people—instead, target people who are well-suited for the job. Clearly identify your requirements, attract high quality candidates, thoroughly assess them, and select only those with the experience and capability to carry out the job.

4. **Delegating.** The challenge is determining which tasks to delegate. This is critical. You don't want to assign a task to a person who isn't qualified—but a possible job mismatch isn't the only risk. Many business owners become exhausted and unhappy because they don't know the right way to delegate their own tasks. Reduce stress by delegating your low-value tasks so you can focus on more important ones.

5. **Supervising.** Spend enough time with your staff to give them constructive feedback and positive direction. As a manager, nothing is more important to your employees than your time and guidance. Provide training and coaching so you can help your staff perform at a higher level.

6. **Measuring.** Make time to set standards and measure results. The only way to determine if your team is performing well is to measure and analyze. Record your sales and output on a regular basis. Evaluate your performance based on quantity and quality, and how your team contributes to the overall success of your business.

7. **Reporting.** Improve accountability by requiring team members to submit reports on their individual contributions and overall performance in certain measurable areas. This will provide a basis for analyzing results, motivating people to perform better, furthering efficiency and productivity.

Spitz continues to serve as sounding board with a wealth of insight on various aspects of business, from legal challenges and financial reporting to personnel policies and day-to-day operating procedures. The relationship with his mentor is something special to Louie Werderich, who said about being mentored by Bill

Spitz: "I've been lucky to receive many blessings from God, and Bill is one of those blessings."

Some of the feedback from roundtable members and mentees included:

- Discussions were applicable to my business. It certainly unveiled a lot of what my business needs.
- Planning and measuring against the plan is key. Be a planner and a strategist. Be aware of market trends in my industry.
- I'm more motivated to make necessary changes. A reminder of things I already know and need to implement.
- Someone else telling you about it gets you going.
- Success is limited if the top does not have the right priorities.
- I've actually been doing more things right than I thought I was. I just need to take the time to document, measure and communicate better.
- I only thought that I was pro-active before. Mentoring helps me understand the many different components of business growth.
- Roundtable approach was good. Learned from group experiences. Much more applied knowledge from experienced people.
- It lets you work with other business people with the same or different problems.
- Sharing of resources, a good open forum. There isn't any business situation they have not seen.

I learned much from Bill Spitz over 40 years. I taught him a few lessons. Sharing of meaningful business ideas with colleagues is so rare and important.

Some of the key points that I gleaned from him include:

- Founders and/or managers are not always leaders and need to be groomed as such.
- Know your strengths and weaknesses.
- Nurture the appreciation of employees.
- The concept of a very frequent measurement keeps the company solidly growing.
- I am not alone in this struggle.
- Adjust incentives in the company.

- Gain a better understanding of the overall market.
- Hiring the right people.
- Have employee communication meetings regularly.
- Importance of planning.
- Importance of leadership.
- Really need to take the discipline to write a business plan and use it.
- Measure your business, even on a weekly basis.
- Being aware of trends in markets outside my own that may affect the way we do business.
- Team with the best. I teamed with the best, including Bill Spitz.

*Hank Moore is pictured with Lady Bird Johnson in 1993,
planning an environmental public festival.*

*Hank Moore with Texas Governor John Connally in 1967.
Also pictured: Patricia Millican McBride.*

Hank Moore with Audrey Hepburn in 1990.
Working together in support of UNICEF.

Hank Moore and Joan Wilhelm Moore posed with Bill Spitz in 2016.

Chapter 13

THE PEOPLE TREE

People Skills Checklist for Business Success.
Talent Acquisition and Management in the Workforce.

T alent Acquisition is the process of attracting and hiring skilled employees to fulfill a company's business needs. Talent Acquisition professionals:

- Build a strong employer brand to attract the right candidates.
- Proactively build applicant pipelines to meet current and future business needs.
- Maintain relationships with past candidates for future opportunities.
- Strategically source potential hires from diverse backgrounds.

Talent Acquisition helps companies build workplaces with skilled employees who drive successful businesses. With good Talent Acquisition strategies, companies will:

- Transform recruiting to a proactive hiring function.
- Create pipelines of candidates for future staffing needs.
- Recruit diverse employees by sourcing candidates from various backgrounds.
- Hire people with the agility to grow beyond their role.

Talent Acquisition teams will identify, attract and hire high-potential people. They:

- Work with hiring managers and executives to forecast staffing needs.
- Improve the recruitment process by conducting candidate experience surveys.
- Participate in recruitment events to grow their network of potential hires.
- Source potential candidates to fill their talent pipelines through social media and searches using Google or other methods.

Talent Management is the ongoing process of developing and retaining employees throughout a company. Talent Management professionals:

- Coach high-potential employees.
- Deliver employee training programs.
- Build hiring and succession plans.
- Mentor, reward and promote employees.

Talent Management helps companies engage employees and prevent turnover. With successful Talent Management strategies, companies:

- Identify internal candidates to fill key positions.
- Increase retention rates through employee career path steps.
- Boost morale to keep employees motivated.
- Model appropriate conflict resolution skills.
- Coach and develop employees to help them achieve their full potential.

Talent Management teams develop new and current employees' skills, making sure they align with their company's organizational structure and overall goals. They:

- On-board new hires by scheduling first-day tasks and check-ins.
- Conduct skills gap analyses and schedule training programs.
- Design an organizational structure and define each position's responsibilities.
- Prepare succession plans for future hiring needs.

The best employees exhibit higher goals and better communications skills. Good behaviors in the workplace show a willingness to work cohesively with teams. Individuals who are part of teams achieve more than they would on their own. Team members deliver outputs that are acceptable and better. Good companies develop keys to increase professionalism.

Social Emotional Learning is the process through which people acquire and apply the knowledge, attitudes and skills necessary to understand and manage emotions. This allows them to set positive goals, feel and share empathy for others, establish and maintain positive relationships and make reasonable decisions.

The basics of good business are rooted in respect. The demonstration of respect is a valuable commodity that caring professionals must nurture and show toward their colleagues, customers, industry, marketplace and stakeholders.

Employee behavior is defined as an employee's reaction to a particular situation at workplace. Employees need to behave sensibly at workplace not only to gain appreciation and respect from others but also to maintain a healthy work culture.

These are examples of good behaviors at work:

- Positive values.
- Relaxed and productive atmosphere.
- Commitment to excellence.
- Open and honest communication.
- Cooperation, support, and empowerment.
- Sense of humor.
- Compassion, respect, and understanding, especially to elders.
- Flexibility.

It is vital to give employees training on people skills. Don't rely upon workers to know all the right things to say to customers. Write service lines. Formal training is a benefit of working there and should be celebrated as leading employees toward more successful careers.

These are the kinds of training programs that would benefit young employees and their upcoming managers:

- Business etiquette.
- The art of building successful relationships.
- Interviewing skills.
- Professional image.
- Meeting and report writing protocols.
- Customer service.
- Telephone etiquette.
- Tradeshow etiquette.
- Representing the company in the community.
- Understanding stakeholders in the company's universe.
- Quality control topics.
- Self-image vs. public perception.
- The polished executive.
- The business leader as community leader.
- Coaching skills.
- Mentoring next generations of company leaders.
- Evolving from manager to leader.
- Working with outside resources, consultants and vendors.
- Working effectively with the news media.
- Writing plans: personal, departmental and company.
- Sustaining cultures of service, gratitude and mission.

Organizations, which click and sustain a track record, must realize that:

- There is nothing more permanent than change.
- Change is 90% beneficial. So, why do people fight what's in their best interests?
- Learn from the past.
- Avoid repeating the same mistakes.
- There exists more knowledge in failure than through repeated successes.
- "Saving face" is not the most important thing.
- Becoming part of an organization involves commitment and responsibility from each of its members.

- Put the customer first, and they will keep you first.
- Get advice from the best consultants, not the wanna-be's.
- Continually research, study, understand and communicate what works well.
- Loyalty and consistency pay off.
- Understand what motivates people to work.
- Reward the traits of professionalism.
- Never stop planning.
- Never stop changing.
- Never stop improving.

Chapter 14

COMMUNITY RELATIONS AND CAUSE RELATED MARKETING FOR BUSINESSES

Thoughtfulness Pays Dividends

For those doing business on a long-term basis, respect and understanding of the company will improve its chances. No matter the size of the organization, goodwill must be banked. Every company must make deposits for those inevitable times in which withdrawals will be made.

To say that business and its communities do not affect each other, is short-sighted and will make business the loser every time. Communities surround business but are not subject to its policies and operations. While business usually caters to its own agenda, the community is flexible, unpredictable and emotional.

When business practices and performance pose potential harm to the community, an expected backlash will occur. Communities used to be passive because company presence meant jobs and economic incentive. The mobility of business has forced communities to compete for other businesses, which makes them very Leary of companies that defy the public's best interests.

Since one cannot market a problem-ridden culture, the communities are addressing the troubles, in order to attract more responsible organizations. In this era, the community has spoken out. Business is on fair notice to get its act together.

Communities are clusters of individuals, each with its own agenda. In order to be minimally successful, business must know the components of its community intimately.

No company can cure community problems by itself, unless it is the problem. But each company has a business stake for doing its part. Community relations is a function of self-interest, rather than just being a good citizen. The art is to identify those constituencies who serve or can harm the company's strongest needs.

To prioritize which spheres or causes to serve, business should list and examine all of the community's problems. Relate business responses to real and perceived wants/needs of the community. Set priorities.

The only constraints upon community relations are regulatory standards and the amount of resources that can be allocated. There can never be a restraint upon creativity.

Every community relations program has five steps:

1. Learn what each community thinks about the company and, therefore, what information needs to be communicated to each public. Conduct focus groups. Maintain community files. Organize an ongoing feedback system.

2. Plan how to best reach each public and which avenues will be the most expedient. Professional strategic planning counsel performs an independent audit and guides the company through the process. Get as many ideas from qualified sources as possible. Find compatible causes to champion. Maintain contingency plans.

3. Develop systems to execute the program, communicating at every step to publics. All employees should have access to the plan, with a mechanism that allows them to contribute. If others understand what the company is doing, they will want to be part of it.

4. Evaluate how well each program and its messages were received. Continue fact-finding efforts, which will yield more good ideas for future projects. Document the findings. Build into all community relations programs some realistic mechanisms by which results can be shown. When planning, reach for feasible evaluation yardsticks.

5. Interpret the results to management in terms that are easy to understand and support. Community relations is difficult to evaluate, unless a procedure for doing so is set. Provide management with information that justifies their confidence. Squarely address goals and concerns.

Companies should support off-duty involvement of employees in pro bono capacities but not take unfair credit. Volunteers are essential to community relations. Companies must show tangible evidence of supporting the community by assigning key executives to high-profile community assignments. Create a formal volunteer guild and allow employees the latitude and creativity to contribute to the common good. Celebrate and reward their efforts.

Community Relations and Cause Related Marketing Are Business Strategies, Not Sales Promotions.

Business marries the community that it settles with. The community has to be given a reason to care for the business. Business owes its well-being and livelihood to its communities.

I recently stopped for lunch at a franchise restaurant. Nobody was at the register. A crew member told me to wait, then later took my order. She started selling donations to some cause, which I declined. When the regular cashier returned, I saw her peddling donation sales, rather than discussing the food customers were attempting to order. People were blindly making donations, without understanding what they supported. The sales of those promotional pieces caused the line to grow out of the restaurant door. People were just buying the promotion in order to get through the line.

I support cause related marketing and have advised many corporations on setting up such programs. However, peddling sales to some "foundation" that is named after your product and which supports only one cause is not appropriate. The store was littered with stickers. The process of selling the stickers made the waiting line longer. As a result, the iced tea had run out, and nobody checked it.

I went to their website, where franchise chains allege, they want customer comments. I stated, "Having a foundation to support the community across the board is great. Who is to say that a sales promotion tied directly to your products is right? I say it is not, and I'm an expert on cause-related marketing. You need to revise your service lines. Peddling the sales of stickers in a tackily littered store is inappropriate. I'm gravely concerned about this practice of badgering customers in support of some phantom charity; how this store does it is not right."

The franchise owner later called. He talked all over me in a defensive manner. His voice was high-pressure, probably the result of sales training classes. Rather than addressing my concerns, he rifled over them and questioned my ability to assess community relations. Still, he questioned my interest in community relations.

"We're a franchise," he admitted. "This was dictated to us by corporate. I'm sorry that you feel that way because we do so much good. You're invited to attend when we present the donation." I replied, "No, I'm not going to be a prop in your photo opportunity, for you to sell product." I reminded him that it was customer donations that enabled the attention, not a corporate initiative for which they were taking the credit.

He was not listening. He was simply rationalizing a corporate marketing initiative. So too was the corporate person who later called to argue with me for daring to state my opinions. Sadly, people like that don't care or even get that re-thinking their strategy is an option.

There are many wonderful ways where companies support the community:

- Give percentages of sales to approved charities.
- Offer certificates for product when people make legitimate donations.
- Coupon book activities with schools.
- Allow non-profit groups to present on their premises.
- Advocate community causes in their advertising.
- Sponsor noteworthy community events.
- Recognize that executive time spent in the community is good for business.

No company can cure community problems by itself. Each company has a business stake for doing its part. To prioritize which spheres or causes to serve, business should list and examine all of the community's problems. Relate business responses to real and perceived wants/needs of the community. Set priorities. There can never be a restraint upon creativity.

My advice to companies as they create charity tie-in, cause-related marketing and community relations activities includes:

- Don't say that you want customer input unless you are prepared to really hear it.
- Franchisers should not sell sure-fire promotions to build sales as part of the worth of the franchise.
- Community support is not a one-cause (vested interest) matter.
- If you seek customer comment, do not talk over the customer.
- Do not keep rationalizing flawed strategies to your customers.
- Realize that customers' opinions matter and that they have more buying choices than just your store.
- If you purport to have a foundation, it cannot or should not be named directly for your product.
- Do not run your "foundation" out of a corporate marketing department.

In some cases, corporations would do well to create stand-alone foundations to bring greater cohesion to their giving strategies and community relations activity.

Community relations is action-oriented and should include one or more of these forms:

1. Creating something necessary that did not exist before.
2. Eliminating something that poses a problem.
3. Developing the means for self-determination.
4. Including citizens who are in need.
5. Sharing professional and technical expertise.
6. Tutoring, counseling and training.
7. Promotion of the community to outside constituencies.
8. Moving others toward action.

Publicity and promotions should support community relations and not be the substitute or smokescreen for the process. Recognition is as desirable for the community as for the business. Good news shows progress and encourages others to participate.

The well-rounded community relations program embodies all elements: accessibility of company officials to citizens, participation by the company in business and civic activities, public service promotions, special events, plant communications materials and open houses, grassroots constituency building and good citizenry.

Never stop evaluating. Facts, values, circumstances and community composition are forever changing. The same community relations posture will not last forever. Use research and follow-up techniques to reassess the position, assure continuity and move in a forward motion.

No business can operate without affecting or being affected by its communities. Business must behave like a guest in its communities…never failing to show or return courtesies. Community acceptance for one project does not mean than the job of community relations has completed.

Community relations is not "insurance" that can be bought overnight. It is tied to the bottom line and must be treated accordingly, with resources and expertise to do it effectively. It is a bond of trust that, if violated, will haunt the business. If steadily built, the trust can be exponentially parlayed into successful long-term business relationships.

Chapter 15

FUTURE WATCH

Growth by Capitalizing Upon Change.
What It Will Take to Sustain and Move Forward.

T his chapter enumerates the benefits of changing and moving forward as a result. Companies must detect problems, create opportunities and assure that planned growth takes place. Those who do so will master change, rather than falling the victim of it.

Businesses cannot exist in a vacuum. They must interact with the outside world. They must predict the trends and master the issues affecting the climate and opportunities in which they function. This includes stimulating "outside-the-box" thinking, building customer coalitions and distinguishing your company from the pack.

The future is a series of journeys along a twisting and turning course, affected by what we choose to do and the priorities that we assign. Along the way, there are warning signs that we either recognize or pay the price later for overlooking. Company futures are determined by choices that we make.

Our present tense and, thus, our future is further influenced by time and resources we spend interacting with other people and the actions of other people, directly or indirectly affecting us. The perspective of future actions is based upon mistakes we make and what we learn from them.

There are several schools of thought on the subject of futurism, depending upon the niche focus of those consultants who embrace the process. Some are marketing focused and say that the marketplace decides and drives all changes. I say that the marketplace cannot guide itself and needs to be steered and educated in order to make reasonable demands and foster achievable results. It is important that we not classify futurism as a champion or a subset of marketing, technology, training or research. This is intended to take futurism out of the esoteric and into the practice of business.

These are nine of my own definitions for the process of capturing and building a shared vision for organizations to chart their next 10+ years. Each one gets progressively more sophisticated.

Futurism is what you will do and become, rather than what it is to be. It is what you can and are committed to accomplishing, rather than what mysteriously lies ahead.

Futurism means leaders and organizations taking personal responsibility and accountability for what happens. Abdicating to someone or something else does not constitute business strategy and, in fact, sets the organization backward.

Futurism learns from and benefits from the past, a powerful teaching tool that I call "yesterday-ism." Giving new definitions to old ideas and new meanings to familiar premises, we should learn from the previous successes of others. We must study the business crises and learn from the failures of others. Business must understand the events, cycles, trends and subtle nuances because they will recur with great regularity.

Futurism means seeing clearly your perspectives and those of others. Growth companies capitalize upon change, rather than becoming a by-product of it. Understand what change is and what it can do for your organization.

Futurism becomes an ongoing quest toward wisdom. The organization commits to learning, which creates knowledge, inspires insights, and culminates in wisdom. It is more than having data that is not interpreted or applied. It is more than just being taught or informed.

Futurism is a mix of ideas that inspire, manage and benchmark change. The ingredients may change management, crisis management and preparedness, streamlining operations, empowerment of people, re-engineering, quality improvement, marketplace development, organizational evolution and vision.

Futurism means developing critical thinking and reasoning skills, rather than dwelling just upon techniques and processes. Sales, technology, re-engineering, marketing, research, training, operations and administration are pieces of a much larger mosaic and should be seen as such. Futurism embodies thought processes that create and energize the mosaic and its pieces.

Futurism results from watching other people changing and capitalizing upon it. Understand from where we came in order to posture where we are headed. Creating organizational vision, setting the stage for all activities, processes, accomplishments and goals. Efforts must be realistic, and all must be held accountable.

Futurism indeed becomes the foresight to develop hindsight that creates insight into the future.

Change Management

Research shows that change is 90% beneficial. So why do people fight what's in their best interest? It occurs because of fears, contexts, decisions and a tendency to second-guess. Change management is an elixir, not a punishment.

People and organizations change at the rate of 71% per year, without always seeing it occur. The secret with planning-based futurism is to benefit from inevitable changes, rather than become victims of an environment that was changed by others. While some in the marketplace do not manage change, the most successful companies read those signs and create opportunities to surpass the others.

Companies driven only by money (making it and keeping it) see business as a game, not a philosophy of productivity. Human beings and the organizations which they inhabit are products of change. The manner in which they accept change has a direct relationship to their future success. The ability to adapt, learn and innovate is the basis of change management. Thriving upon change and mastering it are the fundamentals for Futurism.

Developing sophisticated thinking, reasoning, idea generation and planning skills is the only way in which organizations and their leaders will survive in the future. Today's workforce will need three times the amount of executive development and leadership training that it now gets if the organization intends to stay in business, remain competitive and tackle the future successfully.

Organizations of all sizes must have planning in order to delineate future operations, opportunities, future directions which the company might take and nuggets of wisdom to help get them to new plateaus.

There is a difference between how one is basically educated, and the ingredients needed to succeed in the long-term. Many people never amass those ingredients because they stop learning or don't see the need to go any further. Many people think they are "going further" but otherwise spin their wheels.

There is a large disconnect between indoctrinating people to tools of the trade and the myriad of elements they will need to assimilate for their own futures. Neither teachers nor students have all the necessary ingredients. It is up to both to obtain skills, inspiration, mentoring, processes, accountability, creativity and other components from niche experts.

Companies owe it to themselves to think and plan before launching piecemeal training programs. After carefully articulating and understanding direction, then niche project work within the organization will stand a chance of being successful.

Styles and Approaches to Mastering Change

Low-Power	Entrepreneur	Innovator
Maintain the status quo.	Carve new opportunities.	Create paths.
Technical proficiency skills.	Develop to an art.	Create modules.
Caution, Low-profile.	Take bold steps to lead.	Convictions.
Dependency.	Autonomy.	Self-reliant.
Survival.	Risk and expansion.	Vision.
Bureaucracy.	Customer orientation.	Leading.
Fulfill tasks, schedules.	Honor-exceed commitments.	Value-added.
Live and let live.	Our corner of the world.	Global village.
Learning.	Knowledge.	Wisdom.

Growth Strategies to Succeed in Changing Times

Businesses cannot exist in a vacuum. They must interact with the outside world, predict the trends and master front-burner issues affecting the climate and opportunities in which they function. This includes stimulating "outside-the-box" thinking, building customer coalitions and distinguishing your company from the pack.

There are several good reasons to embrace change management: It beats the alternative. Organizations and professionals who become stuck in ruts and stubbornly cling to the past are dinosaurs, which the marketplace will pass by.

Professionals, specialists and technicians owe their careers and livelihoods to change. Because they are educated and experienced at new techniques, they have market power.

Change is not as high-risk as some people fear. Failure to change costs the company six times more. Lost business, opportunity costs and product failures are signs of neglect, poor management, failure to plan-anticipate and grow the company.

Those who champion change advance their companies and careers. It accelerates the learning curve and success ratio. Those who do not get on the bandwagon will not last in the company. Those who excel develop leadership skills, empowered teams and efficiencies.

Change helps you do business in the present and helps plan for the future. Without mastering the challenges of a changing world, companies will not be optimally successful. The organization which manages change remains successful, ahead of the competition and is a business-industry leader. Meanwhile, other companies will have become victims of change because they stood by and did nothing.

There are many types of businesses in today's global economy. Many factors affect their ability to grow, much less their chances for longevity. The art of business survival lies in distinguishing each tree from the forest, each forest from the environment and each environment from the global village. Trees may exist or even thrive in one forest (business climate).

Everyone must be measured and champion their own accountability. The natural order is chaos. It requires organization and purpose to create order. The art and skill with which order is achieved equates to growth strategies.

Growth does not necessarily mean bigger. Growth can be lateral by moving a company into ancillary businesses or into new business areas. It will be most successful when it is strategic, planned, measured and with applications to the next inevitable plateau. Strategy sustains for business crises. Strategy determines growth, along with opportunities, challenges and methodologies that will address the future, varying with each company. Companies should establish a formal visioning program.

Value Analysis of a Healthy, Nourished Business

Only at such time as the strategic plan is implemented to assure consistency in purpose, then the following components of a company vision may be expected to ring true, per each category of the Business Tree™:

1. **The Business You're In.** Products and services reflect marketplace needs of today and the future. Processes are continually updating themselves. The expansion of your business is a natural outgrowth of carefully planned and well implemented strategy. You give customers what they cannot really get elsewhere.

    Turn crises, trends and disappointments into lessons well learned. When we see the downfalls and comebacks of others, we optimize potential in ourselves. Crystallize your niche and scope. Study and refine your own core business characteristics. Make investments toward quality controls.

2. **Running the Business.** Though company leadership influences vision, the process of implementing it must involve the total organization. Operations continue to streamline and are professional and productive. The company's demonstrated integrity and dependability assure customers that the team will perform magnificently.

    Make objective analyses of how the organization has operated to date. Document practices, procedures, operations and structure in writing. The physical plant is regularly studied, updated and modified. Distribution standards are documented, practiced and measured. Time management and "just in time" concepts are applied. Plans are in writing to address inventories and reducing surplus. Outsourcing, privatizing and collaborating plans are annually updated, with realistic, measurable goals.

    Reduce entrenched fears and defeating characteristics. Make wise use of technology. Maintain quality controls that exceed the specifications. Multiply the number of win-win situations.

3. **Financial.** The company has a fiduciary responsibility to run effectively and profitably. All must respect this, though finance cannot govern all aspects of company activity. Keeping the cash register ringing is not

the only reason for being in business. You always give customers their money's worth. Your charges are fair and reasonable.

Cost containment is one (but not the only) factor of company operations. Each product-service is budgeted. Assets are adequately valued and managed. Cash flow, forecasting and budgeting are consistently monitored.

Business is run economically and efficiently, with excellent accounting procedures, payables-receivables practices and cash management. Basing future projections upon past achievements invites unfair expectations. Reduce opportunity costs. Optimize the book value of the company.

4. **People.** No organization lives or dies by one person. The successful company is people-friendly, improving productivity by making higher investments in human capital. Employees know their jobs, are empowered to make decisions and have high morale in carrying the company banner forward. Every employee must be accountable for their activities and is sufficiently trained.

Collaborations assure that the best talent is assembled. Top management has as a priority the need to develop and practice People skills development and team building responsibilities. Management and employees become highly accountable. The employee teams are empowered, competent and demonstrate initiative and judgment.

Codes of ethics and corporate responsibility are observed. The corporate culture reflects a formal Visioning Program.

5. **Business Development.** Strategic planning gives you a better understanding of the marketplace in which your company competes. External factors of the marketplace must always influence the products produced and services rendered.

Customer input must factor into all long-term planning decisions. Customer service is always the focus. Communications are open, frequent, professional and with a deep sense of caring.

All members of top management have business development responsibilities required of them. The company has and regularly fine-tunes a communications strategy. Components include plans for sales, marketing, advertising, public relations, research, and marketplace development, annually updated, with realistic, measurable goals.

6. **Body of Knowledge.** There is a sound understanding of the relationship of each business function to the other. Every part of the organization must learn more about and how to interact better with each other's. A condition of departments living in a myopic vacuum is not acceptable to your progressive organization.

    The company learns how to benefit from changes, predicting and staying ahead of trends. Management learns and understands the lessons of failure as the basis for future success. The organization takes a more global view. Everything that goes on outside our company affects our business in some way.

    Provide leadership for progress, rather than following along. Create strategies that previously never existed. Go outside the box more than ever before. Develop and champion the tools with which to change.

7. **The Big Picture.** Shared organizational vision is a road map for progressive growth. Things do not just happen without thoughtful planning and strategy. The company leadership approaches business as a lifetime track record of accomplishments. You maintain and regularly benchmark a strategy for the future, reflecting the society in which we live. In the conduct of business, you ethically walk the talk.

    Generating new ideas enables companies to broaden the understanding of what is possible. Sustain a corporate culture that seeks to do right and be our best. Therefore, business becomes more creative, effective and profitable.

8. **Review the progress.** Benchmark the accomplishments, which serves as planning for the next phase. Analyze accomplishments in terms of overall organizational vision and implications for successful achievement of long-term company objectives.

9. **Shared Vision is crafted, articulated and followed.** The ongoing emphasis is upon updating, fine-tuning and improving the corporate culture. The CEO shares strategies and philosophies with employees and stakeholders. Creative business practices are most welcome in such a progressive organization.

    Strategic planning is viewed as vital to business survival and future success. Outside-the-box thinking does indeed apply to us and will be sought. The organization maintains and lives by an ethics statement.

The manner in which one navigates through the rocky times and takes proactive steps to recovering from inevitable setbacks speaks toward long-term success. Taking shortcuts will actually deter the journey toward success.

Chapter 16

COMMUNICATIONS, CORRECTLY POSITIONING YOUR COMPANY

Essential Roles of Corporate Communications and Public Relations

I t's not enough to simply make a good widget. Every organization must be in the widget production, distribution, marketing, selling and deliverability business.

Fundamental to running a successful business is the necessity to craft, fine-tune, perpetuate, benchmark and evolve the organization's image, public posture and the intricately subtle nuances of same. Corporate communications does not just happen all by itself. It must reflect careful forethought toward a changing corporate culture, with layers of sophisticated actions in congruity with that culture.

All too often, service providers in the communications specialty fields are called upon. The result is a patchwork of conflicting images, rather than a tapestry of what best suits the organization. Often, organizational communications image is biased by the slant of the service provider quilt currently being used for cover.

How organizations start out and what they become are different concepts. Mistakes, niche orientation and lack of planning lead businesses to failure.

Processes, trends, fads, perceived stresses and "the system" force managers to make compromises in order to proceed. Often, a fresh look at previous knowledge gives renewed insight.

Underlying tenets for the organization that should be followed through the communications program include:

- Think Big Picture.
- Conceptualize and communicate your company's own goals.
- Understand conflicting societal goals.
- Fit your dreams into the necessities and realities of the real world.
- Find your own niche...do your thing.
- Get satisfactions from doing something well and committing to long-term excellence.
- Seek truths in unusual and unexpected sources.
- Share your knowledge and learn further by virtue of mentoring others.

In many industries and professions, business development has occurred primarily by accident or through market demand. Because of economic realities and the increased numbers of firms providing comparable services, the notion of business development is now a necessity, rather than a luxury. Competition for customers-clients is sharpening. The professions are no longer held on a pedestal...a condition which mandates them to portray or enhance public images.

As companies adjust comfort levels and acquire confidence in the arena of business development, there is a direct relationship of the success of corporate communications to billings, client mix diversity, market share, competitive advantage, stock price and levels of business which enable other planned growth.

Public perceptions are called "credence goods" by economists. Every organization must educate outside publics about what they do and how they do it. This premise also holds true for each corporate operating unit and department. The whole of the business and each sub-set must always educate corporate opinion makers on how it functions and the skill with which the company operates.

Gaining confidence among stakeholders is crucial. Business relationships with customers, collaborators and other professionals are established to be long-term in duration. Each organization or should determine and craft its own corporate culture, character and personality, seeking to differentiate itself from others.

Top management must endorse corporate communications, if your company is to grow and prosper. Few companies can even sustain present levels of sales without some degree of business development.

Some people in your organization will devote much time to promotions, public relations, marketing and advertising. This quality should be recognized and rewarded...since professionals with a sense of business direction play an important part in company growth. Be it a "necessary evil" or not, corporate imaging activity can be accomplished with skill and success.

The professional organization that evokes a consistent image—and backs it up with actions—will prosper in today's rapidly changing marketplace. In image building, the following ideas should be considered:

- Your company and profession fill essential needs of society.
- Each key staff member represents a learned profession.
- Qualities denoting your company include skill, expertise, objectivity and independence.
- Work and abilities of your employees are diverse and creative.
- Your key management team is dynamic, in terms of business issues.
- The marketplace is rapidly expanding and is an excellent career choice for young people.
- Your team encompasses multi-dimensional professionals concerned with much more than the immediate responsibilities of the work at hand.

Ingredients of a Corporate Communications Program

The organization's Visioning Program takes years to develop. It is a hybrid of strategic planning, corporate culture, benchmarks and the dreams of the company. It must embrace top-down and bottom-up support. Producing the Visioning Program requires teamwork from across the organization. Frequent communications about the program's progress may be the arena for qualified communications professionals.

For public companies, a format Investor Relations Program has direct relationship to book value on Wall Street, stock price, stakeholder confidence and applicability toward long-term growth. Its writing and maintenance must encompass professionals from the planning, financial and communications disciplines, working together as a company brain trust.

Every organization must have a formal, written, sustainable and measurable Public Relations Program. Its components should include complete generic press

- Training and testing.
- Timeline for implementation.
- Benchmarks for measurement.

The use of social media has become a major communications vehicle for non-profit organizations. They use it to communicate their services to clients and donors, through such mechanisms as:

- Alerting stakeholders to immediate needs.
- Interacting with the community on a near-daily basis.
- Posting videos.
- Responding to emergencies.
- Communicating with stakeholders
- Bringing awareness to organizational mission.
- Telling human-interest stories.
- Conveying research and supporting documents.
- Providing a forum for comments.
- Building likes tend to increase awareness, understanding and support.
- Replacing other media outlets that have been lost.
- Facilitating on-line fund-raising campaigns.
- Allowing for immediate acknowledgement of public support.
- Inviting contributions from community of stakeholders.

Websites include Facebook, LinkedIn, Twitter, Google+, YouTube, Instagram, Pinterest, Vimeo. Many organizations have blog sites. They include articles, photos, news releases, client testimonials and event reminders.

Chapter 17

INTERNATIONAL BUSINESS

G lobalization increasingly affects every person throughout the world. It is accelerated by the infrastructures of communication, where the transfer of everything from ideas and data to goods and services has become a staple of everyday business.

Globalization impacts the safety of our nations, the value of our currencies, the condition of stock markets, the products we buy, the customers we serve, our jobs and the competition which we face.

Globalization is about breaking down political barriers. Borders are becoming more porous. People are on the move. Governments are nervous, and their tax bases are at risk.

The dynamics of globalization have altered our environment and the fundamental requirements of a complete business education. As technological advances and international trade continue to shrink the world in which we live, cross-cultural experience and understanding becomes not an advantage toward success, but a prerequisite. The globalization process considers different cultures, practices, and dilemmas faced within the realm of international business.

The world is dividing into ancient and modern, conservative and progressive camps. Some see it as the West against the rest of the world, Americanism versus traditionalism, or New Europe against Old Europe. People revert to cultural defenses against new ideas and outside influences.

Key points for developing a global business mindset:

- Every company with sales of more than $2 million should be exporting.
- Business must sell more products and services than its country buys.
- It is more about exporting products and services, rather than the exporting of jobs.
- Trade deficits should not become juggling acts by Wall Street or governments.
- Travel to see what the competition is doing.
- Follow your customers' trade routes.
- Utilize the services of consulates and departments of commerce for contacts.
- Get governments to talk more about exports.

Understand world history:
- It repeats itself.
- World history is far beyond that in which our countries participated.
- Study historical events of other nations.
- Be aware of the bad events and their long-term implications.

Study how the global economy works:
- Relationship of inflation from one country to another.
- Currency issues.
- Trade balances.
- Import and export processes.
- Systems of trade and money flows.
- Activities of international organizations, such as the WTO, IMF and World Bank.

Be familiar with global politics:
- Look beyond the news headlines and what is portrayed as news.
- Trade blocs.

- Geopolitics.
- Strategic alliances and activities.

Understand the world's cultures:
- Gives insights into how people think the way they do.
- Data Based Group, population 600 million.
- Relationship Based Group, population 3.8 billion.
- Group Based Group, population 1.6 billion.

Interact with and help your customers develop their international activity:
- Study their competition.
- Build, negotiate and manage international accounts.
- Build loyal, profitable and lasting overseas customer accounts.

Key Areas in Expanding International Marketplaces

Corporate Strategy. Strategic management, is concerned with the management of the corporation as a whole, as opposed to the functional areas, such as marketing, finance and accounting, all of which look at specific aspects of the firm. Executives are united by a common interest in company performance. Corporate Strategy encompasses an understanding of why some firms do better than others and develop structured theories and explanations of firm performance.

International Negotiations. Understand the processes of negotiation as it is practiced in a variety of settings. While a manager needs analytical skills to develop optimal solutions to problems, a broad array of negotiation skills are needed for these solutions to be accepted and implemented. Components of an effective negotiation include culture, government at the table, currency issues and ethics.

Finance with International Perspective. Topics include stock and bond valuation, the capital-budgeting decision, portfolio theory, the asset-pricing models, raising capital, capital structure, mergers and acquisitions, costs of capital, option pricing, and risk management.

International Competitive Strategy. Focus upon the development of competitive strategies in the global environment-including the identification of internationally relevant strengths and weaknesses, the movement and use of resources to gain competitive advantage, and strategies to confront competitors, both domestic and multinational.

Genies are granted three wishes.

Three represents the Trinity, the soul, the union of body and soul in human in the church.

There were three gifts of the Magi to Christ as God-King-Sacrifice.

Chinese tradition considers three (3) to be a lucky number. It is believed that groups of three in Chinese culture are even luckier. Confucius said: "Three people are walking together. At least one of them is good enough to be my teacher." A Chinese proverb says: "The wisdom of three ordinary people exceeds that of the wisest individual." There were three kingdoms, three Halls of Forbidden City, three emperors and three Moral Guidelines. Three represents potential.

People with the lucky number 3 have strong personalities. They possess mystical abilities, creativity and an instinct for art. They are sociable and talented, with a magnetism that inspires people around them.

Trios in Entertainment

In the Disney cartoons, the Three Little Pigs encountered the Big Bad Wolf. The pigs' names were Browny, Whitey and Blackie.

Famous musical trios included The Bee Gees, Andrews Sisters, Beastie Boys, Jimi Hendrix Experience, Nirvana, The Browns, Rush, Carter Family, The Impressions, Trio Los Panchos, Bachman Turner Overdrive, James Gang, Mandrell Sisters, King Cole Trio, The Stray Cats, The Supremes, The Police, Cream, Destiny's Child, ZZ Top, The Fleetwoods, The Dixie Chicks, Pointer Sisters, Tony Orlando & Dawn, Rascal Flatts, Ramsey Lewis Trio, Genesis, Kingston Trio, Lady Antebellum, Chad Mitchell Trio, Fontane Sisters, Grand Funk Railroad and the Three Tenors.

Movie Trilogies

Back to the Future (Michael J. Fox)

The Godfather (Al Pacino, Robert De Niro)

Lord of the Rings (Elijah Wood, Viggo Mortensen, Ian McKellen)

John Ford's Cavalry Trilogy: *Fort Apache, She Wore a Yellow Ribbon, Rio Grande* (John Wayne)

Jason Bourne (Matt Damon)

Original *Star Wars* trilogy (Mark Hamill, Harrison Ford, Carrie Fisher)

Indiana Jones (Harrison Ford)

Man With No Name, Dollars trilogy (Clint Eastwood)
Matrix trilogy (Keanu Reeves)
Alien trilogy (Sigourney Weaver)
Pirates of the Caribbean (Orlando Bloom, Keira Knightley, Johnny Depp)
Spider-Man (Tobey Maguire, Kirsten Dunst)
Naked Gun (Leslie Nielsen)
X-Men (Hugh Jackman)
The Terminator (Arnold Schwarzenegger)
Hannibal Lechter (Anthony Hopkins, Jodie Foster)
Blade trilogy (Wesley Snipes)
Austin Powers trilogy (Mike Myers)
Mad Max trilogy (Mel Gibson)

TV Show Trilogies

MASH, After-MASH, Trapper John MD
Mary Tyler Moore Show, Rhoda/Phyllis, Lou Grant
December Bride, Pete & Gladys, Cara Williams Show
Perry Mason, New Perry Mason, Perry Mason Movie Mysteries
Danger Man, Secret Agent, The Prisoner
I Love Lucy, The Lucy Show, Here's Lucy
Andy Griffith Show, Gomer Pyle, Mayberry RFD
The Beverly Hillbillies, Petticoat Junction, Green Acres
Four Star Playhouse, Zane Grey Theatre, Dick Powell Theatre
Three's Company, The Ropers, Three's a Crowd
Life with Elizabeth, Date with the Angels, Betty White Show
The Brady Bunch, Brady Brides, The Bradys

Book Trilogies

Bourne Trilogy, by Robert Ludlum
Millenium Trilogy, by Stieg Larsson
King Trilogy, by Stephen Douglass
Hunger Games, by Suzanne Collins
Internal Devices Trilogy, by Cassandra Clare
Graceling Realm, by Kristin Cashore
The Falsifiers, by Antoine Bello

Beyond Trilogy, by Janet Morris
His Dark Materials, by Philip Pullman
Orphan Trilogy, by James and Lance Morgan
Bronze Horseman Trilogy, by Paullina Simons
Trilogy of the *Chosen*, by J.M. LeDuc
African Trilogy, by Chinua Achebe
Bloodlines Trilogy, by Glen Duncan
Sign of Seven Trilogy, by Nora Roberts
The Legends trilogy, by Hank Moore
The Big Picture of Business trilogy, by Hank Moore
Peter Drucker Trilogy: *Effective Executive, Five Most Important Questions, People and Performance*
W. Edwards Deming Trilogy: *Out of the Crisis, New Economics, Best of Deming*
Tom Peters Trilogy: *Thriving on Chaos, A Passion for Excellence, The Excellence Dividend*
Stephen Covey Trilogy: *7 Habits of Highly Effective People, The 8th Habit, The Leader in Me*

Three Stages in Business
Business life cycle: launch-growth, maturity, shake-out & decline.

Three stages of business development: having value, communicating value and delivering value.

Three stages of professional development: building a knowledge base, observing and reflecting, plus gaining and sharing experience.

Three stages of customer service: improving, transforming and sustaining.

Business continuity planning: resolve, respond, rebuild.

Ways of taking action: cautious, medium space, full force.

Human resource management: pre-hiring, training, post-hiring.

Branding: design, value proposition, positioning statement.

Financial accounting: sorting invoices, posting ledgers, closing journal entries.

Change: unfreezing, changing, refreezing.

Leadership levels: public, private, personal.

Leadership development phases: Emerging, developing, strategic.

Human resource management: pre-hiring, training, post-hiring.

Three Rights Offset a Wrong

There is much more good in companies that might be recognized at first glance. Rather than focusing on the negative, we look at the strengths and how they can elevate companies further.

Things in business go wrong. The skill of running business is how you correct the mistakes and move forward. By observing, one obtains perspectives and factors into planning and strategy.

These are the categories of Wrong, in order from accidental to purposeful and worse:

- Inexact.
- Inaccurate.
- Astray.
- Incorrect.
- Mistaken.
- Erroneous.
- Imprecise.
- Off-target.
- Invalid.
- Untrue.
- False.
- Iniquity and Injurious.
- Deceptive.
- Unfair.
- Harmful.
- Dishonest.
- Offensive.
- Discrediting.
- Fraudulent.
- Dishonorable.
- Unacceptable.
- Violations.
- Transgressions.
- Unethical.
- Illegal and Corrupt.

The basics of good business are rooted in respect. The demonstration of respect is a valuable commodity that caring professionals must nurture and show toward their colleagues, customers, industry, marketplace and stakeholders.

Really accomplished professionals reflect back on their early careers as foretelling of great things to come. Secrets to success come from revisiting the early years. Learning from the past allows us to maximize the future.

Chapter 19

FOOD INDUSTRY CASE STUDIES

I have conducted management assessments for many industries and companies. This is a representative growth strategies assessment, conducted on behalf of food manufacturing and processing industries. It is indicative of the way in which overviews and strategies are developed with a Big Picture of Business approach.

Forces driving trade include:
- Consumer preferences.
- Institutions.
- Governments.
- Technology.
- More firms with global reach.
- Consolidation.
- Decreasing producer market power in global economy.
- Access to other markets via e-commerce.

Trends and opportunities:

- U.S. consumers have year-round demand for variety of products.
- Ethnic and regional markets want foods from home.
- E-commerce facilitates trade.
- Emerging economies rely upon agriculture and fiber products for trade balances.
- More retailers familiar with global supply.
- U.S. production will continue to exceed domestic demand.
- International cooperative relationships being formed.

There are four ways to develop business: sell new customers, cross-sell existing customers, create new products and establish alliances. Here are strategies to consider:

- Gain understanding of world markets.
- Develop market intelligence.
- Build trading and distribution capacity.
- Develop more sophisticated marketing philosophy.
- Seek out needed alliances to fill gaps.
- Learn from the most experienced.

Food industry business strategies:

1. Consider members in other countries.
2. Develop alliances with global manufacturers.
3. Alliances with global retailers.
4. Joint ventures with foreign cooperatives.
5. Develop alliances with other suppliers.
6. Build E-commerce capacity.
7. Develop new products and packaging.

The food sector is complex. It is composed of input suppliers, producers, processors, distributors and those at the retail end of the chain. It covers a large number of industries, with many trends and issues impacting on the way it operates. These range from the amalgamation of chemical companies at the input end to the increasing power of the supermarkets at the retail end. A number of issues such as genetic modification could have a profound influence on the food industries.

Trends with a Food Focus

The world's population grows to 8.98 billion by 2040 and then declines to 8.41 billion by 2100.

There will be a tripling in demand for food and animal proteins over the next 50 years, which needs to be satisfied by current available arable land and water.

Global trade barriers are being reduced, which will increase movement of food products globally. Large multinationals are looking to fill their pipelines as they merge and become larger.

Venture capital funds are targeting agriculture and food as an investment opportunity. Rollups will positively impact the industries.

Aging Societies. Fiscal pressures associated with aging societies are set to intensify over the next few years, and even more so beyond. Deficits and debts are on an explosive path in most large countries, as well as in many smaller ones.

Winning the battle against the desert. For less than a dollar a tree, Tunisia is planting 40 million trees a year to combat desertification. The government-sponsored "green wall" project uses military manpower to keep costs low; soldiers are also being deployed to help nomads adapt to farming.

All-day eating. Rigid distinctions among breakfast, lunch, and dinner—and of the times of day they occur—are fading as individuals fit their dining habits around more flexible and fluid work and life schedules. Restaurants accommodating these blurred dining habits will offer a mix of big, little, and medium meals during all hours.

Sustainable Agriculture. To make global agriculture more sustainable, land use zoning and regulations to minimize damage, retiring 5-15% of the most marginal land, farming with nature, eliminating subsidies and market barriers, promoting better management practices, improving certification and eco-labels. Organic agriculture is expanding in most countries to meet increasing demand. The organic sector of agriculture has been growing at 15-30% per year.

Trends affecting the food industries:

- Industry research as a marketing tool.
- Industry campaigns, such as those conducted by the beef industry.
- Food processing technologies.
- Supplies to underdeveloped nations.
- China's feed grain market.

- Supply response of market grain surplus.
- Linkages in markets.
- Government reforms.
- Tobacco industry litigation, punishment and responses.
- Impact of E-Commerce on traditional trading relationships and practices.
- Improving Investment in commodities markets.
- Specialty crops online international trading.

The future is opening up more opportunities. Food industry trends to watch include:

- Gourmet packaged salads.
- Meals ready to eat.
- Sodas losing in popularity. Juices and teas on the rise.
- More ethnic foods to be packaged.
- Custom food manufacturers are more prolific than ever.
- Fortification of preservative-free foods that promote health. The consumer's quest for health is having a great impact on the food processor.
- Restaurant operators are targeting entrees, appetizers, sandwiches and soups that promote menu diversity by using petite portions and ethnic variations.
- Consumer skepticism about healthy food additives. The disappointment in the taste of more-healthful low-calorie or low-fat items has left many food developers feeling cynical when it comes to ingredients touted as being healthier.
- Extend the sweetness of food/beverage products while extending and slowing glycemic response.

Food industry participants chose in this order: consistency, price per serving, convenience, labor savings and sensory quality. Those surveyed also found convenience (35%), offering better quality at the same prices (15%), and healthier foods (14%) to be the top-three most significant trends in the development of prepared foods for foodservice distribution.

Establishing partnerships between the manufacturer and the end user in the early stages of product development gives customers an opportunity to fully explain what they are seeking.

In recent years, the advent of some non-thermal processing systems that pasteurize and/or sterilize have been offered to processors as alternative systems. These systems hold the dual promise of not degrading any product characteristic for enhanced product quality and opening up new markets where new types of products can be developed.

Food safety continues to be the most critical issue. Manufacturers have begun retooling their hazard analysis and critical control points programs, tightening access to plants, improving traceability backward into their supply chain and sealing trailers and bulk storage tanks. Machinery makers are working on delivering lower fat, higher productivity and other food industry demands.

Industry Trends and Opportunities for Business

Food industry hot growth areas for careers:

- Computer information systems.
- Food processing and distribution.
- Outdoor recreation businesses.
- Food and forest product distribution.
- Landscape, horticulture and lawn care.
- Technical service problem solvers.
- Commodity brokers.
- International market representatives.
- Managers for larger farms.
- Intensive livestock production.
- Fruit and vegetable production.
- Ornamental horticulture and turf grass management.

Upstream Issues with producers include the weather, government bans, crop insurance, farm bills in Congress and state legislatures and opening borders. International agricultural industries to watch include Argentina, Australia, Bulgaria, China, France, Germany, Guatemala, Japan, The Philippines and Poland.

Downstream food producers must be competent in:

- Scientific work.
- Co-products and by-products.
- Changing patterns of trade and commercial activity.
- Banking and financial management.

- Technology transfer.
- Problem recognition and solution.
- Marketing.
- Consumer trends and customer service.
- Collaboration building.
- Supply chain management.
- Business planning.

Also, watch trends in related industries, including:
- New directions in the breakfast food market.
- The consumer nutritionist industry.
- The baking industry.
- Fertilizers, pesticides and farm inputs.
- Fiber and apparel.
- Food processing, production and sales.
- Meat, poultry and livestock.
- Pulp and paper.
- Wood and forest products.
- Landscape/nursery industry.
- Demands of food banks.
- Financial Adjustments in the agricultural sector.
- Farm machinery and equipment industry.
- Agricultural chemical use, farm production and the environment.

Factors of efficient management include:
- Financial analysis, tools and ratios.
- Cash flow and profitability analysis.
- Operations effectiveness in Agribusiness
- Evaluation of operations strategy.
- Supply chain management.
- Efficient consumer response.

Chapter 20

SMALL INVENTIONS

Little Things That Make Big Things Work

Household Staples

Refrigerator: The first artificial refrigeration system was invented in 1748. The first system using vapor to cool was invented in 1805. The first ice making machine was invented in 1857. A process of liquefying gas was devised in 1876. The first widely utilized refrigeration system was released in 1927. Freon was used as a lower toxicity alternative to the substances used in previous refrigeration units.

Clothes Hangers: Today's shoulder-shaped wire hanger, was inspired by a coat hook invented in 1869 by O. A. North. In 1906, a men's clothier in Grand Rapids, MI, became the first retailer to display clothing on hangers. In 1932, Schuler Hulett patented a design which used cardboard tubes mounted on the upper and lower parts of the wire to prevent wrinkles. Hangers can be made in wood, wire, plastic, rubber and other materials. Some are padded. A caped hanger is an inexpensive wire clothing hanger covered in paper. Caped hangers are used by dry cleaners to protect garments.

Weed Eater: George Ballas was the inventor of the Weed Eater, a string trimmer company founded in 1971. The idea for the Weed Eater trimmer came to him from the spinning nylon bristles of an automatic car wash. He thought that he could devise a similar technique to protect the bark on trees that he was trimming around. His company was bought by Emerson Electric and merged with Poulan, which was later purchased by Electrolux.

Home Remedies

Epsom Salts: Can ease back pain, smooth the skin, heal cuts and improve sleep. In the early 17th century, a farmer in Epsom, England, was out with his cattle when he saw water filling a cow's hoof-print. Next day, he discovered that the water had a mineral taste. Word of the mineral water spread. Chemists adapted the formula to containing inorganic salt magnesium sulfate.

Milk of Magnesia: As Ireland's first Inspector of Anatomy, James Murray was required to know the circumstances of everybody being dissected by his office. He created a preparation consisting of magnesium hydroxide, an inorganic compound. Mixed with water and ingested, the cloudy liquid acted as an antacid and laxative. Murray was knighted for his invention.

Office Supplies

Stapler: In 1877, the first device to bind documents together was patented by Henry Heyl. In 1879, George McGill created commercial staplers that could drive a half-inch wire through paper. In 1895 came a fastener that was fast and convenient to use. In the 1920s, staplers became smaller, lighter and capable of casing hundreds of staples. In the 1930s, Jack Linsky and the Swingline Company introduced compact staplers where users could open and drop in replacement staples.

Paper Clips: For as long as there have been paper documents, we have needed devices to file them together. In 1855, strong steel was bent into rust-free hooks, hangers and paper clips. In 1899, William Middlebrook received a patent for the machinery that created the clips.

Thumbtacks: In 1900, Edwin Moore, a photo lab technician, created a pin with a handle. His first pushpins had glass handles and steel points. His first big sale was $1,000 worth of tacks to Eastman Kodak Company.

Filing Cabinet: In the early 1800s, shelves and dividers were built inside wooden safes, accommodating ledgers and stacks of papers, safeguarding contents from theft. Letter cabinets had flat file drawers, evolving to meet the needs of newly emerging businesses. Document filing cabinets to hold legal documents were patented in 1868. Originally constructed with mood, the metal filing cabinets began appearing in 1891. The lateral stack was introduced in 1898. The lateral file was developed in 1998.

Writing Instruments: The quill pen was introduced around 700 A.D. John Jacob Parker invented the first self-filling fountain pen in 1831. Lewis Waterman invented the first practical mass-produced fountain pen in 1884. The first ballpoint pen was invented by Laszlo Biro in 1938. A pre-filled disposable ink cartridge was developed in 1950. In 1954, Parker Pen Co. introduced a long-lasting ballpoint pen. In the 1950s, French pen company BIC began widespread distribution of economical pens. Rollerball pens were introduced in the 1980s.

Rulers: The first method of measuring was a rod made of copper alloy in the year 2650 B.C. By 1500 B.C., there were ivory rulers. The first folding ruler was invented by Anton Ullrich, and the first flexible ruler was made in 1902. Rulers come in a different shapes, lengths and sizes. Materials used include plastic, wood and metal.

Automobile Equipment

Windshield Wipers: Mary Anderson was a real estate developer, cattle rancher and winemaker, though not a driver. In 1902, while riding a streetcar in New York City, she noticed the conductor had to open up part of the windshield to create visibility. She sketched a device for a removable "Window Cleaning Device" made of wood and rubber and operated manually via lever. She patented windshield wipers in 1903 but never saw a dime from the equipment that became standard in cars a decade later.

Laminated Glass: In 1903, French writer, artist and scientist Edouard Benedictus invented laminated glass. His assistant accidentally left some cellulose nitrate in a beaker and then stored it on a shelf. The beaker fell on the floor, but instead of shattering, it held together. Benedictus received a patent in 1909, although it didn't make its way into mass production until World War I, when it was used in gas mask goggles, and finally ended up in cars in the 1920s. In 1937, it became a requirement for all new cars. Today, laminated glass consists of multiple layers of glass held together with polyvinyl butyral (PVB) or ethylene-vinyl acetate (EVA), which also has the benefit of staying clearer and helps block more sound and UV rays.

Antifreeze: Ethylene Glycol was first used in dynamite, allowing the explosive to be made in cool, safe surroundings. It was an organic compound synthesized in 1856 by French chemist Charles-Adolph Wurtz. Added to water, it lowers the freezing point and raises the boiling point. In 1926, automakers adapted the compound into antifreeze, now known as coolant.

Cup Holder: By the 1950s, automobiles were extensively used for transportation in a mobile society. Designers made a "snack tray for cars that hangs from the dashboard." The Automobile Seat Article Holder was patented in 1953. The modern slide-out cup holder was designed by Clyde Morgan and introduced in the 1955 Chevrolet models. The 1957 Cadillac introduced a magnetic glove compartment door with metal tumblers. In 1983, Chrysler designed the minivan, with cup holders sunk into the dashboard.

Seat Belts: The first seat belts were invented by British engineer George Cayley and were used in gliders. The first patented seat belts were developed in 1885 by Edward J. Claghorn, used in carriages and taxis, plus by firemen and painters who needed to stay fastened to raised seats or other objects. Volvo engineer Nils Bohlin developed the first three-point seat belt, introduced in the 1959 models. In 1966, seat belts became required by law, with the three-point belts becoming standard in the 1970s. Bohlin also developed side impact protection equipment.

Safety Designs: Béla Barényi was a designer at Mercedes-Benz, developing 2,500 patents and designs for safety. One was the safety cell, which is an enclosed steel compartment inside the car, thus absorbing the force from a collision. He also invented the collapsible steering column, first introduced in the 1959 models.

Air Bags: John Hetrick saw his daughter almost thrown through the windshield in an auto accident. This motivated him to design air bags, with a patent granted in 1953. Alan Breed developed hardware that could sense crashes and in 1968 made the first electromechanical air bag system. In 1988, a law went into effect requiring air bags in driver and front passenger seat positions.

Rearview Cameras: In the 1970s was designed for big construction vehicles. Camera outside the vehicle were attached to monitors on the dashboard. Rearview cameras are now common in passenger cars and trucks.

GPS: In 1973, the U.S. Defense Department's NAVSTAR GPS was built for military use. After an airliner strayed into Soviet air space and was shot down in 1983, the government declassified GPS and made it available for widespread use. GPS was developed for tracking, used in cars and phones.

Communications Equipment

Printing Techniques: The woodblock printing system was developed in the year 200 A.D. Johannes Gutenberg developed a printing press system in 1439. Processes for making etchings came along in 1515. Lithography was invented in 1796. Rotary printing presses were invented in 1843. Offset printing came along in 1875.

Hot metal typesetting was devised in 1884. The mimeograph machine was created in 1886. Innovations included screen printing in 1911, dot matrix printing in 1925, xerography in 1938, inkjet printing in 1967 and laser printing in 1969. Solid ink printing and 3D printing both debuted in 1986, followed by digital printing in 1991.

Typewriters: In 1575, Italian printmaker Francesco Rampazetto devised a machine to impress letters on paper. In 1714, British inventor Henry Mill obtained a patent for the typewriter. In 1802, Agostino Fantoni stylized the braille typewriter. In 1829, the typographer was patented. The first commercial typewriters were introduced in 1874. By 1910, mechanical manual typewriters were standardized. The first electric typewriter was produced in 1900. Remington Rand produced the first electro-magnetic typewriter in 1929. IBM introduced the Selectric typewriter in 1961, ink ribbons replaced by carbon ribbons in later models. In 1973, ink was switched to cartridges. Electronic typewriters came along in 1979, thus transitioning to computers for business office use.

Drum Scanners: Beginning in 1860, the Pantelegraph was introduced, the first facsimile machine to transmit handwriting, signatures and drawings. Thje Belinograph was invented in 1913, housing a photo cell and transmitted over phone lines. The Belinograph transmitted photos to news agencies, with color photos sent as three separate RGB filtered images. Drum scanners capture image information with photomultiplier tubes. The first image scanner for a computer was developed in 1957 at the U.S. National Bureau of Standards. The first image scanned and transmitted was a photo of the child of project coordinator Russell Kirsch.

Fax Machines: In 1880, inventor Sheldon Bidwell improved on the Pantelegraph to scan any two-dimensional original. Fax is short for facsimile. Early systems used direct conversions of image darkness to audio tone in a continuous analog manner. Receiving fax machines receive tones and reconstruct the images, printing paper copies. In 1924, RCA engineer Richard Ranger invented the photoradiogram, a transoceanic forerunner to modern fax machines. Western Union introduced its desk model in 1948. Xerox Corporation introduced the modern model in

1964 under the name Long Distance Xerography. In 1985, Hank Magnuski of GammaLink introduced the first computer fax board.

Flatbed Scanners: These produce good scans from reflective artwork. These feature the Charge Coupled Device arrays. Types of flatbed scanners are CCD, CIS, 3D, planetary, hand document scanner, portable and Smartphone scanner applications.

Entertainment Media and Equipment

Radio: In 1920, the first radio sets were sold by Westinghouse to promote its first station, 8XK in Pittsburgh, PA. In 1926, NBC Radio signed on the air. In 1927, CBS Radio signed on the air. In 1939, NBC covered the opening of the World's Fair and the first football game, baseball game and prize fight were broadcast. The year 1940 saw the first basketball game and hockey match and the first coverage of political conventions broadcast.

Television: In 1898, the first suggestions were made that pictures with sound could be carried across large distances. Movies were introduced in European arcades in 1895. Within three years, research was begun to carry the moving pictures to distant locations. This actually preceded the development of radio. In 1927, the first test television pictures were sent.

The year 1928 saw the first American home got a TV set. the first regularly scheduled TV programs and the first trans-oceanic TV signal sent from London to New York. The first public demonstration of a color TV model was in 1929. The first closed-circuit TV projected on a big screen in a theatre was in 1930. In 1941, the first licensed commercial television station (WNBT-TV) went on the air. The first commercial cost sponsor Bulova Watches a total of nine dollars.

The year 1945 saw the first public demonstration of a TV set in a department store, 25,000 watching. 1947 saw the first mass production of television receivers, the first broadcast of a joint session of Congress and the first broadcast of a World Series baseball championship. In 1951, RCA unveiled the first community TV antenna system (forerunner of cable TV). In 1952, coaxial cable was laid, facilitating national broadcast transmissions.

1953 saw the first worldwide event coverage: the coronation of Queen Elizabeth (film flown from England) and RCA testing the first compatible TV sets. In 1956, video tape was first used on television production. Originally, tape was used for commercials and portions of programs. By 1958, entire programs were taped and edited for later broadcast. This ultimately spelled the beginning of the end of live television (except for news shows).

Record Players: In 1877, Thomas Edison introduced the cylinder, developed originally for business office use. It was the earliest Dictaphone, whereby messages would be recorded by a needle on a rolling tube. In 1888, Emile Berliner invented the phonograph record, for the purpose of transporting music to consumers. Columbia Records (now Sony) was founded in 1898, followed by RCA Victor Records in 1901. Edison missed his chance to influence the recording industry by sticking with the cylinder medium, not converting to phonograph records until 1912 and finally getting out of the recording business in 1929.

Records: In 1931, research into record speeds other than 78RPM ensued. In 1948, Columbia Records first issued long-playing record albums on the market. In 1949, RCA Victor Records first issued 45-RPM singles on the market.

At every juncture, there were transition periods in the adoption and acceptance of new media. For the first 11 years of 45RPM records and LPs being manufactured, there were still 78RPM discs on the market. Throughout the tape formats, there were still records. With the advent of Compact Discs, there were still records and cassette tapes on the market. To now rush to conversion of all music to digital downloads is short-sighted and stands to kill markets and after-markets for CDs that still have another 20 years to run.

45RPM Adapters: These are plastic or metal inserts that go in the middle of 45RPM records, so they can be played on the LP spindle of a turntable. The first adapters were introduced by the Webster-Chicago Corporation. They were made of solid zinc, difficult to insert into a record and almost impossible to remove without breaking the disc. A differently shaped, but similarly difficult-to-use metal adapter was made by Fidelitone. Capitol Records for a time produced what they called "Optional Center" or "O.C. 45" records. These had a triangular cardboard insert with an LP-size spindle hole; the cardboard center could be punched out for playing on 45RPM spindles but could not be replaced.

Audio Tapes: 1946 saw the importing of reel-to-reel recording from Germany to the U.S. 1965 saw the advent of audio cassette tapes. 1968 saw the advent of eight-track tapes. 8-track tapes were only meant to be an interim medium, until CDs were developed.

Video Cassette Tapes: In 1980, the concept of videotape rentals was first introduced. The retail cost of VCRs went below $1,000 for the first time. By 1984, the retail cost of VCRs went below $500 for the first time. In 1985, the cost of blank videotapes dropped below $10.00 for the first time.

Creative Inventions

Horatio Adams knew that his father Thomas had purchased a lot of Mexican chicle with the intent of producing a rubber substitute. Horatio, then 13, found an alternate use, designing chewing gum. He developed gumballs and convinced the local druggist to dispense them.

Alexander Graham Bell was 18 when he began developing a way to transmit speech. His "harmonic telegraph" evolved into the telephone.

Joseph Armand Bombardier was 15 in 1922, living in Quebec, Canada. Spending winters in the snow, he added a sleigh frame and hand-whittled propeller to his father's old model T car. Thus, evolved the snowmobile.

Louis Braille was accidentally blinded as a child. While attending a school for the visually impaired in Paris, Braille was 15 when he created a system using raised dots instead of letters.

Sam Colt was attending a boarding school at age 15. Wishing to get popular with the other kids, he made a firework and discharged it outside. Years later, he adapted the concept, and it became the revolver gun.

Thomas Alva Edison was 17 in 1862, producing as his first invention a telegraphic repeating instrument, while working as a telegraph operator.

Frank Epperson was 11 in 1905 when he left his drink, a mixture of water and powdered soda on the porch overnight, during which time it froze in the cold weather. He called this delicacy the "Epsicle." 18 years later, Frank made it for his kids, and they called it "Pop's Sicle." In 1923, he commercialized the product, developing various flavors (30 now on the market, with orange being the most popular).

Benjamin Franklin loved to swim and was 11 years old when he invented flippers for the hands. The device was later adapted as flippers for the feet.

Chester Greenwood was 15 in 1874 when creating his first invention, earmuffs, which were made by his factory for the next 60 years. Greenwood created more than 100 other inventions.

Cyrus Hall McCormick was 15 in 1824 when he developed a lightweight cradle for carting harvested grain. In 1831, he invented a horse-drawn device to cut small grain crops, known as the reaper.

Robert Patch was 6 when in 1957 he invented a toy truck that can be disassembled and can be rebuilt into different kinds of trucks.

Theresa Thompson (age 8) and her sister Mary (age 9) in 1960 invented a solar tepee for a science fair project, calling it the Wigwarm. They are the youngest sisters ever to receive a U.S. Patent.

Anton van Leeuwenhoek was 16 in 1648 when he developed improvements to the microscope.

George Westinghouse was 19 when he got his first patent in 1865, for the rotary steam engine.

High-Tech Inventions

The space program has brought modern life many inventions. There are 1,800 spin-offs in NASA's Technology Transfer Program, including CAT scanners, computer microchips, cordless tools, ear thermometers, freeze-dried food, insulation reflective techniques, invisible braces for teeth, enriched baby food, the joy stick, light-emitting diodes, memory foam, microwave ovens, scratch resistant lenses, shoe insoles, smoke detectors, solar energy, the swimsuit, powdered lubricants, water filters, space blankets, land mine removal, the soap soaker, flame resistant textiles, the ingestible thermometer pill, workout machines for conditioning, highway safety grooving, artificial limbs, pollution remediation, radial tires, ventricular assist devices, software catalogs and much more.

The 21st century, in business and in lifestyles, is dominated by technology, from cell phones to wi-fi, from the internet to social media and from modern adaptations of technologies from two earlier centuries.

Technology has influenced so many devices and niche industries, including aircraft navigation, alarm systems, analyzers, automated attendants, automobiles, broadband communications, cable fiber optics, call systems, cellular mobile station equipment, clocks, cloud storage, computers, converters, data management systems, digital test equipment, distributors, earth stations, educational and training systems, fiber optic tools, hardware, headsets, HVAC equipment, key systems, lighting systems, message systems, modems, monitoring systems, paging systems, power supplies, radio telephone equipment, railroad systems, receivers, revenue and billing systems, routers, security systems, semiconductors, signaling systems, storage systems, surge protectors, switches, telecommunications devices, teleconferencing, test equipment, towers, transformers, trucks, video games, video

Often, technology is a "bells and whistles" project that companies readily put money behind, rather than first addressing total-organizational issues, problems and opportunities. It does not solve all problems, nor should it be blamed for creating all problems.

To many, technology is still "fun and games" and is not fully utilized as a productivity tool. The more that we learn it, the more that technology works.

The focus always needs to go back to understanding what business you're really in, what you become, how you exist and many other unanswered questions. Applying "band aid surgery" is not the answer and is more costly in the long-run.

People need more than technology to be productive. Yet, without adequate technology, they are handicapped. We must not give a disproportionate amount of attention to technology and leave people (any organization's best resource) the short end of the stick.

Organizations often adopt a "we versus they" attitude toward technology. "We" make the policies and decisions. "They" are the technology providers and implementers, who support us but do not participate in corporate decisions. Often, technology becomes utilized primarily by the rank and file. Management does not see a reason to embrace technology. In minds of many managers, technocrats are not in the decision-making loop. This is an unfortunate flaw of corporate thinking.

Each year, companies spend billions of dollars on the latest technology but do not reward their people for creative thinking. People are trained in the use of technology but are not trained adequately in other aspects of business operation… notably in the powers of reason, communications and the people skills necessary to work optimally with each other.

Shifting paradigms toward accepting modern technology must be accompanied by modified behaviors. Thinking that technology will cure all ills is another version of burying one's head in the sand to the truths around us.

Technology proponents say that those who do not embrace it are dinosaurs, out of touch and computer illiterate, three distinct categories, one of which has to do with technology.

Certainly, every executive should learn how to operate a computer. More importantly, technology professionals should learn more management skills and must have more exposure to non-tech aspects of their business.

The bigger priority is to apply creative thinking to all aspects of company operation. Use technology as a tool. Utilize people as the masters of that tool.

Encompass planning and bigger-picture thinking into all business operations. Therefore, those who use technology do so with a bigger understanding of its place in the Big Picture.

When technology is thought of as a component in the "macro," rather than a "micro" world unto itself, it will have mature utilization. Otherwise, it will be viewed as a bunch of high-priced toys that are played out of context to the main game.

7 Levels of Technology in Corporate Usage

1. **Basic Operations.** Necessary equipment to do basic jobs. Telephones, word processors, fax machines, time-tracking mechanisms. Along with furniture and basic equipment, these are minimums for running a business.

2. **Tools of the Trade.** Contemporary technology, per area of departmental usage. Technology of the energy industry, for example, has customized design and usage. Every industry niche develops and perfects its own necessary-operations technology.

3. **Accountability Systems.** These include infrastructures which track, report, acknowledge and prioritize. Used primarily to crunch numbers, track dollars, count heads and generate reports.

4. **Process Systems.** An extension of industry-specific technology, it logs wells, charts flow of product through pipelines, projects demands and counts production statistics (per the example of the energy industry).

5. **Meet the Marketplace.** Technology of selling, marketing and serving clients. Databases, solicitation call sheets, customer tracking data, initiatives for follow-up, customer service data. Used to project markets, make sales and provide after-sale service.

6. **Knowing Where Technology Ends.** Understanding its true place in operations. Realistic appraisal of what it can and cannot do…how it supports core business operations.

7. **Company Operations**. Commitment to technology in terms of company functions…not as the driving force. Greater commitment is given to people, philosophies of doing business, strategic planning, ethical operations and future-directed vision.

7 Misconceptions and Mis-Uses of Technology

1. **Buy the Marketing Hype.** Vested interests sell technology as the primary answer to life's questions. Because sellers say it is a brave new world, consumers purchase pieces of equipment (which by themselves do not constitute "technology"). The worst travesty is buying something for the "bells and whistles" and not knowing what to do with it.

2. **Kids with Toys Syndrome.** He with the most elaborate arsenal of equipment has the flashiest business. Sadly, this is the downfall of many a business.

3. **Divert Focus from the Rest of the Organization.** Showcasing our hardware and hyping all our software will entertain people, who will want to do business. That's more important than fixing the organization, top to bottom. Another fatal flaw of corporate thinking.

4. **Think It Will Solve All Problems.** Because a "consulting" firm recommended it, then it must be all things to all people. Organizations often cling to technology as their "only savior" because they feel frustrated with processes and systems that don't work. Technology gets unfairly hyped and then criticized when unfixed processes-systems continue "business as usual."

5. **Hucksterism.** The Internet by itself is not the future of the world…it is how we use it that counts. For many, it represents huge dollar signs… like a carnival side show. For a much smaller percentage, it is the world's largest library. The choice of realizing its potential is yours.

6. **Instant Gratification.** To the under-educated, one just punches a button, and it's all there before you. Life does not work that way, with or without modern technology.

7. **Thinking About Machines.** There is no substitute for steady, planned growth, company vision and clear focus of operations.

7 Realities of Technology

1. It constitutes one tenth of 1% of organizational emphasis. Keep it important, but pay attention to the remaining 99.9%, notably people and long-term planning.

2. It is one tool of your trade…not your main business. Understand what business you are really in, why your company operates as it does,

where your customers are, and use various mechanisms to do business effectively.

3. See technology as a library, not a game-room. Let the Internet put a research focus into your business. Start charting trends, acquiring data and seeing how competitors are focused. With more information, you'll make more informed choices and practical business decisions.

4. Don't abandon the old technology and processes. Integrate them with the new.

5. Learn to use and use to learn. Continuing education and professional development make the organization's most important resource—its people—more productive, challenged and effective. Technology-supported distanced learning and training are now available and should be utilized for professional development.

6. Generations see technology differently. There are five generations in the workforce. Teaching, learning and usage must be tailored to all ages, job classifications and developmental stages. Respect what senior workers did with technology of their d, and they are embracing modern technology. Young and mid-level workers can learn much by watching and modeling their seniors.

7. Technology is a factor of efficiencies, savings and expediencies. Technology is not a source of creative thought, values, ethics and vision for the organization. Technology is a tool, which feeds into tactics. Sales is a tactic. There are dozens of other tactics that a successful organization must pursue. Tactics feed into objectives, which feed into goals, which feed into strategy, which feeds into Vision.

The printed versions of books are often much cheaper than the eBook version. This is a big part of the reason why students buy hardbacks. Also, they can sometimes profit from the notes made in the books by previous students.

1. It's much easier to quickly find what you want in a print book—especially something like a dictionary.
2. You don't have to wait for a print book to boot up, and you don't have to charge it.
3. It's easier to lend (or borrow) a print book.
4. There's also a vanity / signaling advantage to a printed book. Visitors to your home can glance through your shelves and see what kind of a person you are by the books you keep.

About Emails

These are statistics and information on the flow of electronic mail messages to computers:

- How many emails are sent per day: 269 billion.
- How many emails are sent per year: 74 trillion.
- Average number of emails a worker receives per day: 121.
- Open rate for emails: 34%.
- Open rate for attachments within emails: 19%.
- Average open rate for retail emails: 21%.
- How many people use emails: 4.3 billion users.
- Percentage of emails that are opened on mobile devices: 55.6%.
- Percentage of emails that are opened on a desktop computer: 16%.
- Percentage of attachments that are actually read: 12%.

Why is email called spam? Before the internet became commercialized and unsolicited commercial e-mail was sent the name spam was given to sending the same mail several times for no good reason. This is the amount of email that is spam: 59.8%. The largest source of unsolicited email is China, 14.36% of global spam volume.

These are tips on how to stop spam emails:
- Try to avoid opening spam emails and clicking on links in spam messages.

- Don't buy anything from a spammer.
- Don't be tempted to reply.
- Don't threaten the spammer.
- Avoid 'unsubscribe' options.
- Use a disposable email address.
- Be wary about giving out your main email address.

These are some reasons why people do not read attachments:
- Unrecognizable file format.
- Bad file association or problem with program.
- Compressed files.
- Anti-virus program preventing files being opened.
- The sender has an Apple computer, and you have a PC.
- Outlook add-ins.
- Corrupt files.
- Word is proprietary software and is not cross-platform.
- Word documents can often carry viruses.

Email attachments may negatively affect your deliverability. The main purpose of your email should be to get a reply. Don't flood prospects with too much data at once. Intrigue them. Once you catch their attention, use all the data while talking to them.

Why Digital Reading Is No Substitute for Print

A number of researchers have sought to measure learning by asking people to read a passage of text, either in print or on a digital device, and then testing for comprehension.

Students reported that print was aesthetically more enjoyable, saying things such as "I like the smell of paper" or that reading in print is "real reading." What's more, print gave them a sense of where they were in the book—they could "see" and "feel" where they were in the text.

Print was judged to be easier on the eyes and less likely to encourage multitasking. Almost half the participants complained about eyestrain from reading digitally ("my eyes burn"). 67% indicated they were likely to multi-task while reading digitally (compared with 41% when reading print).

By contrast, 28% of Americans have read an e-book, and 14% have listened to an audio book—in the last year. In addition to being less popular than print books overall, the share of Americans who read e-books or listen to audio books has remained fairly stable in recent years.

40% of Americans read print books exclusively; just 6% are digital-only book readers. 34% of Americans have either read an e-book or listened to an audio book in the last year, but relatively few Americans read books in these digital formats to the exclusion of print books.

Young adults—80% of 18- to 29-year-olds have read a book in the last year, compared with 67% of those 65 and older. These young adults are more likely than their elders to read books in various digital formats but are also more likely to read print books as well: 72% have read a print book in the last year, compared with 61% of seniors.[1]

Women are more likely than men to read books in general and also more likely to read print books. The share of Americans who read books on tablets or cellphones has increased substantially since 2011, while the share using dedicated e-readers has remained stable.

What percentage of information do we retain? 30% of what they SEE. 50% of what they SEE and HEAR. 70% of what they SAY and WRITE. 90 percent of what they DO.

Below are seven of the most practical techniques for retaining information:
1. Take notes on the page.
2. Ask yourself questions about the material.
3. Skim the text first.
4. Impress, associate and repeat.
5. Introduce the information to others.
6. Read out loud.
7. Read on paper.

These are ways to better retain what you hear:
1. Read actively. You won't retain information if you just casually read the material.
2. Summarize chapters after reading them. You shouldn't study in one big session.

3. Take notes. Many students take notes during class.
4. Explain the material to someone else.

These are ways to absorb and retain Information:
1. Abbreviate words while taking notes.
2. Record a video of yourself summarizing your notes.
3. Review your notes right after class & later that same day.
4. Teach someone what you have learned.
5. Look for book summaries.
6. First read the whole page. Then, underline important points.

- Bars on the windows. (metal pipes, for safety and protection from intruders)

Older Name for It	Modern Name for It
Parasol	Umbrella
Ice box	Refrigerator
Horseless carriage	Automobile
Constantinoble	Istanbul
Yugoslavia	Kosovo
New Amsterdam	New York
French Indochina	Vietnam
Pocketbook	Purse
Handbag	Backpack
Stove	Range
Toilet	Commode
Toilet paper	Bathroom tissue
Tin foil	Aluminum foil
Refuge receptacle	Trash can, garbage can

Concepts for which the names changed names over the years

Peep show—film arcade—silent films—talkies—movies—cinema—video

Mexican—Chicano—Mexican-American—Latino—Hispanic

Soda—fountain drink—coke—pop—soft drink—mixer—diet drink

Janitor—custodian—sanitation engineer

Washroom attendant—maid—domestic—steward

Housewife—homemaker—domestic engineer

Sheriff—marshal—constable—bobby—COP—law enforcer—peace officer

Militia—rangers—soldiers—battalions—regiments—army—military forces—peace keeping forces

Categories of Words and Terms

Anomaly—Something different, irregular, of uncertain nature, peculiar or not easily classified.

Contronyms—Words that have opposite meanings, depending upon usage.

Heteronyms—Words that are spelled identically but have different meanings when pronounced differently.

Oxymoron's—Combination of contradictory or incongruous words, pointedly foolish.

Paradox—A tenet that is contrary to expectation or received opinion. Self-contradictory statement that at first seems true. Something with seemingly contradictory qualities or phrases.

Pleonasms—Two concepts (usually two words) that are redundant, needless repetition of an idea in a different word, phrase, or sentence.

Homonyms—Words pronounced alike but different in meanings, connotations or significance.

Synonyms—Words with the same or nearly the same meanings.

Antonymns—Words with opposite meanings.

Homograph—One of two or more words spelled alike but different in meaning or pronunciation (as the bow of a ship, a bow and arrow). The word "set" has more definitions than any other word in the English language.

Homonyms—Words pronounced alike but different in meanings, connotations or significance. The ant is an insect. Your aunt is a relative. A bat is sports equipment in baseball. A bat flies around in the dark Chips are units of snack food (potato, corn). Chips are components of computers

Business Meanings Via the Perspectives of Words

To most people, the **milkman** brings bottles of milk products to your door. (At least, they did in the old days.) On the farms, the **milkman** is the one who takes cans of milk away to the dairy for processing.

Marketing can be either inward or outward. Companies undergo **marketing** campaigns to promote products and services to potential customers. Those same consumers do their own **marketing** when they shop at grocery stores.

People define **music** according to their personal tastes, experiences and backgrounds. What may be entertainment to one person may be noise or objectionable content to another. **Music** to one's ears is defined as what they want to hear or choose to acknowledge.

Service is a term that constitutes more hype than actual practice. Companies say they pride themselves on customer service. In reality, they see **service** as a sales vehicle or an add-on product. When customers ask for non-paid **service** such as politeness, consideration, follow-up and manners, that's a totally different situation, and customers are often disappointed. Sadly, full-scope customer **service** in business is poor, declining or nonexistent, per company.

Change is a wonderful phenomenon that people hate and fight to their detriments. Research shows that **change** is 90% positive and that people and organizations **change** at the rate of 71% per year. Yet, out of fear, they fight, resist and are combative toward **change** and to those who are **change** agents. It is inevitable, and one should benefit from **change,** rather than become a victim of it.

When some people hear the term **consultant**, they run. Research shows that only 2% of all **consultants** are really veteran business advisors. Most **consultants** are vendors who sell packages of products and services, displaced executives, computer vendors or people in transition. There really is an art to quality **consulting**, which requires years of experience, finesse, discipline and talent to amass…few have it.

Futurism is seen as an esoteric term. Some say they have no control over their destiny. In reality, thoughtful planning for **future** eventualities enables one to prevent tragedies 85% of the time. **Futurism** is a series of thinking and reasoning skills, backed by planning. To deny, ignore or fight the **future** is foolhardy. To prepare for it means steady growth and success.

Diversity is a concept that encompasses ideas, cultures, philosophies and behaviors. Sadly, some people see **diversity** as a punishment, when associated with training. To the contrary, it is a gift because all of us are living examples of **diversity**.

Technology is a tool of the trade, not an ideology or a mantra. Some people mistakenly believe that technology creates the future, or they are willing to abdicate control of their own destinies to outside forces. Such an extreme position is not fair to technology because it sets up mechanical processes to get blamed later for thinking not done today. Thought processes need many avenues in which to be successful. Thereafter, tools of the trade (including technology) may be applied.

Food is a means of survival for some…a base source of nutrition, sustenance and nourishment. **Food** becomes a creative expression of artistry for gourmets. For many people, **food** equates to a reward system. Mealtimes are prime business development and networking events. Social occasions have quality **food** and beverage components.

Transportation is necessary to get people from here to there. **Transportation** is a vital component of the economy, conveying goods throughout intricate networks to marketplaces. **Transportation** is a status symbol to some people.

Business is a livelihood for some. It is a cut-throat game for others. It is a creative expression for still others. For most people, the team becomes an extended family. Business is really a grouping of wants, needs, objectives, outcomes and much more. The way in which priorities and stresses are juggled depends upon how successful the business becomes.

Communication is something that all of us utilize yet is one of the most misdirected concepts. Many people see **communication** is a one-way process…it is only effective if it is two-way and continually refined. Many businesses put out messages that they want to be heard, yet do not test for effectiveness of messages received. Many organizations seek out response from audiences, and many others set roadblocks to dissenting messages getting within earshot.

Communication is the barrier that causes misunderstanding, strife, unrest and productive shutdown in organizations. Depending entirely upon the mindset of human beings in charge, **communication** can also be the "breath of fresh air" or information source that widens opportunities for understanding, action, support and interactive participation.

Chapter 24

THE BUSY WORK TREE, THE LEARNING TREE AND THE EXECUTIVE TREE

7 Major Parts of a Person's Job, Profession and Career

Any individual working in their business life is analogous to a tree. He-she seemingly looks the same each day but sheds leaves, lets the limbs rot and applies "band aid surgery" to the branches later in life. Those who nurture later rather than sooner have less value, success and profitability to the company or organization for whom he-she works. Some people do not grow and bloom to their full potential and do not achieve job-profession- career success for which they are capable.

Give it nourishment, and the individual's Business Tree will grow. If properly nourished, the tree's growth process is planned, steady, optimally profitable and a pleasure to watch it bloom.

Neglect it, and any tree will wither and eventually die. The declining tree is a blight on the environment, harming its components and the neighboring grounds and flowers.

Understand your true business purpose. Trees (jobs, professions, careers) seemingly look the same, but they're all different. Trees are composed differently, with parts and structures relative to the environment in which they attempt to grow.

Without proper care, trees (individuals) wither. With proper care, they blossom. Address problems in every realm that comes up, rather than selectively ignore some. With continued care, they sprout deep roots and live a richer life.

The opportunity costs of remediating malnourishment, deterioration or damage are six times that of properly feeding the tree on the front end. Human beings being like we are, few of us do everything perfectly on the front end. The art and skill with which we remediate difficulties constitutes success in business.

People Have Trees: The Busy Work Tree
The Business Tree has five branches, a trunk and the base, with their percentages per role-function-activity:

Branch 1. The business you're in (10%).
Branch 2. Running the business (14%).
Branch 3. Financial (10%).
Branch 4. People (28%).
Branch 5. Business development (23%).

Category 6 (trunk). Body of Knowledge (8%).
Category 7 (roots). The Big Picture (7%).

Categories 1-5 are primary branches (business functions) on the tree (company), listed in the priority order that most companies pay attention, time and resources. Branch 1 is merely a starting point. Companies then mature their Business Tree by nurturing the other branches.

People (Branch 4) comprise the organization's most important and under-nourished resource, comprising 28%. People in the work force are trees as well, whether they are employed by a corporation, health care institution, school, small business, non-profit agency, retailer, professional services firm, community volunteer group, professional association, partnership or collaborative joint venture.

On the job, their time and activities may be classified as The Busy Work Tree. Their development as individuals may be reflected in The Learning Tree. Both of these trees are included in this monograph, showing the diverse ways in which people are expected to divide their time on the job and the factors that build them as individuals.

Most individuals address only three categories at any given time, some effectively and others not. This is why businesses experience recurring problems, requiring various activities to enrich, improve and empower their employees. The tree (individual) that does not address at least six components cannot remain standing (succeed in the long-run).

No single branch (area of business emphasis) constitutes a healthy tree. None of the limbs (responsibilities), twigs (assignments) and leaves on each branch (duties) provide all the nourishment required to breed a healthy tree (individual in the workplace). Each branch has its proper responsibility and should learn to interface with the others.

The Busy Work Tree will not stand without a trunk and base. These keep the branches, limbs twigs and leaves on a growth curve. Trees with thicker bases and deeper roots will sprout greener (be profitable), shed less often (fewer failures) and live longer (cultivate a Body of Work).

Sometimes, people say: "I could do my job if I didn't have to do all this other stuff." In reality that "other stuff" is all part of doing the job. We offer allocations of percentages to activities necessary to fully "do the job."

The Busy Work Tree represents the components of a person's job, profession and career, with their percentages per role, function and activity:

Branch 1. Core business (18%).
- Doing what the organization is supposed to do. (13%).
- Adding your own professional abilities, specialties, skills and expertise (5%).

Branch 2. Deliverability of the product-service (23%).
- Administrative practices, procedures, operations, structure, review (4%).
- Office maintenance and support (3%).
- Working with technologies (1%),
- Preparation (2%).
- Production and distribution of product-service to clients-customers (13%).

Branch 3. Accountability (10%).
- Reporting, tabulating and interpreting (6%).
- Projections and planning (3%).
- Fiduciary responsibilities (1%).

Branch 4. People (23%).
- Working with supervisors and colleagues (4%).
- Working with clients and customers (10%).
- Working with other constituencies (3%).
- Training, empowerment, team building to do your job better (6%).

Branch 5. Company goals, needs and vision (16%).
- Meetings (4%).
- Document production (3%).
- Preparation to deliver the core product-service (7%).
- Representing the company outside your office (2%).

Category 6 (trunk). Professional development (5%).
Category 7 (roots). Body of work: Your long-term goals and contributions (5%).

The Learning Tree

This embodies the major components of an individual's life experiences. The successful professional person takes the time and appropriates the resources to develop a Body of Work, rather than just hold jobs. Business is approached as a lifetime track record of accomplishments. This sophisticated and vital category includes:

- Building a clear, cohesive, operational Vision for the individual.
- Conceptualizing a specific action plan to be effective on all branches of the tree.
- Facilitating programs where progress is measured and maintained.
- Attentiveness to company obligations.
- Maintaining a well-earned reputation.
- Contributing to the economy and communities in which one lives and works.

- Taking concepts such as quality management, ethics and outside-the-box thinking out of the esoteric and into daily operation.
- Recommending new ideas and business practices which surpass the niches of others.

The Big Picture provides leadership for progress, rather than following along. The successful person develops and champions the tools to change. The quest is to manage change, rather than falling the victim of it.

Leadership development embodies mentoring lessons and creative ways of retreading old knowledge to enable executives to master change, rather than feel as they are victims of it. Executives' value to organizations, employees, customers, influential constituencies and ascendancy to management is a direct reflection of mastering the life skills listed on The Learning Tree:

1. **Life**
   - Environment, family.
   - Acceptable and unacceptable behaviors.
   - Meeting physical needs.
   - Street wiseness.
   - Food, water, clothing, shelter.
   - Safety and preparedness.
   - Knowing how to get by.
   - Interfacing with others who know.
   - Rules and regulations.

2. **Living Well**
   - Personal management.
   - Behavior.
   - Home administration, upkeep.
   - Communication skills.
   - Health and wellness.
   - Subtleties and niceties of life.
   - Meeting social needs.
   - Fine wine (the process of living well).
   - Entertainment.

3. **Working Well**
   - Economic survival.
   - Time, skills and energy management.

- Fiduciary responsibilities.
- Training, organizational development.
- Meeting needs to create, achieve, excel.
- Areas of expertise.
- Talents and skills.
- Change management.
- Professional orientation and demeanor.

4. **Education**
   - Meeting intellectual needs.
   - Literacy skills enhancement.
   - Multiple interests.
   - Arts appreciation, support.
   - Formal schooling.
   - Non-credit learning for fun.
   - Technical training.
   - Hobbies.
   - Professional development.

5. **Philosophy**
   - Viewpoint (senses and mind connected together).
   - Inspiration.
   - Meeting spiritual, moral, ethical needs.
   - Common sense.
   - Maintain focus and perspective.
   - Committed to amassing knowledge and life insights.
   - Perceptions and realities.
   - Adaptabilities and flexibilities.

6. **Self-Fulfillment**
   - Meeting emotional needs.
   - Psychological enhancement.
   - Comfort from within.
   - Interpersonal relationship building.
   - Self-growth.
   - Trust, caring, sharing, tenderness, empathy and sensitivity.
   - Thinking and feeling concepts.
   - Seeks-fulfills balance in life.
   - Learning from failure and success.

Professional Seasoning

It is a fallacy to assume that one becomes a seasoned executive simply because he-she wears several hats in a small organization. Executive seasoning is time-tested. Only experience brings wisdom. One cannot fast-forward to the executive tracks without having laid steady groundwork.

The purpose of this chapter is to show young professionals the path to the top:

- As years progress, one's responsibilities do not decrease.
- Nothing meaningful is ever lost. Important things are worth remembering by those who know the value of knowledge.
- Things do not always work out as planned. But they do work out. Planning assures a better outcome. Things never work out by themselves.
- Stay organized and focused, especially when the company is not in crisis.
- The Business Tree is all interrelated. No single piece can or should stand alone.
- Power sharing = Empowerment must be real. Make all involved a part of the solution.
- Work as though your name were on the door.
- Be paid what the marketplace thinks you are worth.
- Organizations do not have bad people. They have bad policies that encourage people to behave badly.
- Greater society must help organizations maintain values, communicating consistent messages.

The scope and complexity of a top executive's career are multiplied higher than the worker. One cannot fathom being at the top until they have paid dues, learned from the journey and amassed wisdom to handle the duties, responsibilities and accountabilities.

A professional must examine the context in which they work, pursue a career and operate their business. To be valued as professionals, we must continually enrich ourselves, covering all five major branches of the tree, plus the trunk and base.

As with trees, people do not look, act and behave the same, but they have common cultural needs. Like organizations, people trees possess qualities relative to the environment in which they attempt to grow. Without proper care, they wither. Without continued care, they die. With proper care, they blossom. With continued care, they sprout deep roots and live a richer life.

What Motivates People to Work and Achieve

Per each category of The Business Tree™:

1. **The business you're in**
   Doing good work, with standards of professionalism.
   Producing products/services that make a difference.
2. **Running the business**
   Maintaining high productivity.
   Ability to control and influence.
   Making correct decisions.
3. **Financial**
   Receiving adequate compensation.
   Maintain standards of accountability.
4. **People**
   Being accepted and acknowledged.
   Being part of a motivated team.
   Receiving praise, recognition and advancement.
   Having a certain amount of freedom on the job.
   Learning new things
   Enjoying work relationships and having fun with the job
   Achieving balance in life, thus becoming a more valuable employee
   Working with good managers and leaders.
   Being perceived as a role model.
5. **Business Development**
   Direct involvement in important projects.
   Doing work that empowers customers.
   Integrity, with customers and ourselves.
6. **Body of Knowledge**
   Exemplifying standards of quality.
   Remaining confident about work.
   Exemplifying value and excellence.
   Need for personal and professional growth.

7. **The Big Picture**
   Feeling like you've made a positive contribution.
   Accomplishing worthwhile things.
   Being in an organization that makes a difference.

Quotations About and For Business Leaders

"Hitch your wagon to a star."
–Ralph Waldo Emerson

"He who rides a tiger is afraid to dismount."
–Proverb

"There is always room at the top."
–Daniel Webster

"A man's reach should exceed his grasp.
Man partly is and wholly hopes to be."
–Robert Browning, 19th Century British poet

"If you would hit the mark, you must aim a little above it.
Every arrow that flies feels the attraction of earth."
–Henry Wadsworth Longfellow

"There is no such thing as a free lunch."
–Milton Friedman, 20th Century U.S. economist

"If two men on the same job agree all the time, then one is useless.
If they disagree all the time, them both are useless."
–Darryl F. Zanuck, film producer (1949)

"A great man is always willing to be little. To be great is to be misunderstood.
The essence of greatness is the perception that virtue is enough."
–Ralph Waldo Emerson

"Great deeds are usually wrought at great risks."
–Herodotus

"A truly great man never puts away the simplicity of a child."
–Chinese proverb

"There are no gains without pains."
–Adlai Stevenson

*"Be nice to people on your way up because
you'll need them on your way down."*
–Wilson Mizner

"Success has killed more men than bullets."
–Texas Guinan

"Success is counted sweetest by those who never succeed."
–Emily Dickinson

*"Success is relative. It is what we can
make of the mess we have made of things."*
–T.S. Eliot, poet

*"People are in-exterminable, like flies and bed-bugs.
There will always be some that survive in cracks and crevices."*
–Robert Frost, poet (1959)

"When you get to the end of your rope, tie a knot and hang on."
–Franklin D. Roosevelt

"Talent develops in quiet places, character in the full current of human life."
–Goethe, 19th Century German poet and dramatist

"There is no substitute for talent. Industry and all the virtues are of no avail."
–Aldous Huxley

Chapter 25

THE POWER OF IDEAS

My Tribute to Larry Sachnowitz

One of the most unforgettable people in my life was Larry Sachnowitz. He was creative, an advertising-marketing guru constant source of creativity and a visionary.

He championed the Eight Great Understandings:

1. It's not important what you think people think. It's what they think that's important.
2. It's not what people say that's important. It's what they do.
3. Simplicity is power.
4. Most people in business don't understand business.
5. People are interested in themselves.
6. Think and feel like the other person.
7. It's not just what you say but how you say it.
8. How you end a relationship is just as important as how you begin a relationship.

He began his career with Gulf State Advertising in 1962 and purchased the firm in 1978. He had a quest for intellectual stimulation, was clever with words, was bold with ideas and gave back to the community continually.

Some of Larry's great advertising campaigns included:

- "Take Good Care of Yourself" for the Institute for Preventive Medicine.
- "All Over America" for the National Roofing Contractors Association.
- "What Do You Say, The Broadway" for Broadway National Bank in San Antonio.
- "Bless Their Little Soles" for Bill Douglas' Shoe Box.
- "Changing Minds" and "Learning, Leading" for the University of Houston.
- "Some Stores Have All the Fun" for Oshman's Sporting Goods.

Burma-Shave created a unique form of national advertising in the 1930s to appeal to highway motorists. Every few miles, a placard carried clever phrases, often plays on words. The aim was to intrigue viewers and keep them anticipating more. By recognizing the concept, audiences often created slogans of their own and submitted them to a willing company. Some of the classic Burma-Shave slogans included:

- "Half a pound for half a dollar. Spread on thin above the collar."
- "We can't provide you with a date. But we do supply the best darn bait."
- "His tomato was the mushy type…until his beard grew over-ripe.
- "Better try less speed per mile. That car may have to last a while."
- "To steal a kiss, he had the knack…but lacked the cheek to get one back."
- "It gave McDonald that needed charm. Hello Hollywood. Good-by farm."
- "Around the curve…lickety-split. It's a beautiful car…wasn't it?"
- "If Crusoe'd kept his chin more tidy, he might have found a lady Friday."
- "If anything will please your Jill, a little jack for this jar will."
- "That barefoot chap with cheeks of tan. Won't let him chap when he's a man."

Larry was a big fan of the Burma-Shave campaign. His client was Sage Department Stores, a local discount chain that competed with Fedmart, Woolco,

Eagle, Gibson's and Globe. This was the era before Walmart's dominance and the popularity of dollar stores.

In the 1970s, Larry designed a campaign for Sage Stores. Media utilized included outdoor, television and signage. He paid tribute to Burma-Shave with comparable witty and creative slogans for Sage:

- "Pinocchio saved at Sage. Pinocchio knows!"
- "Clark Kent saved at Sage. Super, man!"
- "Alec Saved at Sage. Smart Alec!"
- "Joe Sambito saved at Sage—What a relief!" (Joe Sambito was a relief pitcher for the Houston Astros baseball team in the 70's).

I worked in the 1980s with two of the best jingle creators. Dick Marx (father of rock star Richard Marx) had created jingles for hundreds of products, including Kellogg's ('best to you") and Malboro. Larry Sachnowitz was a master of the retail psyche, the intellect and the heart…all combining fuel for his potent lyrics.

Our client was a troubled city with an unemployment rate of 28%. On the U.S. side of the Mexican border, they were devastated by devaluation of the peso, energy woes and ranching downturns. Communitywide mistrust and a sense of hopelessness existed. My long-term recommendation was that the community actively solicit manufacturing operations to bolster the economy. The Maquiladora program did indeed drop the unemployment rate from 28% to 13% in three years.

But, for the moment, hope needed to be restored. A bank commissioned Marx and Sachnowitz to write a song of encouragement, "You Can Believe/Puede Creer." In what came to be the city song, these excerpts said it all: "If you believe in the brotherhood of people. If you believe in a strong and helping hand. If you believe in warm and friendly faces. If you believe in the better side of man. You can believe… you can be sure. You can be certain and secure. You Can Believe/Puede Creer."

I personally observed the team's genius with other local advertising campaigns, including Star Furniture, Elliott's Men & Boys Shops, Broadway National Bank ("what do ya' say, the Broadway") and others. Great advertising is not just national in scope. Every community creates memorable and effective advertising. The national jingle writers assist talents in every locality to meet the marks, exceed the goals and weave some art into a business format.

Larry once took me to a meeting with the power structure of a restaurant chain. Larry was visionary and always right, and they were bent on self-destruction. Larry said, "You only have three problems: your food is terrible. Your prices are too high. And your customer service is terrible. Other than that, you don't have any problems." Their response was oblivious. I was there as the adjudicator, the voice of reason. Sadly, the chain went bankrupt.

Some of Larry's favorite sayings were:

- "You cannot stay in business if you're not selling something."
- "Protect the business."
- "Now is the time to buy."
- "Now is the time to sell."

He Loved Community Service

From the joy, accomplishment and glow that we get from pro-bono activity come the glimmers of the potential within. We pick community service projects based upon the good that it will do for others. The passion from within must fuel every task that we voluntarily perform. The body of accomplishments are in the heart, not on the awards in plaques.

Larry advised me that when recognition for volunteer service comes, you are propelled to do more the next time for other causes, in unique ways and to light the torch for others.

He served as president of the Houston Advertising Federation, chairman of the Texas Southern University Foundation, a member of the Dean's Executive Advisory Board for the University of Houston College of Business, chairman-elect of The National Conference of Christians and Jews and a member of The Houston Philosophical Society. He served as president of Congregation Emanu El in Houston, a member of the National Board of Religion in American Life, Inc., and on the Board of Advisors for the Brooklyn College Conservatory of Music. He was also an Adjunct Professor at the Jones School of Business at Rice University and Executive Professor at the University of Houston College of Business in its Entrepreneurial and Innovation Program.

As I meet people in the business world, they recall activities that I performed in community service. They recall boards that you served on or causes associated with your name. I respond by recounting the commitment and how it touched me or made me a better person. On that subject, Larry told me, "You often receive credit for good deeds that others did. Be sure to spread the credit around."

Successful people are products of mentorship. So are our communities. I've remembered and recorded most of the worthwhile advice that I've been given. Again, thinking about volunteerism as Larry did, we make and honor our commitments… nurtured by our responsibility to mentor others. If we're going to be called role models, we show it without fanfare and inspire others to lead.

The Power of Ideas

This material is the brainchild of Larry Sachnowitz. This was a series of magazine articles that were prototypes of a manuscript. I encouraged him to write books. He died in 2001 and would have published books, at the urging of myself and others.

I now take this chapter to proudly showcase his wise, insightful ideas.

"We want people to think of us as a marketing service organization. Marketing is defined in the most complicated ways by all kinds of people, but it is really very simple. Marketing is everything you do to get and keep a customer." Sachnowitz explained. "One of the greatest things I have heard said was that most companies believe that it is the decisions they make that will determine how successful they will be. Well, it is not the decisions a company makes, but the possibilities they have to choose from. We are a company that brings possibilities to the table."

It was Sachnowitz's philosophy that business people really know their business, but sometimes lose or overlook a perspective that is critical for success. "Most people don't know what they don't know," he said. "When it comes to generating powerful ideas, you can either do it or you can't. An advertising agency that can, has a special place in the world. There is a difference between ideas and powerful ideas. Clever is one thing, but powerful ideas can change a business. Most of our ideas are powerful because of their dramatic simplicity. A lot of the communication in America is complicated but the most powerful symbols in the world are simple."

Creativity Takes Courage and Leadership

Larry's key points:

- There's a mistaken notion about creativity and about creative people."
- "Change requires creativity. Creativity requires courage."
- "The mood for creative courage is more critical than ever."

- "Creativity is a matter of ability and instant linkage, not prolonged thinking."
- "The world is full of creative people, mostly undisciplined and unfocused."
- "Too many marketing ideas intended to sell something to somebody don't."
- "Be especially aware and resistant lo ideas that are clever, meaningless, foolish, naïve, ill-conceived, incredulous, tasteless, embarrassing, innocuous, impotent, powerless, egocentric, confusing, complicated and immeasurable."
- "Maximize your potential. Whatever you do, don't limit the potential of your business by surrounding yourself with safe, frightened, narrow, boxed-in, corporate, tuning fork thinkers. You just can't afford it. Have the courage to create. Develop that courage in your people. Have inside and outside courageous creators close to you in every area of your business."

The Most Dangerous Excuse in Business Today
Larry's key points:

- "People see and hear the same things differently."
- "If you want to be in business tomorrow, you gotta wanna learn like never before."
- "The most dangerous excuse is not having enough time."
- "Picking and choosing what to pay attention to is a major problem."

Where the Buck Really Starts and Stops
Larry's key points:

- "Most business owners and managers are like the squirrel in the spinning cage."
- "Don't fix it if it ain't broken has broken a lot of businesses. Not realizing that something is seriously wrong is like a fatal disease undetected."
- "Inside, management may be paying attention to the wrong things."
- "The business starts and stops with the customer."

- "You need your heads examined and the heads of your customer."
- "Ask a lot. Listen a lot more."
- "We must remember what we forgot."
- "Without strategic customer focused marketing, you can easily lose your most vital asset."

Corn Flakes vs. Political Flakes

Larry's key points:

- "Powerful advertising is one of the greatest safeguards the American consumer has."
- "The problem is you can't return or throw away an inferior politician instantly."
- "Put the spin on political flakes, and we eat them all up."
- "Political advertising on television has become more destructive than instructive."

Keeping the Eye and the Mind on Business

Larry's key points:

- "You're either in the business, or you're out of business."
- "What is the critical element, the key ingredient to a successful business? Without a customer, there is no business."
- "A customer by any other name is still a customer."
- "Effective business leaders recognize the right ideas."
- "Embrace the courage to create and the willingness to change and do things differently."

Larry Sachnowitz was a great visionary, and I loved and respected him for it. Remembering creative visionary Larry Sachnowitz, the advertising—marketing guru.

Chapter 26

ADVERTISING SLOGANS

**Texture for Perspectives on Life and Motivations to Buy.
The Witty, the Glib and the Pertinent.**

Advertising jingles exist in our psyche. We recall them at a moment's notice. We quote them to our kids. We use them in memos and meetings. They are the brain waves for our lives. Thus, they were effective in creating recall value.

Advertising jingles are more than cute lyrics and catchy tunes. They are designed to market the worth of the sponsoring organization and its products. By hearing a jingle at least seven times, we have a familiarity of the product. Through repetition, we increase loyalty to the point that buying patterns commence.

Commercial messages weave into the fabric of classic television. Where such mini-songs are as vital as TV themes, promotional slogans and programming strategies in developing and exploiting public tastes, preferences and behaviors.

"Good for life," Dr. Pepper. The American Medical Association sued Dr. Pepper, charging that the slogan wrongly promoted the product as a health remedy. The case went all the way to the U.S. Supreme Court. Dr. Pepper lost and had to remove the slogan from public consumption. It replaced "Good for life" with "10-2-4."

"When you're Number Two, you try harder or else," Avis Rent-a-Car. This campaign pulled the company out of the red and subsequently set the tone for customer-friendly campaigns by other emerging car rental companies.

"The end of the plain plane," Braniff Airways. This campaign utilized a fashion designer motif to catapult a regional airline from Dallas, Texas, into a national air carrier.

"Take it off. Take it all off," Noxema shaving cream. This campaign helped triple Noxema's business.

"I hate Qantas for bringing so many people to Australia," Qantas koala bear. During the ad's first eight years, airline sales tripled.

"To look sharp every time you shave. To feel sharp and be on the ball. Just be sharp. Use Gillette Blue Blades for the quickest slickest shaves of all." This jingle was written in 1953 by Mahlon Merrick, who was Jack Benny's television conductor.

Advertising is a profession that encompasses several specialties, including campaign strategy, planning, buying, specialties, point-of-purchase and sub-specialties per media.

Composers of advertising jingles are a rare breed. Pop music superstar Barry Manilow cut his teeth on ad jingles (State Farm Insurance, Band-Aid, McDonald's, etc.) in the early 1970s. Manilow ably learned the secrets of commercial hit records as having comparable traits as commercial jingles, including clever slogans, sense of humor, pertinence to the product, musical hooks, sing-a-long potential, memorability and mass-market appeal.

Some of the Best Advertising Slogans of the 20th Century

"You never outgrow your need for milk." –**American Dairy Association**
"We make money the old-fashioned way…we earn it." –**Smith Barney**
"Please be kind…rewind." –**Video rental stores**
"Which twin has the Toni?" –**Toni home permanent**
"They're G-R-E-A-T." (Tony the Tiger) –**Kellogg's Frosted Flakes**
"The beer that made Milwaukee famous." –**Schlitz Beer**
"A little dab'll do you. Use more…only if you dare. The girls will all pursue you. They love to get their fingers in your hair." –**Brylcreem**
"You deserve a break today." –**McDonald's**

"50 million times a day…at home, at work or on the way. There's nothing like a Coca-Cola."

"I'd like to teach the world to sing in perfect harmony." –**Coca-Cola**

"It's the real thing…in the back of your mind…like you're hoping to find." –**Coca-Cola**

"Things go better with Coca-Cola."

"Raid kills bugs dead." –**S.C. Johnson Co.**

"If you've got the time, we've got the beer." –**Miller High Life**

"When you care enough to send the very best." –**Hallmark Cards**

"I can't believe I ate the whole thing. Try it…you'll like it." –**Alka-Seltzer**

"Let's get Mikey. He won't eat it. He hates everything. He likes it." –**Quaker Oats**

"The milk from contented cows." –**Carnation**

"See the USA in your Chevrolet. America is asking you to call. Drive the USA in your Chevrolet. America…the greatest land of all." –**Chevrolet**

"Better things for better living through chemistry." –**Dupont**

"The disadvantages of length. A silly millimeter longer." –**Benson & Hedges cigarettes**

"You'll wonder where the yellow went when you brush your teeth with Pepsodent."

"Look mom, no cavities." –**Crest toothpaste**

"You're in good hands with Allstate." –**Allstate Insurance Co.**

"Like a good neighbor, State Farm is there." –**State Farm Insurance Co.**

"Now it's Pepsi, for those who think young." –**Pepsi-Cola**

"Wet and wild. Seven Up is first against thirst. So crisp, so smooth."

"How about a nice Hawaiian punch?"

"Hey, big spender, spend a little dime on me." –**Muriel Cigars**

"You meet the nicest people on a Honda." –**Honda motorcycles**

"The closer you get…the better you look." –**Clairol hair coloring**

"No matter what shape your stomach is in." –**Alka-Seltzer**

"Takes a licking and keeps on ticking." –**Timex Watches**

"Look sharp. Feel sharp. Be sharp." –**Gillette razors and blades**

"Good to the last drop." –**Maxwell House Coffee**

"When you say Bud, you've said it all. The King of Beers." –**Budweiser Beer**

"Everything you ever wanted in a beer…and less." –**Miller Lite Beer**

"What this commercial is trying to sell you won't make your breath any sweeter, your clothes any whiter or your acid indigestion any better. It'll just make you more human." –**Business Committee for the Arts**

"Extinct is forever." –**Friends of Animals**

"Be all that you can be." –**U.S. Army**

"Just say no." –**Drug abuse prevention**

Advertising Icons and Personalities

Speedy, for Alka-Seltzer, introduced in 1958.

Mr. Clean, introduced in 1958.

Choo-Choo Charlie, for Good & Plenty Candy, introduced in 1959.

Charlie the Tuna, for Star Kist Tuna, introduced in 1962.

Ronald McDonald, introduced in 1963, becoming the official company spokesman in 1967.

Mr. Whipple (played by actor Dick Wilson), for Charmin, introduced in 1965.

Josephine the Plumber (played by actress Jane Withers), for Comet, introduced in 1965.

The Malboro Man, introduced in 1965.

The Pillsbury dough boy, introduced in 1966.

Madge the Manicurist (played by actress Jan Miner), for Palmolive, introduced in 1966.

The Maytag Repairman (played by actor Jesse White), introduced in 1967.

O.J. Simpson racing through an airport, demonstrating speed of service for Hertz Rent-a-Car.

Joe Namath wearing Beautymist Panty Hose.

Brother Dominic, the monk who photocopies his manuscripts, for Xerox.

Clara Peller as the "Where's the beef?" lady, for Wendy's, introduced in 1980.

The Energizer Bunny, for Eveready Batteries, introduced in 1980.

Chapter 27

FOREIGN WORDS AND TERMS USED IN ENGLISH

A la carte, from French, from the menu.

Ad hoc, from Latin, for a particular purpose.

Ad lib, from Latin, improvised.

Ad nauseam, from Latin meaning *to a sickening degree*.

Addenda, from Latin, a list of additions.

Aficionado, from Spanish, an ardent devotee.

Alfresco, from Italian, outdoors, fresh air.

Allegro, from Italian, joyful musical tempo.

Alma mater, from Latin, former school.

Alter ego, from Latin, the other self.

Alto, from Italian, singer with a lower voice.

Au jus, from French, a beef sauce.

Avant-garde, from French, experimental.

Babushka, from Russian, wearing a scarf or head covering.

Ballet, from French, a form of dance performance.

Bete noire, from French, someone or something disliked.

Bon vivant, from French, someone who lives luxuriously.

Bon voyage, from French meaning *have a nice trip*.

Bossa nova, from Portuguese, style of music developed in Brazil.

Bric-a-brac, from French, a collection of small decorative objects.

Buffet, from French, a system of serving meals.

Bona fide, rom Latin meaning *genuine*.

Café, from French, an elegant restaurant.

Carpe diem, from Latin, means seize the day.

Carte blanche, *unlimited authority*.

Caveat emptor, from Latin meaning *let the buyer beware*.

Chevrolet, a popular automobile.

Chin-chin, from Chinese, drinking toast.

Chocolate, from Native American language.

Cobra, from Portugene, means snake with hood.

Comme ci, comme ca, from French, means so-so.

Coup de gras, from French, the finishing blow.

Croissant, from French, a flaky roll or bread.

Dachschund, from German, breed of dog.

Delicatessen, from German

Dim sum, from Chinese, food served family style.

Dolce vita, from Italian, meaning the sweet life.

En masse, from French meaning *in a large group*.

Entre nous, from French, between ourselves.

Entrepreneur, from French

Espionage

Fait accompli, from French meaning *established fact*.

Faux pas, from French meaning *a social blunder*.

Fest, from German, a party, festival, celebration or event.

Genre, from French, meaning categories of concepts or services.

Gesundheit, from German, a blessing when someone sneezes.

Glitch, from Yiddish, a small problem.

Guerrilla, from Spanish, a warrior or fighter.

Gung-ho, from Chinese, enthusiastically working together on something.

Hoi Polloi, from Greek, the masses, common people.

Honcho, from Japanese, means chief or leader.

Hors d'oeuvres, from French, food appetizers.

Hubris, from Greek, meaning overly conceited, self-centered and ego-maniacal.

ipso facto, from Latin meaning *by the fact itself.*

Karaoke, from Japanese

Karate, from Japanese, a martial arts sport.

Kindergarten, from German, early schooling for children.

Kitschy, from Yiddish and German, something lowbrow.

Klutz, from Yiddish, someone prone to accidents or mistakes.

Kung fu, from Chinese, a martial arts sport.

Lingerie, from French, intimate apparel.

Macho, from Spanish, very strong and masculine.

Mano a mano, from Spanish, directly, hand to hand.

Margarita, from Spanish, fruit drink made with tequila.

Mea culpa, from Latin, I am to blame, apology.

Menage a trois, from French, a household of three.

Mensche, from Yiddish

Mitzvah, from Yiddish, meaning doing good deeds.

Moccasin, from Native American language.

Modus operandi, rom Latin meaning *method of operating.*

Mopez, from Swedish, a bicycle with a motor.

Ninja, from Japanese, a spy or skilled warrior.

Nom de plume, from French, pen name.

Origami, from Japanese, assembling paper into works of art.

Paparazzi, from Italian, the corps of photographers who follow celebrities.

Patio, from Spanish, an outdoor area or square.

Persona non grata, from Latin meaning *an unacceptable person.*

Pinata, from Spanish,

Prima donna, from Latin meaning *a temperamental and spoiled person.*

Pro bono, from Latin meaning *done or donated without charge.*

Quid pro quo, from Latin meaning *an equal exchange.*

Rendezvous, from French

Rucksack, from German, also known as a backpack.

Savoire-faire, from French, the ability to say and do the correct things.

Schmooze, from Yiddish, to talk in a friendly way.

Shaman, from Russian, means tribal priest.

Sheikh, from Arabic, ruler of group of people in Arab cultures.

Sic transit, from Latin, thus passes.

Siesta, from Spanish, a nap.

Sine qua non, from Latin, indispensable element or condition.

Soprano, from Italian, style of singing voice.

Spiel, from Yiddish and German, a quick speech or story.

Status quo, from Latin meaning *the existing condition*.

Taekwondo, from Korean, a martial arts sport.

Terra incognita, from Latin, unknown or uncharted territory.

Tofu, from Chinese, a food additive.

Tsunami, from Japanese, a giant sea wave or earthquake.

Veni, vidi, vici, From Italian, I came, I Saw, I conquered.

Verboten, from German, forbidden.

Waltz, from German, a dance.

Yenta, from Yiddish, someone who complains or whines a lot.

Yin and yang, from Chinese, forces that are opposites.

Zeitgeist, from German, characteristic of a period in time.

Chapter 28

PUTTING BUDGETING INTO PERSPECTIVE

The Bigger Picture of Strategic Planning

F rame of reference is everything in business. Different people within the same organization have contrasting views as to the Core Business They're Really In (discussed in Chapter 3).

The term Budgeting gets tossed around in many ways. Budgets get blamed for gridlock. Budgets get politicized. Budgets get more attention than the umbrellas under which they rightfully belong: Strategic Planning and Visioning.

Budgeting by itself is a minor piece of business strategy. By itself, Budgeting does not constitute full-scope planning and business strategy. Budgeting is an important part in the process.

Questions to follow in Budgeting as part of Strategic Planning and Visioning processes include:

- Does this process increase your accountability to funding sources and to the public?
- Are budgeting measures used to manage performance?

- Is the performance management system focused upon outcomes?
- Are the key measures the best representation of progress of the institution?
- Can the benchmarking information be accessed regularly?
- How well can management effectively interpret and apply findings to the decision process?
- Does your strategic plan adequately describe what you do?
- Does the strategic plan provide necessary guidance to the activities you will measure?
- How diverse is the planning committee?
- Do performance measures provide an early warning system for problems?
- How do you handle crisis management and preparedness?
- Have you prioritized and fully defined key measures and non-key measures?
- Have you done scenario planning of measures beyond your immediate control, i.e. external factors which profoundly impact your livelihood?
- Do the measures address both internal management and external perceptions and accountabilities?
- Performance measures should be included in contracts with all resources, such as adjuncts, vendors, suppliers. Supply chain management should be implemented. Quality management should be implemented.
- Adjustments must be periodically made to target markets, definition of terms and modification of strategies.

Organizations start out to be one thing, but they evolve into something else. In their mind, they're one thing. Other people think they are something else. Priorities change. Dedicated providers of the service stated in the original company mission become frustrated when they don't understand the reasons for shifting priorities.

Most often, what organizations say they do in external promotions to potential customers actually ranks low on the actual priority list. That occurs due to the agendas of individuals who guide the organization, departing from the core business for which founders were presumably educated and experienced. Add to that the harsh realities of doing business and staying competitive.

Here is an average priority ranking for companies-organizations:

1. Revenue volume and its rewards (bonuses for key management).
2. Growth, defined as increasing revenues each year (rather than improving the quality of company operations).
3. Doing the things necessary to assure revenue (billings, sales, add-on's, marketing). Keeping the cash register ringing…rather than focusing upon what is being sold, how it is made and the kind of company they need to be.
4. Running a bureaucracy.
5. Maintaining the status quo. Keeping things churning. Making adjustments, corrections or improvements only when crises warrant (band aid surgery).
6. Glory, gratification and recognition (for the company and for certain leaders).
7. Furthering stated corporate agendas.
8. Furthering unwritten corporate agendas.
9. Courting favor with opinion leaders.
10. Actually, delivering the core business. Making the widget itself. Doing what you started in business to do…what you tell the customers that you do.
11. Doing the things that a company should do to be a good company. Processes, policies and procedures to make better widgets and a better organization.
12. Customer service, consideration or follow-up beyond the sale.
13. Looking after the people, in terms of training, empowerment, resources and rewards.
14. Giving back to those who support the company.
15. Advancing conditions in which core business is delivered.
16. Walking the Talk: ethics, values, quality, vision.
17. Giving back to the community, industry, Body of Knowledge.

People in the organization who do things below the top nine priorities have vastly different perceptions of the organization, its mission, their role and the parts to be played by others:

- Some jockey for position to make their priority seem to advance higher.
- Some keep people on the low rungs in check, assuring that their priorities remain low.
- Some become frustrated because others' priorities are not theirs.
- Some build fiefdoms within the organization to solidify their ranking.
- Some do their job as well as possible, hoping that others will recognize and reward their contributions.
- Some don't think that they're noticed and simply occupy space within the organizational structure.
- Some try to take advantage of the system.
- Some are clueless as to the existence of a system, pecking order, corporate agendas, company vision or other realities.

7 Steps Toward Getting Budgets Accepted More Readily

1. Commitment toward strategic planning for your function, department and company.
2. Know your values.
3. Refine your values.
4. Control your values.
5. Add value via internal services.
6. Take ownership of your values.
7. Continue raising the bar on the company's values.

7 Stages in Making a Case for Business Funding

1. Link to a strategic business objective.
2. Diagnose a competitively disadvantaging problem or an unrealized opportunity for competitive advantage.
3. Prescribe a more competitively advantaged outcome.
4. Cost the benefits of the improved cash flows and diagram the improved work flows that contribute to them.
5. Collaborate with others.
6. Maintain accountability and communications toward top management.
7. Contribute to the organization's Big Picture.

Rules for Budgeting and Planning

1. Use indicators and indices wherever they can be used.

2. Use common indicators where categories are similar and use special indicators for special jobs.
3. Let your people participate in devising the indicators.
4. Make all indicators meaningful and retest them periodically.
5. Use past results as only one indicator for the future.
6. Have a reason for setting all indicators in place.
7. Indicators are not ends in themselves but are only a means of getting where the organization needs to go. Indicators must promote action. Discard those that stifle action.

Base Budgets on Value, Not on Cost

1. Readily measurable values:
   - Time and cost of product development-service delivery cycles.
   - Reject, rework and make-good rates.
   - Downtime rates and meantime between downtimes.
   - Meantime between billings and collections.
   - Product-service movement at business-to-business levels.
   - Product-service movement at retail levels.
   - Product-service movement in the aftermarket (re-sales, repeat business, referrals, follow-up engagements).
2. Values in terms of savings:
   - Time and motion savings.
   - Inventory costs.
   - Speed of order entry.
3. Values in terms of efficiencies:
   - Meantime between new product introductions.
   - Forecast accuracy, compared to actual results.
   - Speed, accuracy and efficiency of project fulfillment.
   - Productivity gained.
   - Continuous quality improvement within your own operation.
4. Values that will benefit other aspects of the company operation:
   - Quality improved on behalf of the overall organization.
   - Creative new ideas generated.
   - Empowerment of employees and colleagues to do better jobs.
   - Information learned.
   - Applications of your work toward other departments' objectives.

- Satisfaction in your service elevated.
- Voiced-written confidence, recognition, referrals, endorsements, etc.
- Capabilities enhanced to work within the total organization.
- Reflections upon the organization's Big Picture.
- Contributions toward the organization's Big Picture (corporate vision).

Chapter 29

BOARD DEVELOPMENT

Keepers of the Flame.
Briefing for Board of Directors Members.

Board members represent the best and brightest in their own organizations. Serving corporations, associations and community organizations is an obligation and trust. If service is best rendered, then all involved will benefit.

Persons who are recruited for and commit to service on boards of directors have several important responsibilities, per categories on my Business Tree™, including:

1. **The business you're in.** Visit programs and become knowledgeable about the organization's work. Don't spend all your board time in meetings. Get to know senior staff, in your areas of expertise. Become an informed advocate.

2. **Running the business**. Study the organization's reason for being and how it operates. Be sure that you are committed to its mission and have

abilities to expand it. Boards provide counsel to management but should not get involved in the day-to-day affairs of running the organization.

3. **Financial**. Board members have fiduciary responsibility, authority and liability for all business operations. Learn to read and understand budgets. Understand the internal controls, unrelated business income tax and accountability.

4. **People.** Your time is your most precious commodity. Spend it wisely, doing homework about the organization that you represent. Factor in support time by your family and business colleagues. When all share in the responsibilities, then all can share in the pride of achievement.

5. **Business development.** Realize that board participation is, likewise, a commitment of your company. Understand that necessary out-of-pocket expenses and time expenditures of your employees will be borne by you and/or your company. Board service benefits your business, your association and your industry. Strategize that all are impacted optimally.

6. **Body of Knowledge.** Understand "the competition." Every organization competes with others, in some shape or fashion. Study the competition in the marketplace, so that opportunities to exchange ideas, collaborate or meet newly identified community niches may be feasible.

7. **The Big Picture.** Strategic planning and building a shared vision are prerequisites for every board of directors. To succeed in trying times, every board member must contribute to the organization's future and advocate actions that assure that pro-active change occurs.

Boards must represent the shareholders and all other stakeholders. They have the ultimate authority in guiding the affairs of the corporation. They are responsible for corporate affairs and the selection and supervision of officers. Boards set the policies and work with management in conducting the strategic planning and visioning. Officers are responsible for the procedures and actions. The power and authority lie within the entire board.

Board members are required to act within their authority, exercise due care and observe fiduciary responsibilities. Breach of any of these duties could result in liabilities on the part of the directors and the overall organization.

Challenges for Boards of Directors

Since the corporate scandals, board members have been under a microscope with brighter lights aimed at them. Some corporations have had a difficult time in recruiting the best possible board members. That's in part because they sought the same types of people from limited niches where board members were chosen in the first place.

It is vital for corporations to reach out to new constituencies for their boards. This means going outside the organization's own executive committee. It means recruiting enlightened individuals with vision and the inclination to inspire others toward creative business approaches. Outside directors should reflect all aspects of the business, not just core business and financial.

The ideal board member should:

- Have a bias for action.
- Communicate ideas to diverse constituencies.
- Draw upon business background for making decisions.
- Maintain objectivity at all times.
- Devote time and energies toward board service.
- Have insights into people and problems.
- Be a team player.
- Understand the art of compromise.
- Take action, even on controversial matters.
- Have the ability to inspire.
- Prepare for all board meetings.
- Attend all board meetings.
- Support and promote the organization at every possible occasion.

As part of the corporate reform movement, boards of directors, once recruited and organized, should operate as efficiently and professionally as the business units of the company in question.

To that end, a thorough briefing book should be prepared for and by the board's executive committee. The ideal board manual should include:

- Board roles and responsibilities policy statement.
- Ethics statement.

- Job descriptions for each member.
- Delineation of board and staff roles.
- Legal and insurance considerations.
- Articles of Incorporation.
- Corporate bylaws.
- Board policies, including guidelines for working together, attending meetings, setting agendas, hiring executives, etc.
- Guidelines for recruitment of board members.
- Policies for orientation, training and development of board members.
- Guidelines for removal of board members.
- Procedures for sustaining a high-quality relationship between the board and the chief executive officer.
- Work plan for the board, with relevant goals from the strategic plan.
- Description, roles, responsibilities and work plan for board committees.
- Annual calendar for the board.
- Sample meeting agenda and minutes.
- Statement about the manner in which meetings will be held, including time, place, Parliamentary Procedure, option for on-line meetings, attendance policies and executive sessions.
- Guidelines for evaluating the Chief Executive.
- Delineation of board and staff roles.
- Procedures for developing advisory boards and advisory committees, including their roles and responsibilities.
- Corporate survival guide, including directions and recommendations from the board's outside advisors.

Board Self-Evaluation Process

There should exist a deliberate board evaluation initiative, with the specific goal of identifying ways to do a better job of governing and protecting the shareholders. Policies and procedures should encompass the Board Self-Evaluation, including checklists and principles on evaluating activities and effectiveness of the board.

Questions to ask in self-evaluation might include:

- Are we constructively engaged with management in determining corporate strategy and does management think so?

- Have we shown leadership and vision at creating that strategy?
- Are we providing the necessary strategic thinking, oversight and advice?
- Are we effectively monitoring and supporting management's execution of the strategy?
- Is the board able to respond in a timely way to indications that a change in strategy is needed?
- How are we structured to be agents of change?
- The evaluation can focus on board structure, asking questions such as whether the board has the right skill set, profile and committee structure.
- The evaluation can focus on board meetings, asking such questions as whether the materials prepare the board for necessary discussions and whether there is sufficient time for directors to meet independently of management.

The evaluation can focus on board responsibilities, asking questions such as whether board members are satisfied with the CEO performance review process.

Responsibilities of Board Members

Directors may have specific responsibilities that are unique to the business or industry in which they perform service. The directors will also have a variety of responsibilities which are defined in the bylaws of the organization and in numerous federal and state statutes and regulations.

One should consult with a qualified outside business advisor when defining the specific responsibilities for the board members. Every board shares a set of general responsibilities that members should be prepared to assume when they serve. The following checklist may be helpful to consider when the board conducts its self-assessment.

1. **Organizational Governance.** The Board is responsible for setting the strategic directions. The board, in conjunction with the executive staff, defines the directions, programs, services and outreach efforts of the organization.

   The Board has responsibility for developing and approving updates to the strategic plan and the associated budget, which defines the programs and initiatives for each fiscal year. Board members have the ultimate fiduciary responsibility and are responsible to assure that the organization is fiscally sound and operated within procedures and policies that are prudent and ethical.

The Board should create and modify the written governing policies of the organization. These include the definition of goals, definition of executive limitations and responsibilities, financial planning, asset protection, code of conduct, Board operations and performance.

The entire Board will review and approve any and all actions of the Executive Committee of the Board, which is empowered to act between Board meetings, and under circumstances when a full Board meeting is not possible.

2. **Assurance of Executive Performance.** The Board does not conduct the work of the organization, but it must assure that the necessary work is done, through delegation to the Chief Executive Officer.

   The performance of the organization is monitored by the Board with internal and external reports and through the ongoing performance appraisals of the CEO. It is important that all Board members recognize that management is the responsibility of the staff. The Board's primary roles are to define policy and to set direction for the organization.

3. **Board Governance.** The directors create policies and procedures for the governance of the Board. The Board takes the necessary steps to assure that its members are knowledgeable about the organization, including its culture and norms, the profession, the marketplaces it serves, and the roles, responsibilities and performance as a body. The Board nurtures the development of members as a cohesive working group and regularly monitors its performance as a Board.

4. **Linkage with the Organization.** The Board must develop and maintain healthy relationships with the organization, stay in touch with current issues and set strategic directions. Their role is to act in the broad best interest of the organization, supporting directions that serve all of its facets.

Directors should not act in a limited or representative role reflective of a given constituency with which they are or have been affiliated. Board members should function as emissaries for their organization.

The ideal board member would have many of the following competencies and abilities as part of their talent arsenal for director service. Such talents apply to corporate, non-profit, association and volunteer boards:

- Advising-coaching skill.
- Business understanding.
- Cost-benefit analysis knowledge.
- Feedback expertise.
- Group process experience.
- Intellectual versatility.
- Negotiation skills.
- Observation techniques.
- Organizational development theories familiarity.
- Personal and professional development commitment.
- Presentation skills.
- Questioning abilities.
- Relationship building experience.
- Self-knowledge about core businesses.
- Strategic Planning and Visioning commitment.

No board member has all of these skills and talents. Most board candidates have a handful of these skills, in part because most were drawn from the same pool as the others. Thus, the limited scope of myopia that plagued the boards of Enron and other troubled corporations.

We must select directors with complimenting skills as well as counter-balanced opposites. Those of us with most or all of the above talents relish our generalist position, and we enjoy the balance with niche-specialty directors.

Recommendations to Directors

Given the need to recruit board members from all professional niches and to delineate their roles and responsibilities. there are specific activities which they could pursue. Here is my suggested briefing to board members, per branch on The Business Tree™:

1. **The Business You're In**. Know the programs and how they work. Get to know senior staff. Become an informed advocate for the organization and its industry.

2. **Running the Business.** Employ and supervise the Executive Director. Approve annual plan of work and goals submitted by committees. Adopt rules and procedures for conduct of meetings. Recommend and approve necessary changes to by-laws or governing documents. Attend board meetings. Serve on committees and task forces to carry out objectives. Attend the annual meeting.

3. **Financial.** Maintain and champion fiduciary responsibility for all organizational actions. Approve and oversee the annual budget. Approve quarterly and year-end financial statements. Oversee financial transactions.

4. **People.** Serve as an elected member of a leadership team. Address the needs and problems of the staff in policy decisions. Maintain communication with designated members as Board liaison. Bring aboard new people and new ideas.

5. **Business Development, External Relations.** Serve as delegate to other organizations. Participate in marketing.

6. **Body of Knowledge.** Research and understand the competition. Employ lobbyist representatives. Research and understand regulators and other outside influences. Take part in guiding, monitoring and evaluating organizational performance and effectiveness. Champion change. Accommodate growing pains as a company evolves from startup to growth toward maturity, the responsibilities and character of its board of directors will evolve as well.

7. **The Big Picture.** Participate in and champion Strategic Planning and Visioning. Define the mission and participate in strategic planning to review the purposes, priorities, financial standing and goals. Uphold high standards, serving as role models to the organization. Create, interpret and measure policies and strategies. Evaluate how well the board is performing and maintain an effective organization, procedures and recruitment.

In this era following the corporate scandals and anticipating years of corporate reform initiatives, challenges and opportunities for boards and their directors still far outweigh the downsizes. The secret to success is the order in which one prioritizes and maximizes windows of opportunity.

Remember these essential realities about your business, if you wish it to sustain and meaningfully grow:

- You have more strengths than the others.
- Yours is a "demand" industry.
- The opportunities far outweigh the threats.
- Turn others' weaknesses into your threats.
- Many of life's great secrets are in the earth.
- Nothing can grow without proper nurturing, care and attention.
- Everyone has to market and promote the cause.
- Seek board members from more diverse strata.
- Use experts from outside your industry.
- Champion change.
- Board service is an honorable trust.
- Being a role model, you become a better executive.
- Board service is more about building and sustaining relationships.

Service on boards is a culmination of a senior business executive's career. It is more than a line on a resume. If conducted correctly, board service will round out the professional and should have spin-off effects for his-her company.

Identification-recruitment of board prospects is an ongoing process. Seek those who have served other organizations well, especially in the non-profit realm. Get referrals from all strata of the community, to assure a diverse board (career orientation, expertise, interests). Determine each board member's true intentions and best capabilities for service.

Offer training for the boards, including an annual retreat (professionally facilitated). Provide a complete manual. Board members should attend staff training and community functions. Education and professional enhancement are the non-profit organization's stock in trade. Keep the communication flow open, sent well in advance of deadlines for action.

Board members who are most successful will budget their time and spend it wisely on behalf of their organizations. Requirements for board meeting attendance and committee participation quotas should be articulated from the outset. The board chair should monitor each board member's activities, to get maximum value for their time, talents and resources.

Board members maintain relationships with the organization, the board itself, the staff, committees and task forces, outside resources and the public. All relationships should be nurtured.

Chapter 30

ETHICS, CORPORATE SUSTAINABILITY AND GOVERNANCE

I t is important to look at the whole of business, rather than only at the micro-niche parts. Depending upon whose definition of Corporate Responsibility we hear, it could currently symbolize:

- Political agendas for both parties in upcoming elections.
- Committee hearings by Congress.
- Brief moments of glory for whistle blowers and watchdog groups.
- A total obsession with accounting (which only occupies 2% of a company's Big Picture).
- Media circuses, focusing upon selective business issues but not the Big Picture.
- Opportunities for non-business experts to opine and mandate behaviors.

In reality, Ethics has long been with us, though some companies did not observe, designate or prioritize it Ethics in business come from the shadows when crises

sales and customer loyalty, positive reactions to brand image and reputation, heightened productivity, employee commitments to quality, empowered loyal workforces and reduced regulatory oversight.

Corporate Social Responsibility is concerned with treating stakeholders of the company ethically or in a socially responsible manner. Consequently, behaving socially responsibly will increase the human development of stakeholders both within and outside the corporation.

Corporate Sustainability aligns an organization's products and services with stakeholder expectations, thereby adding economic, environmental and social value. This looks at how good companies become better.

Corporate Governance constitutes a balance between economic and social goals and between individual and community goals. The corporate governance framework is there to encourage the efficient use of resources and equally to require accountability for community stewardship of those resources.

Ethical priorities for your company in the New Order of Business may likely be addressed in the event that you:

- Create a corporate code of ethics.
- Create the role of Corporate Ethics Officer.
- Learn to identify issues involved in making corporate ethical decisions.
- Recognize the considerations in the analysis and resolution of ethical dilemmas.
- Apply ethical rules and guidelines toward corporate workplace situations.
- Refine your company's complaint process and investigation procedures.
- Adjudicate employee conduct arising under the corporate Code of Ethics.
- Widen the sensitivity toward issues which may lead toward legal liabilities.
- Embrace standard ethical reporting and compliance procedures.
- Increase the frequency of corporate and personal ethical judgments and decisions.

Burst Bubbles Being Refilled

Perception is reality. It is no longer sufficient to pay lip service to ethical issues, such as investor protection, consumer accountability, issues management, protecting the environment and diversity. Concern must be demonstrated. The public needs to see action on every company's part. The same holds true for public sector institutions.

Credibility is formed by the ability to impact all other issues. Total quality means that we must communicate cross-culturally. Find out what people need to know, when they need it and then deliver it.

Organizations who fail to address ethical issues of the day are endangered species. Whatever the public expects of companies, then those companies should expect the same of themselves. My concerns revolve around these areas:

1. **Society that Produced the Business Scandals.** If we decry the scandals and wrong doing, then modern society must accept our roles in letting them happen.

Too many artificial measurements abound and are based upon flash, sizzle and hucksterism. Having the weekend movie box office grosses for movies on TV and in newspapers every Monday is bogus. Momentary box office grosses are not accurate measures of a film's worth. So much coverage of sales volumes leads media pundits to use ludicrous terms like "X knocked off Y this weekend." When the public hears that misleading statements, they start talking that way too. The public consciousness needs to get away from teasers and slogans.

Anybody who hangs their hats on changeable, temporary rankings is headed for a fall. Top rankings as the ultimate measure of worth and value lead to cottage industries that manipulate the numbers. Bogus research gets purchased. Inflated production reports, unrealistic market shares and improvement quotes receive the spin of those vested in perpetuating the myths.

Projecting futures by past momentary successes will escalate the sweepstakes mentality. As long as the media keeps posting movie box office receipts as the only measure of films' standing, then films will be made to match those criteria.

Business has turned into a smoke and mirrors aura. When perceptions matter more than realities and hype more than substance, then the stakes keep escalating to a frenzy. They parlayed the hype to the media, who conveyed to the public, who re-conveyed to each other via idol chatter. The buzz created an unrealistic stock marketed, populated by get-rich-quick day traders.

The frenzy for slogans and clever quips has anointed the word "solutions" into the business lexicon. Solutions are vendor commodities that appeal to purchasers who don't know any better. We keep investing in technology, rather than developing "human intelligence." We buy "solutions" from providers rather than address real, systemic and long-term challenges and opportunities for the company.

The computer consulting industry gave us the Y2K event in 1999, a fever frenzy that was designed to generate billings for consulting, training and sales of technology. American business spent more than $600 billion on Y2K consulting, paying for it by cutting such more important activities as strategic planning, training, employee compensation and marketing. Research shows that 91-99% of those problems never would have occurred. The vendors perpetuated the spin that their work kept the problems from occurring, with unsuspecting buyers believing and perpetuating the justifications.

2. **Accounting.** Too much emphasis and control of business has been placed in the hands of accountants. Their focus is micro-niche (only about 2% of the Big Picture of business), and to turn over all framing of business issues to accountants is shortsighted. Large accounting firms have influenced the system in their favor. Public companies must be audited by one of them, thus creating as monopoly situation that cuts qualified mid-sized and local accounting firms out of public company work.

Accountants see business through the financial dimension. To pick most the top management from the financial ranks tends to perpetuate the myopic viewpoint. Accounting firms are notorious at not wanting to collaborate with other consultants and professional disciplines. By not allowing other perspectives on their radars and controlling the business model in their favor, a continuum of sameness has occurred. It will continue to occur until business widens its scope and perspective.

3. **CEOs.** Too much romanticism has been placed upon the term CEO by others who want to be rewarded by them. No Chief Executive Officer by himself or herself can make or break a company. They need codependents in order to do damage. The company that lays down all the gold to one CEO in hopes of magical results is inviting being ripped off.

Conversely, as a reaction to corporate scandals the term CEO is currently in disfavor. The public decries CEOs for the same reasons that we canonize them. People envy the power, status and wealth and cannot fathom the endless behind-the-scenes work conducted by reputable CEOs and management teams.

Most CEOs are not adequately groomed for their roles as company role model and leader. They come from the ranks of core business or financial, without proper exposure to other facets that make a winning company. Thus, they surround themselves with like minds or yes-men. Many CEOs do not take counsel of qualified experts, thus remaining isolated, partially-focused and lonely at the top.

A CEO is only as good as the team that he-she leads. A top CEO fulfills roles and responsibilities across every business unit. The CEO must amass people skills, marketing savvy, planning expertise, quality orientation, leadership tenets, marketplace championing and much more. The days of the internal, bottom-line-only-focused CEO are long obsolete.

4. **Boards of Directors.** Companies must hold boards of directors, management teams, mid-manager ranks and line directors more accountable. These folks expect financial rewards and must be more accountable. They must work in collaboration with the CEO, not as pawns of his-her ideology. Chapter 10 covered the dynamics of board service and the myriad of responsibilities that good directors undertake.

Widening the Frame of Business Reference

Ethics is the science of morals, rightness and obligations in human affairs. Institutions must conduct many activities which impact their general welfare. Ethical issues go beyond nice rhetoric and must encompass duties, principles, values, processes, responsibilities and governing methodologies.

Organizations who fail to address ethical issues of the day are endangered species. Whatever the public expects of companies, then those companies should expect the same of themselves.

The Ethics Statement must be more than a terse branding slogan. Like the Mission Statement in the Strategic Plan, it is the amalgamation of careful thought, weighed insights and tests for fairness and durability. The Ethics Statement must be a part of the Strategic Plan, as are such other fundamental statements covering customer-focused management, diversity, valuing stakeholders, quality management and an empowered workforce.

Every organization differs in how it will implement Corporate Responsibility and Ethics programs. The differences are factored by the company's size, sector, culture and the commitment of its leadership. Some companies focus on a single area of operation. The Code of Ethics may include Fundamental Canons, Rules of Practice and Professional Obligations.

the extra length to which the company goes to become a model. It becomes a good marketing mailing, and it's the right thing to do.

As part of strategic planning, corporate ethics helps the organization to adapt to rapid change, regulatory changes, mergers and global competition. It helps to manage relations with stakeholders. It enlightens partners and suppliers about a company's own standards. It reassures other stakeholders as to the company's intent.

Chapter 31

LESSONS LEARNED BUT
NOT SOON FORGOTTEN

100 Ways for Executives to Succeed Long-term

Everything we are in business stems from what we've been taught or not taught to date. A career is all about devoting resources to amplifying talents and abilities, with relevancy toward a viable end result.

Amassing a **Body of Knowledge** which leads to **Wisdom** is a long and enjoyable process. It is the first step toward a career-life **Strategy**, which evolves into a **Vision**. Using a corporate analogy, a Mission Statement is 1% of a Strategic Plan, which is 20% of a Visioning Program.

Business evolution is an amalgamation of thoughts, technologies, approaches and commitment of the people, asking such tough questions as:

1. What would you like for you and your organization to become?
2. How important is it to build an organization well, rather than constantly spend time in managing conflict?
3. Who are the customers?

4. Do successful corporations operate without a strategy-vision?
5. Do you and your organization presently have a strategy-vision?
6. Are businesses really looking for creative ideas? Why?
7. If no change occurs, is the research and self-reflection worth anything?

Most of us learned about business (which is a compendium of life relationships) "in the streets." Today's business leaders entered and pursued careers without a strategic plan or service manual.

Professionals pursue many approaches to garnering information and, ultimately, to unlocking the answers that inevitably lie within. Methods include seminars, books, consultations, professional association involvement, training, organizational development, executive roundtables, civic activities, etc.

Failure to prepare for the future spells certain death for businesses and industries in which they function. The same analogies apply to personal lives, careers and Body of Work. Greater business awareness and heightened self-awareness are compatible and part of a holistic journey of growth.

None of us can escape those pervasive influences that have affected our lives. Like sponges, we absorbed information and perceptions of life that have helped mold our business and personal relationships.

What I Learned

The most significant lessons that I learned in my life from mentors, verified with experience, include:

1. You cannot go through life as a carbon copy of someone else.
2. You must establish your own identity, which is a long process.
3. As you establish a unique identity, others will criticize. Being different, you become a moving target.
4. People criticize you because of what you represent, not who you are. It is rarely personal against you. Your success may bring out insecurities within others. You might be what they cannot or are not willing to become.
5. If you cannot take the dirtiest job in any company and do it yourself, then you will never become "management."
6. Approach your career as a Body of Life's Work. This requires planning, purpose and commitment. It's a career, not a series of jobs.

7. The person who is only identified with one career accomplishment or by the identity of one company for whom he-she formerly worked is a one-hit wonder and, thus, has no Body of Work.

8. The management that takes steps to "fix themselves" rather than always projecting problems upon other people will have a successful organization.

9. It's not when you learn. It's that you learn.

10. Most people do without thinking because they don't really develop thinking skills.

11. Analytical and reasoning skills are extensions of thinking skills.

12. You perform your best work for free.

13. People worry so much what others think about them. If they knew how little others thought, they wouldn't worry so much.

14. Fame is fleeting and artificial. The public is fickle and quick to jump on the newest flavor, without showing loyalty to the old ones, especially those who are truly original. Working in radio, I was taught, "They only care about you when you're behind the microphone."

15. The pioneer and "one of a kind" professional has a tough lot in life. It is tough to be first or so far ahead of the curve that others cannot see it. Few will understand you. Others will attain success with portions of what you did. None will do it as well.

16. Consumers are under-educated and don't know the true substance of a pioneer. Our society takes more to the copycats and latest fads. Only the pioneer knows and appreciates what he-she really accomplished. That reassurance will have to be enough.

17. Life and career include peaks and valleys. It's how one copes with the "down times" that is the true measure of success.

18. Long-term success must be earned. It is not automatic and is worthless if ill-gotten. The more dues one pays, the more you must continue paying.

19. The next best achievement is the one you're working on now, inspired by the Body of Knowledge to date.

20. The person who never has aggressively pursued a dream or mounted a series of achievements cannot understand the quest-mission of one with a deeply committed dream.

21. A great percentage of the population does not achieve...but admires and learns from those who do persevere and succeed. The achiever thus becomes a lifelong mentor to others.

22. Achievement is a continuum, but it must be benchmarked and enjoyed along the way.

Lessons Which Can Only Come from Wisdom

These are some of the lessons that I learned after age 40 but wish I had learned earlier:

23. The more that you know, the more you need to know. The more you learn, the more you want to learn.

24. It is a true professional who can tell people what he-she does not know and points in the direction of niche experts. Wanna-be's say they always know more than the next person and can do it all.

25. People who often say, "Been there, done that" usually have not.

26. There will be no peace, empowerment or true professional cooperation unless there is a willingness to try and make collaborations work.

27. All of us agree on 95% of the issues. It's that 5% where we disagree that gets reasonable people into conflict.

28. When you squeeze the lemon into a glass of tea or water, cup it with one hand, and squeeze at an angle toward you. When you squeeze straight down, juice flies outward and usually hits someone else.

29. The best quick cure for clothing stains from food is to squeeze a few drops of lemon.

30. The worst violators of "restaurant etiquette" are the people who work there. It's sad when you have to dodge them and be subjected to poor people skills, then be expected to give a large tip.

31. In "telephone etiquette," the person who opens the conversation by asking how you are is trying to sell you something.

32. In "telephone etiquette," the worst violator is the person who answers after hours, usually the boss.

33. Most people are not paid what they're really worth. If they were paid what the marketplace says they're worth and had to live by benchmarks, they would do a much better job. Thus, one must act as though their name is on the door.

34. People who hold jobs and people who pursue careers are different breeds. The twain rarely meet.

35. People don't really "win" lotteries. The money goes toward their administration and feathering their political nest. The same is true for many other quick-fix or hype public sector projects.

36. Full equality, justice and fairness does not exist in society. It can only exist in your heart.

37. When you leave something for repair, write and leave a full description of the problems. Do not give long, rambling explanations to repair people because they will reduce your comments to two words which do not adequately diagnose the situation.

38. Most people who call themselves "consultants" are ill-prepared, have never really "been there" and charge you to get them some experience or dollars. Look beyond the obvious in evaluating consultants.

39. Don't expect clerical people to run your issue, comment or concern up the flagpole. It is not their job because they are busy administering the office. Either speak to the supervisor or put it in writing to his-her supervisor.

40. Government and public sector bureaucracies do not want new ideas or more effective ways to operate. It's nothing personal against you or your expertise. Bureaucracies are predicated upon protecting their turf and their jobs.

41. Change is 90% positive. So why do people fight what is most beneficial to them?

42. The worst line spoken is: "It ain't broke, don't fix it." The next worse is: "We must be doing something right." People use these to rationalize the status quo and avoid confronting their own shortcomings. There is no organization that cannot be improved.

43. There is no such thing as perfection. The better philosophy is Continuous Quality Improvement. Set and exceed standards. Move the yardstick farther each time.

44. The only kind of conflict resolution that lasts is a win-win.

Lessons Learned but Not Soon Forgotten

Fine-tuning one's career is an admirable and necessary process. It is not torture but, indeed, is quite illuminating. Imagine going back to reflect upon all you were taught. Along the way, you reapply old knowledge, find some new nuggets and create your own philosophies.

To help in re-treading old lessons and augmenting with new ones, these are some pieces of advice to mid-level and upper executives:

45. Executive development is a finely tuned art. It is a tireless yet energizing process.

46. People who rise in upper corporate ranks do so for reasons other than themselves. The art is to understand and work with those factors, rather than to become a pawn of them.

47. The old ways of rising to the top have changed. The savvy executive masters the new ways.

48. Don't become a "flavor of the month." Trends and fads in business and in people will subside. Posture yourself for the long-run.

49. Develop and trust your gut instinct. It's right most of the time.

50. Senior level consulting is not something that one retires into. It is not a part-time profession or something that one does in between jobs. Few corporate executives have what it takes to be a consultant.

51. One is not a full-fledged consultant until they have done this and only this for 10 years. One does not become "senior" until they have at least a 20-year consulting track record, not counting working at jobs for someone else.

52. Preventive actions pay back original investments, 6-10 times. Remediate downward spirals, sooner rather than later, to remediate The High Cost of Doing Nothing™.

53. Organizations get blamed for all consequences, including abuse, neglect, suffering and mistakes.

54. Management always wants to assign blame to someone else and success to themselves. They say, "Fix those people." The organization will not grow and mature until management realizes they are "those people."

55. People don't know why they believe in something. They just believe.

56. Never forget where you came from.

57. A fast-lane relief for stress is to slow down.

58. A house divided against itself will fall.

59. Society builds up idols only to shoot them down.

60. People believe lies more readily than they comprehend and absorb truths.

61. We mostly control our own destiny. Each time we abdicate, blame, relinquish or do nothing, opportunities pass by, known as The High Cost of Doing Nothing™. Missed opportunities compound and can never be fully regained.

Teachings Available to All of Us

There have been many truisms of life within our own consciousness. Most were taught to us at early ages. Going back to reflect puts them into today's perspective and utilization:

62. Do unto others, as they do unto you.
63. It's as important how you end a relationship as how you begin it.
64. There is nothing more permanent than change.
65. Not everything changes at once. There's an orderly transition.
66. What's old becomes new again.
67. As things change, they meld with those which do not change. This new equation still constitutes change.
68. You get out of something what you put into it.
69. In order to get, you have to give.
70. You cannot always pick your family members.
71. Caring and sharing is a lifetime art.
72. Nothing worth having comes easy.
73. Plan to make mistakes and how you will handle them.
74. Everyone makes mistakes. It's more important how you correct problems that counts.
75. Sticking one's head in the sand is not an option.

Slogans in Daily Life

Along the way, we heard many song lyrics, slogans and concepts that have deeper implications for business and life:

76. Drive to stay alive.
77. Drive friendly.
78. Let the sunshine in.
79. Please be kind. Rewind.
80. Life is a song worth living. Why don't you sing it!

81. The pause that refreshes.
82. My mama told me you better shop around.
83. The show must go on.
84. There's a sucker born every minute.
85. The beat goes on.
86. Try to remember.

Behaviors, Per Ideologies

There is a distinction between the things people instinctively know to do and the things they choose to do in daily transactions:

87. People know to shake packets of sugar-sweetener before adding to coffee-tea but forget to offer a drink to others before consuming.
88. Insincere respectful language and behavior toward one's elders is inconsistent, forced and comes across as contrived. Good manners should be an ongoing art of social behavior and courtesy to others…second nature, not an act.
89. The people who complain about customer service in retail establishments often give the worst considerations themselves to others in the workplace.
90. Customers who have been legitimately wronged usually do not or cannot speak up for themselves. When some do, it baffles businesses and makes them uneasy. Customers must find the confidence to challenge vendors for poor service.
91. People believe in speaking the truth. As it fits the purposes, the truth sometimes gets skewed.
92. People believe lies more quickly than they recognize the truth.
93. Truth is not always easy to recognize and not always pretty.
94. The bigger the lie, the more likely are more people to believe it.
95. Fight for and with the truth.
96. Citizens do not give as much back to their communities as they claim they do.
97. People who do not place a high value on their own time will not value others' time.
98. People judge others just as harshly as they appraise themselves.

99. Professionals who bill highly by the hour are the worst at getting other professionals to do "extra work" for free, not according the same professional courtesy.

100. Those who complain the most about not getting their "just deserved" (money, respect, power) have not paid enough dues to "get theirs" and likely never will.

Chapter 32

WHAT'S IN A NAME OR LABEL?

Nuances, Shades of Meaning, Usages Not the Same.
Discern the Differences and Semantics

Judge for yourself the relationship of the terms in each set to the other:

Sales—Service	Medicine—Health Care
Fame—Fortune	Business—Finance
Law—Order	Wealth—Riches
Learning—Knowledge	Banking—Finance
Pencil—Pen	Expert—Expertise
Government—Bureaucracy	Worker—Laborer
Career—Profession	Sales—Marketing
Ideas—Ideologies	Chairman—President
Rights—Privileges	Car—Truck
Technology—Equipment	Hearing—Listening
Oil—Water	Management—Labor
Breakfast—Brunch	Audio—Video

Advertising—Public Relations	Culture—Class
Street—Road	Avenue—Boulevard
Health—Wellness	Consult—Advise
Bookkeeping—Accounting	Science—Technology
Own—Rent	Lease—Buy
Concepts—Philosophies	Cassette—CD
Knowledge—Wisdom	Words—Grammar
Today—This Day	History—The Past
Sunlight—Moonlight	Comfort—Ease
Ignorance—Stupidity	Caring—Convictions
Parts—Labor	Air Conditioner—Fan
Education—Training	Lake—Bay
Thinker—Strategist	Watcher—Doer
Parts—Whole	Champagne—Wine
Trade—Skill	Art—Science
Empathy—Sympathy	Planning—Execution
Goals—Tactics	Researching—Benchmarking
Mission—Vision	Food—Groceries
Violator—Perpetrator	Advertising—Promotion
Before—After	Advocate—Activist
Teaching—Learning	Fun—Games
Closets—Storage	Honest—Truthful
Start—Embark	The FBI—The CIA
Barber—Hair Stylist	Allow—Enable
Insurance—Assurance	Ethnic—Multicultural
Bake—Broil	Driver—Chauffeur
Bus—Trolley	Cook—Chef
Athlete—Sportsman	Explain—Convey
Lies—Deceptions	Confidence—Self-esteem
Need—Want	Sip—Gulp
Compliance—Agreement	Couch—Loveseat
Drink—Slurp	Business—Marketplace
Garden—Forest	Read—Absorb
Non-smoker—Ex-smoker	Wealthy—Rich

Try—Attempt	Award—Reward
Problem—Dilemma	Brief—Short
Terminal—Hangar	Prisoner—Hostage
Time—Space	Manager—Leader
Progress—Progression	Resolve—Solve
Dinner—Supper	Genetics—Heredity
See—View	Believe—Perceive
Weather—Environment	Picture—Photo
Police—Highway Patrol	Fiction—Nonfiction
Peace—Calm	News—Entertainment
Carport—Garage	Van—Bus
Thinking—Intuiting	Multiply—Divide
Book—Novel	Store—Dealer
Birthday—Anniversary	Cow—Bull
Misunderstanding—Disagreement	Mailing—Shipping
Legend—Icon	Grocery Shopping—Marketing
Product Selling—Marketing	Seeing—Believing
Collaboration—Cooperation	Research—Development
Jumbo—Shrimp	Lighting—Illumination
Advise—Consent	Music—Lyrics
Crime—Criminal Justice	Clinic—Hospital
Gun—Rifle	Diplomat—Ambassador
Speaking—Talking	Look—See
Mis-statement—Un-truth	Study—Investigate
Right—Correct	Volunteerism—Stewardship
Competent—Proficient	Rain—Humidity
Tollway—Turnpike	Potential—Likely
Tire—Wheel	Business Trip—Vacation
Tablets—Caplets	Illness—Disease
Film—Slide Show	Teacher—Mentor
Time—Motion	Space—Cyberspace
Gasoline—Petroleum	Think—Believe
Habit—Fixation	Warranty—Guarantee
Deny—Disallow	Heredity—Environment

Child Care—Day Care	Sense—Fear
Upstream—Downstream	Friend—Supporter
Respect—Trust	Write-down—Bad Debt
Payables—Receivables	Credit—Debit
Baseball—Softball	Reading—Literacy
Restaurant—Cafe	Sickness—Disability
Friends—Associates	Movie—Cinema
Neglect—Company Dysfunction	Detergent—Clean Laundry
Words—Ideas	Book Learning—Common Sense
Futurism—Evolution	Mental—Physical
Dependable—Reliable	Ratio—Proportion
Reward—Punish	Grocery Store—Supermarket
Package—Container	Bottle—Jar
Instructor—Professor	Arts—Entertainment
Process—System	Coordinate—Expedite
Booklet—Brochure	House—Home
Overpass—Bridge	Language—Grammar
Sauce—Gravy	Decisions—Consequences
Police—Sheriff	Test—Quiz
Corp. Culture—Employee Attitude	Ideas—Innovations
Rain—Rainbows	Confidence—Arrogance
Cool—Cold	Desire—Covet
Warm—Hot	Mad—Angry
Trivet—Potholder	Buy—Sell
Dawn—Daybreak	Rain—Drizzle
Cup—Mug	Hobby—Avocation
TV Set—Monitor	Oil—Energy
Instinct—Behavior	Hills—Mountains
Pamphlet—Guide	Collaborate—Cooperate
Business—Commerce	Request—Demand
Analysis—Assessment	Flowers—Plants
Mind—Behave	Picture—Painting
Trees—Bushes	Box—Container
Reporter—Correspondent	Height—Stature

Sack—Bag	Dead End Street—Cul de Sac
Community—Society	City—Town
Private Sector—Business	Safety—Protection
Solids—Liquid	Public Sector—Government
Probable—Possible	Noise—Sounds
Witness—Observer	Soap—Shampoo
Light—Lamp	Violin—Fiddle
River—Stream	Pets—Strays
Briefcase—Satchel	Hero—Martyr
File—Folder	Scene—Scenario
Consciousness—Awareness	Battle—War
Diagnose—Prescribe	Grass—Weeds
Group—Team	Symptoms—Problems
Stress—Pressure	Cause—Effect
Pleasure—Pain	Originator—Follower
Pan—Skillet	Thrills—Excitement
Create—Initiate	Report—Memo
Socks—Stockings	Diamond—Jewel
Medicine—Pills	Earnings Statement—Annual Report
Floor—Ground	Letter—Note
Facilitator—Implementer	Employee—Colleague
Contender—Winner	Rebate—Discount
Bookshelf—Bookcase	Horn—Siren
Refund—Make-good	Remember—Reflect
Live—Exist	Sugar—Sweetener
Manage—Control	Give—Receive
Alarm—Frighten	Order—Empower
Show—Play	Eating—Dining
Opera—Operetta	Theater—Auditorium
Adjudicate—Solve	Fan—Supporter
Consulting—Visioning	Newsletter—Direct Mail
Groupie—Star	Training—Planning
Tami—Limousine	Jail—Prison
The IRS—Treasury Dept.	Resident—Citizen

Coffee—Tea	Eyesight—Vision
Doctor—Nurse	Bath—Shower
Financial Planning—Banking	Lawyer—Paralegal
Store—Shop	Advise—Supervise
M.D.—Ph.D.—Ed.D.	Ice Cream—Yogurt
Sales Goals—Business Plan	Compliant—Obedient
Furnace—Stove	Heart Attack—Stroke
Library—The Internet	Delete—Destroy
Notebook—Reference File	Wastebasket—Trash Can
Message—Medium	Loudspeaker—Sound System
Limitations—Realities	Catalog—Brochure
Screaming—Discussing	Tastes—Preferences
Hotel—Motel	Change—Resistance
Flavors—Fragrances	Smile—Enthusiasm
Telephone Etiquette—Manners	Capitalism—Opportunism
Mystery—Suspense	Spokesperson—Decision Maker
Expense—Investment	Account—Compute
Human Resources—Leadership	Differences—Barriers
Think—Feel	Professional—Vendor
Associate—Hanger-on	Dial—Knob
Obvious—Subtle	Interpret—Modify
Stop—Cease	Roles—Responsibilities
Priorities—Agendas	Start—Commence
Entrepreneur—Employee	Mimi-series—Soap Opera
Boss—Staff	Plant—Equipment
Seasoning—Experiences	Attitude—Success
Labels—Mindset	Improvement—Results
Wheels—Motion	Telephone Solicitor—Nuisance
Healthy Lifestyle—Longevity	Diameter—Circle
Planning—Achieving	Review—Future Planning
Facts—Figures	Forms—Processes
Experiences—Philosophies	Shirt—Sweater
Lack of Planning—Failure	Ethics—Responsibility
Chair—Stool	Cash Flow—Market Trends

Insurance Premiums—Claims	Research—Planning
Brochure—Communications Plan	Company History—Future Plan
Youth—Mistakes	Transportation—Distribution
Discipline—Work Ethics	Flash—Sizzle
Inputting—Database Accuracy	Discipline—Behaviors
Quality—Success	Plate—Platter
Separate—Distinctive	Earn—Receive

The genesis of this started in the 1960s with two influential schoolteachers. My junior high school speech teacher, Thelma Henslee, used to quiz us with the phrase, "Author or Arthur?" Her point was to discern sound-alike expressions and think through their differences, similarities, correct usage and applicability.

My high school speech teacher, Terri Flynn, used to ask people, "How are you doing?" The typical response was, "Real good." She would then probe, "How good?" She wanted you to use correct grammar, such as "really well." More importantly, she wanted you to choose less-trite expressions, such as "outstandingly fine today" or, more honestly, how you really were doing.

From those teachers and subsequent professional mentors, I learned the value of:

- Using specific, imaginative language to express ideas.
- Saying what you mean and meaning what you say.
- Calling the elephant what it really is.
- Writing for the eye is different from writing for the ear.
- Not settling for trite expressions, slang jargon and other people's quotes.
- Taking the time to educate people on subtle nuances and meanings of words.
- Believing that listeners and readers are more intelligent than others might believe.
- Using vocabulary that expresses thoughts and rises to higher levels.
- Challenging people to read new meanings into old words, phrases and ideas.
- Compelling people to discern ideas for themselves, based upon insights and ideas.

In business (a mirror of everyday life), terms are used interchangeably and out of context. The public doesn't discern differences. With the passage of time, as people and companies "market the hype," they begin to believe the blurred usages of expressions they use.

Improper semantics perpetuate in the mass culture. Constituents accept what they hear. If they hear it enough times, it must be true. They believe what they are familiar with. Getting them to modify familiar patterns is difficult but still must be done.

Cases in point:

- Retailers offer "service" as an enticer to close sales of products. Sales support and follow-p customer service are light years away. Whereas, they'll say anything to make a sale, true-quality customer service is presently at an all-time low. There are many tiers of service, with service to make the sale merely the lowest rung on the ladder.
- Business "consultants" often misrepresent what they do. Accounting firms believe themselves to be full-scope business advisors and sell themselves as such. Training companies tell clients that they also conduct strategic planning and consulting, believing all of those professional disciplines are the same thing.
- There are many differences in business. Sales and marketing are not the same thing. Advertising and public relations are different services. Financial projections do not constitute business planning. Sales quotas do not produce an empowered staff. Edicts by management do not directly lead to behavioral modification. Selling more products does not solve the manufacturing and distribution problems. Career workers and seasoned professionals are different breeds. Grumbling by workers does not constitute discontent and mutiny.

People place labels on everything and everybody, without distinguishing the subtle differences. People and companies believe the labels, without looking into the subtle nuances. Society was not acclimated into discerning differences.

All differences in semantics become opportunities to educate each other about the subtle nuances of labels, terms, phrases and categories.

Chapter 33

VISIONING SCOPE

Creating and Applying Vision Toward Your Organization's Progress

M ost organizations know why they exist and their purpose. Those fundamental elements constitute a Mission Statement.

Most organizations never go past the Mission Statement. Thus, they fail to realize potential. Having a purpose by itself does not make the organization materialize, much less be successful.

Visioning is the process where good ideas become something more. Visioning is a catalyst toward long-term evaluation, planning and implementation. Visioning is a jump-off point by which forward thinking organizations ask themselves:

- What will we look like in the future?
- What do we want to become?
- How will we evolve?

Businesses, communities and organizations will succeed by having, communicating and garnering support for a Shared Vision. Visioning sets the stage for necessary processes, such as growth strategies, re-engineering, training, enhancing shareholder value and organizational development. Without visioning, the community simply performs band aid surgery on problems as they occur. The Vision provides continuous guidance to employees at every level as to how they should manage their respective responsibilities.

Vision is a realistic picture of what is possible. Visioning must be Big Picture in perspective. It must creatively focus upon the whole and then the parts of the organization, as they relate to the whole. It is a process by which a Strategic Plan and Visioning program components come off the shelf and alive into action, relative to all levels of the organization:

1. **Resource.** Equipment, tools, materials, schedules.
2. **Skills-Tasks.** Duties, activities, tasks, behaviors, attitudes, contracting, project fulfillment.
3. **Role-Job.** Assignments, responsibilities, functions, relationships, accountability.
4. **Systems-Processes.** Structure, hiring, control, work design, supervision, decisions.
5. **Strategy.** Planning, tactics, organizational development.
6. **Culture-Mission.** Values, customs, beliefs, goals, objectives, benchmarking.
7. **Philosophy.** Organizational purpose, vision, quality of life, ethics, long-term growth.

The Vision describes what can and will happen, once everyone's energies are focused. Vision is not a financial forecast or a market analysis. Vision is less of a dream and more of a realistic picture of what is possible.

When there is a genuine Vision (as compared to a terse "vision statement"), people are compelled to learn and excel, not because they are told to but because they want to.

Most leaders have personal visions that rarely get communicated to the organization. By default, Vision has resolved around the values and positioning of one leader. Often, a crisis will rally the organization, but that tends to be short-lived.

Given the choice, most people and their organizations will pursue high goals. Visioning is a process that melds individual visions into a recipe for success, a shared set of guiding practices. When different constituencies have common visions (or at least applications of them), they will bond together for purpose and cause.

Personal visions are driven by an individual's deep caring. Shared visions derive their power via common caring. Truly, people want to be connected together.

Shared visions take time to emerge. They grow as a result of successful showcasing of individual visions, with benchmarks for success that are understood. Ongoing conversation is required to foster shared visions. From listening, insights of what is possible shall emerge.

The key elements of Strategic Vision are:

1. Business scope and scale.
2. Product and market focus.
3. Competitive focus.
4. Orientation toward image and relationships.
5. Applicability to organization and culture.

Visioning needs to take place within each business unit, as well as at the larger organizational level.

Too often, management fails to articulate its values or does so imperfectly.

- The purposes and expected benefits of Visioning include:
- Taking hold of the future.
- Setting something in motion that will honor those who have built the organization.
- Involving the widest base of support in pro-active change and growth.
- Benchmarking the progress made and communicating it to constituencies.
- Nurturing the organization's image.
- Understanding the difference between good and bad handling of crises.
- Crises follow-ups that help heal and rebuild after problems versus those that fester and bring destruction to organizations.
- Study and ready the organization to make best advantage of bridge-building and problem remediation concepts.
- Methodologies to address problems sooner, rather than later.
- Establishing safeguards against future trouble.
- Putting more emphasis upon the positive ingredients and happenings.

Visioning is not revenue forecasting or quotas. It is not a marketing campaign. It is not an academic exercise in mumbo jumbo, or a group facilitated activity.

Questions to Ask in Developing Visioning Scope

Investment and expansion opportunities:

What is your company's most important asset?

Who placed the value on it? What was their basis?

Why might others want the assets of your organization?

Entrepreneurship:

What are the pros and cons of the entrepreneur?

How can the entrepreneur amass the more sophisticated business skills?

What is the value of mentorship for aspiring entrepreneurs?

What are the most important things that you learned in life?

Who were your teachers and mentors?

What did they teach you that you use now?

Collaborations-partnering:

What valuable lessons did you learn from competitors, colleagues and consultants?

What circumstances led you toward successful collaborations?

How important is the concept of partnering in today's business climate?

Business development:

Who are a company's stakeholders?

What are some factors outside your company which affect your ability to do business?

How do you go about navigating your future success?

How do you define proper business planning?

How should businesses be players in the global market of the future?

Tackling the future:

Where do you expect to be in another 10 years? How will your company get there?

If you don't plan for the future, what will likely happen?

7 Steps Toward Strategic Vision

1. Analyze the company's future environment, resources and capabilities. Determine where the Big Picture existed before, if it did at all. Crystallize the core business in terms of viabilities to move successfully forward to some discernible point.
2. Clarify management values. Growth must be conducted in concert with core values. Often, senior management have not yet fully articulated their own individual values, let alone those of the organization. This process helps to define and further develop value systems to carry the organization toward success.
3. Develop a Mission Statement. It is a starting point, not an end in itself. The Mission Statement is rewritten several times, as the planning process ensues. The last draft of the statement will be an executive summary of collective ideas and works of the Visioning team.
4. Identify strategic objectives and goals. I ask clients to do so without using three words: "technology," "sales," and "solutions." Most businesses fail to grow because they get stuck in buzzwords and trite phrases that they hear in others' marketing hype. Objectives and goals must be germane to your company and its unique position.
5. Generate select strategic options. There are many ways to succeed, and your game plan should have at least five viable options. When the Visioning program matures and gets to its second generation, you'll find that winning formulas stem from a hybrid of the original strategic options. Creative thinking moves the company into the future, not rehashes of the earliest ideas.
6. Develop the vision statement. It will be action-oriented and speaks from the facts, as well as from the passion of company leaders. It will include a series of convictions why your organization will work smarter, be its best, stand for important things and be accountable.
7. Measure and review the progress. By benchmarking activities and accomplishments against planned objectives, then the company has a barometer of its previous phase and an indicator of its next phase.

The 7 Traits of a Successful Visioning Program

1. Effective visions are inspiring. They must touch the chords of what the company started out to become. They may compel leaders to renew or

multiply their commitments for the future. Their messages apply to every sector of the company.

2. Effective visions are clear and challenging. There is no such thing as perfection, but incremental levels of excellence are to be attained and bested. Every message must be communicated throughout the organization, acquiring feedback and additional commitments from the rank and file. Thereafter, visions become their brainchildren.

3. Effective visions have marketplace purpose, savvy and flexibility. It is not enough to look good on paper or touch the hearts of some. Visions must squarely place the company in the forefront of its market niche, customer base, industry perspective and economic realm. It's all about doing good business and then being a good organization.

4. Effective visions must be stable, yet prudently updated. No "pie in the sky" tenets or trite restatements of other companies' promotions are acceptable. Show how planned, controlled growth will maintain stability for investors, hold interest for the marketplace and propel the organization to break further new ground.

5. Effective visions are role models, when all else is in turmoil. Research shows that only 2% of the world's companies have strategic plans. Visioning programs go far beyond the plan and root the corporate culture into something real and breathing. While most companies meander, your visionary company can chart its own course.

6. Effective visions empower the organization's people first and the customers secondly. People constitute the largest component (28%) of a successful organization. They are neglected because they are not consulted or considered. By nurturing the company's best resource (its people), then productivity, creativity and profitability soar. At all times, what is done and accomplished must focus upon the customer base.

7. Effective visions honor the past and prepare for the future. There are good reasons why the company started. By weathering change and taking new turns, the organization matures. With futures constantly changing, then the art of success comes from re-examining the journey. From the subtlest nuances come gems of gold in the organization's bank.

The 7 Pitfalls to Avoid

1. Settle short-term problems. Otherwise, they will fester and grow. Many organizations fail because they deny the problems, seek to place blame elsewhere or hope against hope that things will miraculously get better. Unsolved problems turn into larger roadblocks to growth.

2. Never let the vision lapse. Keep the vision grounded in reality through benchmarked measurements. Keep the communication open, and the people will keep the enthusiasm alive. Renew the vision every five years with a formal process, thus including newer employees, the latest in business strategies and, thus, the advantage over emerging competitors.

3. Effective visions are lived in details, not in broad strokes. If the mission evolves from the process, then so do the goals and objectives reformulate by changing tactics. The smallest tactics and creative new ways of performing them tend to blossom into grand new visions.

4. Be sure that all sectors of the organization participate. The Big Picture cannot be top-down, nor can the embracement of corporate culture be only from the bottom-up. The Visioning committee should represent all strata of the organization.

5. Periodically, test and review the process. We learn three times more from failures than from successes. Understanding why the organization ticks, rather than just what it produces, makes the really big gains possible. Success is a track record of periodic reflections.

6. Never stop planning for the next phase. The review and benchmarking phases of one process constitute the pre-work and research for the next. From careful study (not whims or gut instincts) stem true strategic planning. From a track record of planning stem organizations of exceptional and profitable visions.

7. Change is inevitable. Research shows that change is 90% positive. Individuals and organizations change at the rate of 71% per year. The secret is in benefiting from change, rather than becoming a victim of it.

7 Levels of Visioning Programs, Determining How Far Organizations Evolve

1. **Was Someone's Pet Idea.** A program was initiated to fit a personal or political agenda. It was sold and accepted as such. Therefore, it will be pursued partially because its motivation is transparent or limited.

Visioning is more than a "program." It is a process, encompassing change, behavioral modification, focus on growth and positive reinforcement.

2. **Done Because It Was Forced or Mandated.** A crisis, litigation, merger, loss of market share, government edict, competition with others or a combination of outside factors caused this to begin. Visioning here is a response, not a choice. The amounts of support and participation depends upon the circumstances and the spirit with which the mandate is carried out.

3. **Done for Show or Image.** Some organizations think that Visioning will make organizations look good. Actually, it makes them good. Visioning is not a substitute for public relations or marketing. It guides the organization which those other functions support. Visioning must focus upon substance, not just flash-and-sizzle.

4. **With Partial Support and Resources.** It is accorded just enough to begin the process but not quite enough to do it right. It is either the domain of top management or is delegated to the middle of the organization. Visioning must be a team effort and well-communicated in order to hit its stride, gather additional support and sustain.

5. **Well Planned.** The Visioning process begins with forethought, continues with research and culminates in a Strategic Plan…including mission, core values, goals, objectives (per each key results area), tactics to address and accomplish, timeline and benchmarking criteria.

6. **Well Executed.** Visioning goes beyond the Strategic Plan. It sculpts how the organization will progress, its character and spirit, participation of its people and steps that will carry the organization to the next tiers of desired achievement, involvement and quality.

7. **Well Followed and Benchmarked.** Both the Strategic Plan and the Visioning process must be followed through. This investment is one-sixth that of later performing band aid surgery on an ailing organization.

Areas of Visioning Focus
7 Steps Toward Vision:

1. **Information**…What We Know, Technologies-Tasks to Gather.
2. **Education**…Teaching, Processing Information, Modeling.
3. **Learning**…Mission, Absorbing Information, Techniques.

4. **Insights**...Synthesizing Information, Values, Strategies.
5. **Knowledge**...Direction, Experience Bank, Inspired Thoughts.
6. **Strategy**...Actions, Goals & Objectives, Viabilities, Creativity.
7. **Vision**...Qualities, Strengths, Realizations, Big Picture Scope.

7 Levels of Organizational Visioning:

1. Planning, Controls, Reorganization.
2. Team Building, Empowerment, Mastering the Political Process.
3. Fiscal Management, Economic Development.
4. Community Input-Output.
5. Communications Image, Services, Accountability.
6. Enhance the Organization's Book Value.
7. Successfully Moving the Company Forward.

First volume in this series…

THE BIG PICTURE OF BUSINESS, BOOK 1
Big Ideas and Strategies
7 Steps Toward Business Success

Digest of Excerpts from the Author's Other Books

THE BIG PICTURE OF BUSINESS, BOOK 2
Comprehensive Reference for Business Success
Doing Business in a Distracted World

Appendix: Classic Hank Moore Magazine Articles

Third volume in this series…

THE BIG PICTURE OF BUSINESS, BOOK 3
Business Strategies and Legends
Encyclopedic Knowledge Bank

APPENDIX
OTHER WRITINGS BY HANK MOORE
Classic Hank Moore Magazine Articles

Behind the Scenes at the TV Soap Operas, TV-Radio Mirror, August 1969

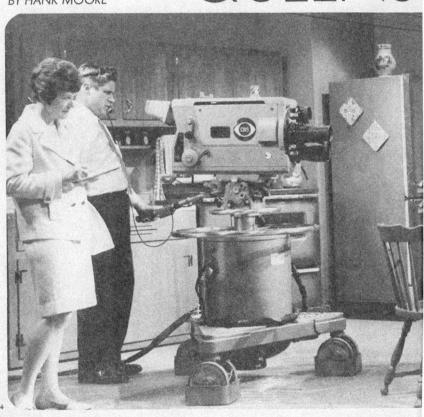

HERE'S THE EXCITING VIEW FROM THE OTHER SIDE OF THE CAMERA!

I SPENT A WEEK WITH THE

SOAP OPERA KINGS 'N' QUEENS

BY HANK MOORE

44

I had been aware of soap operas for many years, catching episodes of various series off and on but never following the plots intently. A remodeling job on our house changed all that a few months back, when I was practically confined to the living room to eat my lunch, any time from 12:30 to 2:30, to the tune of daytime serials.

I became particularly interested in *Love Is A Many-Splendored Thing*, CBS-TV's glamour show, in which things were really happening storywise! Technically, it was a marvel. Dramatically, it was unlike the *Ma Perkins* days—for the better. The plot and the characters really swung! For weeks, I would find myself racing home to see this show, along with my perennial favorite, *As The World Turns*. Appointments just weren't scheduled in conflict with "my" shows, nor were lunches limited to a mere sandwich.

Deciding to parlay this interest into research—and further into an interesting assignment— I recently set out to visit the people who make daytime dramas in New York, doing a six-part series for the Austin (Texas) *American-Statesman*, for which I am a columnist. The producers of *Many-Splendored* arranged a thoroughly delightful weeklong visit with the soap opera

Above: Helen Wagner and Eileen Fulton look very much like you've seen them on your set, playing Nancy and Lisa in "As The World Turns." At left: This is the way camera and crew see young Don Hastings and Don MacLaughlin enacting their roles as Bob and Chris Hughes in this same highly popular daytime serial. As all good viewers know, Bob is the son of Chris and Nancy—and the ex-husband of Lisa. Though the family tree gets a bit tangled, over the long run of any worthwhile soap opera, its fans can name every branch and twig. But only our writer can tell what's going to happen next year on three of your favorite dramas!

What happens next on
"As The World Turns,"
"Search For Tomorrow"
and "Love Is A Many-Splendored Thing"?
Can you keep a secret?

One dominant male among a fascinating variety of women on "Love Is A Many-Splendored Thing": Spence Garrison (as played by Ed Power), seen at right with his ex-wife Nancy (Susan Browning)—who's seldom in such a friendly mood! Two of the top girls are sisters: Laura Elliott (Donna Mills, at left below) and Iris Donnelly (Leslie Charleson). At near right on facing page, it's Spence again, with Iris—whose literal blindness seems fated to continue complicating their one-time "engagement." At far right: Jean Garrison (Jane Manning), who is Spence's stepmother and the drama's chief villainess. Seen here with William Post Jr. as Chandler, actress Jane admits she has studied hard to find out what makes Jean tick like such a time-bomb on the show!

kings and queens at the CBS 57th Street studios. The first day, we were guided through the CBS physical plant by producer Charles Weiss and associate producer John Conboy. We sat in on dress rehearsal and chatted with the stars afterward. Come showtime, we watched it on TV while enjoying a catered lunch in the production offices.

Each day saw conferences with still other producers and stars, and lots of rehearsals. We viewed the casts and crews of such series as World and Search For Tomorrow, two of TV's most popular series, working together as closely as a family. Both actors and directors suggest ways to polish the finished performance; it cannot be done, day after day, without teamwork!

Down the CBS corridors strolled such heroes of the daytime viewer as Don Hastings, instantly recognizable to millions as World's Bob Hughes. He stopped to ask about the weather in Texas, noting that he had taken an embarrassing fall that morning on a slippery New York sidewalk. He recalled looking up sheepishly to find a busload of people all recognizing him, yet taking a certain comfort in the fact that they knew his TV character and probably felt a common sympathy for him!

As a child, personable Hastings toured with the national company of Life With Father in the 1940s. Later, he played Broadway and was the Ranger on TV's Captain Video for six years. He starred on The Edge Of Night for four and a half years before taking the role of Bob Hughes —which he has now played for twice that length of time.

Playing his series ex-wife, Lisa, is Eileen Fulton, who is actually a very quiet and reserved person. "I make Lisa scatterbrained to justify her problems," she confided to me. During a sabbatical leave of one year from the series, Eileen toured the nation in a singing nightclub act, and she still hums pretty tunes while memorizing scripts on the set.

Dagne Crane, who plays Bob's second wife, Sandy, once thought of becoming a nun and studied at both Cleveland's Covenant of the Word Incarnate and at the Southern Seminary finishing school. She switched her studies in order to be a teacher of English literature but became an actress, instead, when a talent scout spotted her in a restaurant. At lunch in the CBS commissary, Dagne proved very interested in health foods—and admitted she is probably even more excited about reading her fan mail than her fans are in writing it!

Don MacLaughlin, papa Chris Hughes on the series, is a witty conversationalist in real life. He has done such diverse things career-wise as teaching English, starring

Undisputed queen of the soap operas is Mary Stuart, who's played Joanne Tate ever since "Search For Tomorrow" debuted in September, 1951. Despite her eminence as an actress, Mary has a right to sing only sad songs, considering what's already happened to Joanne all these years. (Or maybe she's had a glimpse of our author's notes and seen what still lies ahead for Joanne? Picture a well known geometrical figure with three points—then color one of them "vindictive"!)

"As The World Turns": Above, Helen Wagner & Don MacLaughlin as Nancy & Chris. At left, Santos Ortega as Grandpa Hughes and Eileen Fulton as Lisa ("I make her scatterbrained to justify her problems," Eileen confides off-camera).

47

From the beginning—like all serials—"Many-Splendored Thing" could reveal its plot to the cast only a week or so ahead. Storylines may be planned a year or two in advance but the scripts are usually written less than a month before airtime.

Since radio days, organ music has been almost synonymous with soap opera, heightening the emotional drama with the most effective "vibrations" known to the human ear (or heart). On "Love Is A Many-Splendored Thing," it's been played by Eddie Layton, seen here with director John J. Desmond and Donna Mills, who are among his sincerest fans—and there are many such admirers!

Besides striving to keep pace
with today's changing moral climate,
the modern-day "soaps" plan to replace
organ or "canned" music with
specially-orchestrated musical scores

on radio in the long-run *Counterspy*, and doing free-lance photography for national magazines. Helen Wagner, who seems very much like her character of Nancy Hughes, came into show business via music recitals in her native Lubbock, Texas.

Barbara Berjer, *World*'s Claire Cassen, holds a master's degree in drama. Roy Shuman—Dr. Michael Shea, the villain on the show—is quite a jokester on the set. Playing Claire's daughter Ellen Stewart is Patricia Bruder, who was a member of radio's *Juvenile Jury* as a child.

The warmest heart in the *World* family belongs to Santos Ortega, its Grandpa Hughes. He recalled for us a fascinating career of singing in vaudeville, starring as *Ellery Queen* on radio and playing top parts in such as *Charlie Chan*, *Perry Mason* and *The Shadow*. He is quite fluent at faking a Spanish accent, as might be expected from his name.

Over at *Love Is A Many-Splendored Thing*, the show's villainess, Jean Garrison, is actually a most charming actress named Jane Manning: "I get here each day and wonder what horrible, wicked things Jean is up to. She really should be locked away in a penitentiary!"

Miss Manning worked out an analysis of the role so she can play it to perfection. "Jean never had anything and came up from the dumps to struggle for all she could get," she said, summing up the career of a woman who has had an affair with a professional "protege" and was blackmailed for it by her ex-husband.

One of Miss Manning's most embarrassing moments came in a recent episode when she entered the set on camera and fell—because the rug had not been taped to the concrete surface. "I thought of several different things on the way down, but had to figure out a way to change the scene to make the fall fit in," she chuckled. The show, you see, is broadcast *live*.

Playing Jean's stepson Spence is Ed Power, who talks rather academically, as befits a former professor of philosophy and English literature at Emory University in Atlanta, Georgia. Dr. Charles Hartshorne, now professor of philosophy at the University of Texas (our alma mater), remembers Power as a colleague at Emory, "a studious, dedicated scholar."

Power told me more things about U.T. than I knew after studying there. "It is known in my circles for excellent teaching," he said, causing me to wince rather guiltily. He admitted turning to television (first as emcee of a kiddie show, later as a sportscaster) for the money (higher than his teaching salary), but still regrets that he has never returned to school to earn his nearly completed doctorate degree. (Perhaps he will "work it in," someday.)

A screaming maniac on *Splendored* is Spence's ex-wife Nancy! But Susan Browning, who plays her, is a quiet and refined actress who sincerely wanted to know *why* I was such a fan of the show. "In my fan mail," she told me, "so many viewers cannot articulate what they *like* about the role I play. I am dying to know how they feel, so I can improve the character accordingly!"

During the rehearsals I saw, the two pretty "sisters" of *Splendored* were intently studying their roles for overall conception, as well as the daily lines. Leslie Charleson (who plays Iris Donnelly) was an award-winning dramatist at Bennett College. Donna Mills (Laura Elliott) was trained as a dancer and has even staged a ballet on the show as a "dream" dance sequence. Both are obviously serious about the theatre.

Absolute queen of the soaps is Mary Stuart, who has been Joanne Tate in *Search For Tomorrow* ever since it premiered September 3, 1951. She has appeared continuously on more shows for more years than any other day-time serial star! Miss Stuart told us of her love for designing children's books, but said she will stick with *Search* for good.

We asked producer Mary Harris if Rosemary Prinz would return to *World* in the role of Penny Hughes. Miss Harris said Rosemary had simply let her contract run out in May, 1968, and did not renegotiate with the preceding producer. The youthful "veteran" of twelve years with the series had not feuded with management but simply wanted to get into musical comedy work for a while.

We contacted Rosemary when she was appearing in *The Apple Tree* in our hometown, and she told us then that she did not know, one way or the other, if and when she would return to *World*. Miss Harris verified this, noting that both parties (she has never met Rosemary) would have to negotiate Penny's return. "One consideration would be if there was a place in the story for Penny, which there is not at present," she added.

Like viewers themselves, the stars are keenly interested in the characters they play, but are only posted on the plot a week ahead of time, when they get their scripts. An actress on *Splendored* asked for an advance text in view of a long vacation before her next call. "All the information you get out of me, that is where I draw the line," joked producer Weiss, who is even keeping his own mother in the dark on future episodes!

We were sitting in the *World* control room, screening some of the show's many rerun sequences from earlier years which are used as flashbacks. John Colenback, who plays young Dr. Dan Stewart, (Continued on page 92) 49

blues! And she has nowhere to go but up. This time, friends believe, she will make it—for keeps. This time she's old enough to handle her career maturely . . . not just as a little girl who had to grow up too

SOAP OPERAS

(Continued from page 49)

turned to Cort Steen, director, in confusion. "Did Ellen know at that point in the story that David knew Dan was her son?" he asked—prompting Steen to stop the proceedings and engage the other six crew members in a discussion on just what *was* happening on that old show. Steen had directed it six years previously. (Henderson Forsythe, who plays papa David Stewart, settled the question with an emphatic "Yes.")

Over at *Splendored*, we noticed the technical crew in the control room getting absorbed in the emotion of each scene, while the director's cues and instructions became more frenetic and crisper, as the action heated up.

Storylines for all daytime serials are mapped out by writer and producer a year or more in advance (two or three years, on some of the older shows). A month ahead of broadcast, they are finalized as to what actions occur on what days. Actual script writing is only two weeks ahead of broadcast date.

Incidentally, base pay for actors is $165 a day, though most get more than that and are on contracts guaranteeing three days' pay a week, whether or not they are in the story.

Viewer mail is definitely considered in "reinforcing or disproving what we are writing," noted Bob Driscoll, producer of *Search*. It can cause small characters to become more prominent in the story (like Barnabas in *Dark Shadows*), but a majority of writers cannot change the storyline completely. "I find that viewers in their fan letters are generally pretty shrewd in guessing about what will happen tomorrow," Miss Harris added.

Each show takes a full day's work, as witness the *World Turns* schedule: 1:30—show on the air live; 2:30-5:30—read lines and block out scenes for next day's show; 7:30-9:30 the next morning—rehearse; 9:30-10:30—costumes, makeup and hairdressing; 10:30-11—show first goes before the cameras; noon—dress rehearsal with commercials and music; 1:30—show again on the air live, ending one day's ritual and beginning the perennial next.

Most actors prefer to do the shows live to get the best performance. Weiss feels they build up the quality to a climax when on the air and that actors would tend to falter more if the show were being taped in expectation of redoing scenes.

Production studios for the soaps are rather small (averaging about 100 x 200 feet) for quick and easy movement. Sets are arranged in each corner, and the three cameras and two microphone booms must be shuttled about the room. In *World*'s rectangular studio (100 x 350 feet), two men are required to literally run with the monstrous camera for transferring scenes.

soon and make too many decisions! Lauren, wherever you go, whatever you do, we wish you happiness—the happiness you brought so many viewers when you were only a child. —TONY BOWEN

Daytime serials are "grown up" today, as increasing numbers of viewers have noticed. In addition to housewives, their regular audiences (some 200 million a day for all shows) include students, businessmen, career women and professors. They are successful because they touch human emotion in a much broader-based audience than the old-fashioned stereotype of "soap opera" fans.

"We now gear toward the intelligent, and approach our stories like a nighttime show," observed Conboy of *Splendored*. He feels the soaps can no longer afford to deceive viewers with outmoded or downright improbable views on life.

"Viewers can find the frankest material seen during the day," added Weiss. "It is truer to what people go through, and the public is already asking for more."

The various producers' opinions as to whether viewers select special favorites—or simply leave the TV set on all day—are about equally divided. All agree that there is a decided asset in today's writing—far superior to most radio serials, which were often mass-produced by a single team. Each is now independently done by such skilled craftsmen as James Lipton (*Splendored*), who is author of the current bestseller *An Exaltation Of Larks*, and Henry Slesar (*The Edge Of Night*), whose short stories regularly appear in *Alfred Hitchcock's Mystery Magazine*.

Families like the Hugheses (*World*), the Bauers (*The Guiding Light*) and the Ameses (*Secret Storm*) have become American institutions, embracing all that is virtuous and quite a bit of human frailty, too.

The viewer who asks about soap operas' future will find it rosy. Ratings show that every serial on every network outrates any other type of show at competing times. (Most of the top shows are telecast over CBS, but such dramas as NBC's *Another World* have vast audiences, too.)

Full-hour serials are already being contemplated, as are longer acts between commercials (average now, about 4 or 5 minutes). The future may also see specially orchestrated musical scores replacing the organ or "canned" music so long associated with this type of show.

All producers we interviewed dream of *nighttime* soap operas, all viewing with regret the sad fate of the spin-off series launched by *World* in "prime time" a few seasons ago. They still hope—and find encouragement in those television markets which delay broadcasting their shows until late afternoon spots or even late at night (as will soon be tried with ABC's popular *Dark Shadows*).

As for the advance storylines:

Present stories on *World* in the coming year (as of this writing) will be extended to include further closeness between Ellen Stewart and her illegitimate son Dan, reunited last March. Dr. Michael Shea, the series' villain, will be shown to have had a very sad background, and viewers will begin to understand his defense of people who treat him poorly. Shea will take on more warmth and become a hero!

An interesting romantic triangle will explode between brothers Paul and Dan Stewart over romantic interest in Elizabeth Talbot, whose sad background is keeping her from going home to England. Dan's wife will be the pivotal figure.

Search For Tomorrow will open up a sticky triangle in the troubled affair between Joanne Tate and Sam Reynolds—thanks to Sam's wife, who will not let him go so he can marry Joanne.

Love Is A Many-Splendored Thing will have repercussions of the Steve Hurley murder, with the wrong man "framed." Storylines will explore Iris Donnelly's definite blindness and a new relationship for her and fiance Spence Garrison, whose wedding she first broke off last January.

Jean Garrison will have a new affair. And former lover Mark Elliott will unbelievably have a new relationship with estranged wife Laura. Explicit enough!

Although the producers were most gracious in divulging their storylines to me, I will not reveal the endings—most of them surprises *a la* Hitchcock. One trick to remember in second-guessing soap operas is: "Nobody will ever be completely happy. Otherwise, there will be no story," as Weiss pointed out.

I was one of the rare people getting more than hints from the producers, but the main inspiration I brought home was the way daytime dramas are so thoughtfully put together by dedicated professionals who take their work seriously. The soaps are now better artistically because they are created by people with pride and huge talents.

I saw the sets, read the scripts, and met—not the characters—but topnotch actors who are, without exception, even warmer off screen than on . . . especially the villains! In fact, all who make these serials are young, creative, and the nicest people one would ever want in a circle of friends. ●

JACKIE KENNEDY

(Continued from page 32)

In the days and weeks following the wedding, Jackie and Ari commuted between the yacht and Scorpios without experiencing a single intrusion or incursion by an unwanted visitor. The Greeks from the neighboring islands and the mainland had no design to mar the tranquility and peace the newlyweds sought. Ari and Jackie were left alone.

To their small coterie of friends who visited the couple, the idyll seemed complete. They noted that even the Secret Service men—who had been Jackie's inseparable shadows for all the years since her late husband had been elected President of the United States—were no longer on the scene. Her marriage to Onassis terminated the American government's obligation to provide protection to John F. Kennedy's widow.

Even on the two occasions in the latter part of the year—in November and again just before Christmas—when Jackie flew to the U. S. for brief visits, she traveled without a protective escort. There seemed to be no reason for one. Her only peril

Train for exciting career in medical, dental fields

Career Academy graduates enjoy high paying positions in these prestige fields. Train in our fully equipped laboratories in major cities or at home in your spare time. Nationally recognized courses supervised by leading physicians and dentists. NATIONWIDE PLACEMENT ASSISTANCE at No Extra Cost. Accredited Member National Home Study Council and National Association of Trade and Technical Schools. Write for FREE booklet now.

PERMANENT HAIR REMOVER

SAFELY REMOVES UNWANTED HAIR FOREVER

Making the Unknown Familiar, Jefferson Chemical Company.
Austin Magazine 1968

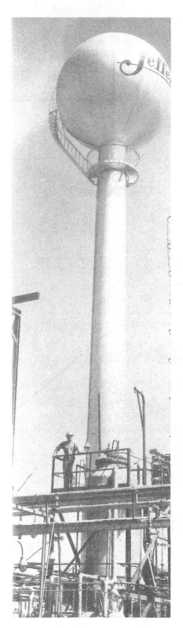

Making The Unknown Familiar

By Hank Moore

Twenty Years Ago Jefferson Blazed A Trail To Austin As One Of The First In Our Growing Colony Of Research & Science Industries

Austin's growing reputation as a center for research and scientific development, had its beginning with Jefferson Chemical Company, one of the first science-oriented firms to discover this town. Occupying a 50-acre plant site at 7114 North Lamar Blvd., products for an international petrochemical operation are conceived and perfected within the north Austin domain.

Petrochemicals are oil mixtures, especially the natural and synthetic hydrocarbon derivatives. The industry has experienced an 11 per cent yearly growth, with an overall 10 per cent rise expected in the next decade. The petrochemical field is of vital interest to business in that its products and research serve all industries.

Jefferson was formed in 1944 as a joint enterprise by Texaco Inc. and the American Cynamid Company. Its first plant was located in Port Neches, Jefferson County, Texas, accounting for the company name. Ethylene, ethylene oxide, and ethylene glycol were selected as main products when the first units began operating by 1947.

In 1949, research and development laboratories were estab-

lished in Austin after negotiating with the Austin Area Economic Development Council. The city was selected with the idea that the scenic beauty would attract new research personnel more immune to undesirable industrial communities. The University of Texas offered a vast technical library and reservoir of highly trained personnel for consultation on company projects. Austin was noted by company officials as ideal for calm working conditions and rich in family cultural environment.

That first Austin installation housed 50 employees in two major buildings. Laboratories have since grown to nine buildings (central complex constructed in 1953) employing 200 persons. At this site are developed and perfected new chemicals and chemical products.

Jefferson's customers rely on the Austin plant as a center for technical assistance to analyze and test products and to update them on scientific methods and production processes.

Main production plant is still at Port Neches and has undergone numerous expansions since it opened in 1948. A second plant was acquired at Conroe, Texas, in 1960, producing some 50 products, many in multimillion pound quantities. Company headquarters moved from New York to Houston in 1955.

As a result of all this expansion and diversification from plant to plant, Jefferson Chem-

(See UNKNOWN Page 18)

11

Behind the Scenes at Mission Impossible, TV Digest Magazine, January 1970

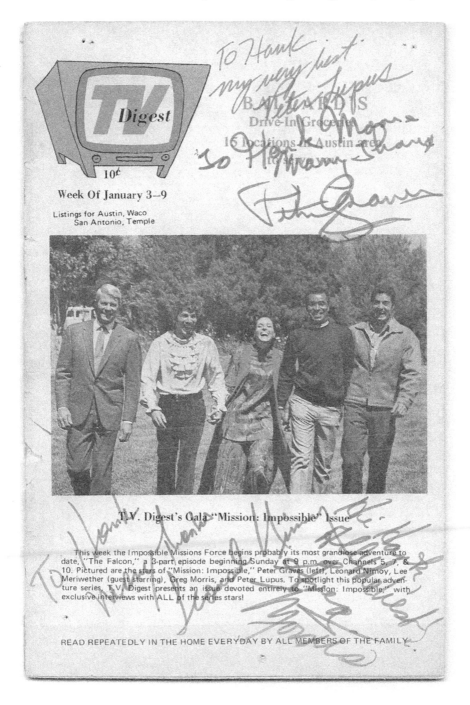

T.V. Digest's Gala "Mission: Impossible" Issue

This week the Impossible Missions Force begins probably its most grandiose adventure to date, "The Falcon," a 3-part episode beginning Sunday at 9 p.m. over Channels 5, 7, & 10. Pictured are the stars of "Mission: Impossible," Peter Graves (left), Leonard Nimoy, Lee Meriwether (guest starring), Greg Morris, and Peter Lupus. To spotlight this popular adventure series, T.V. Digest presents an issue devoted entirely to "Mission: Impossible," with exclusive interviews with ALL of the series stars!

READ REPEATEDLY IN THE HOME EVERYDAY BY ALL MEMBERS OF THE FAMILY

Measurement and Evaluation, Alcalde Magazine, September 1972

SEPT., 1972

Measurement and Evaluation

How students can get credit without going to class and how professors can find out what happens when they're in class

By Hank Moore

CONTINUING ENROLLMENT SWELLS are making it important to know as much as possible about what's in a student's head when he checks in at Gregory Gym for registration. Why register for a class in chemistry when the course covers material he may have mastered in high school? No reason, except how can the student know how much of the course content he has already covered or just where along the learning line he needs to plug in? Equally efficient is knowing how much the student may gain from a classroom tour with a particular professor. Answers to these and other questions are the work of The University's Measurement and Evaluation Center.

Keeping accurate tabs on University students is more than a full-time assignment for the Center. Located at 2616 Wichita Street, it has been called upon as a clearing house for data, and its resources and analytical skills fill a wide variety of campus needs.

Back in 1967 The University's Testing & Counseling Center was divided, the feeling being that the huge case load would be better handled under segmented administration. Dr. Ira Iscoe was appointed director of the Counseling Center and Dr. H. Paul Kelley was named head of the Measurement & Evaluation Center. Both still head their respective divisions and Counseling still makes use of test information furnished by M & E.

Dr. Kelley had coordinated measurement services for the old Testing and Counseling Center from 1958 to 1964. He left to become regional director of the College Entrance Examination Board, returning to the campus again in 1967. Now the largest responsibility of Kelley's organization is the administration of myriad national tests (on contract with College Board and other national agencies) and advanced placement examinations (given by UT) to allow students credit for course material already mastered before college.

Kelley points out that two-thirds of all entering freshmen come to The University with some advanced credit via exams. As there is no limit to the amount of hours to be surpassed (some students have entered school with 40-plus semester hours of credit), more students are figuring they haven't anything to lose by taking the tests. All of which keeps the Center's 30 staffers and computer facilities working longer hours every semester.

A very large percentage of students are placing out of English, Spanish and French courses. The chemistry and biology tests are enabling more and more students to place out as high schools add advanced placement courses in these subjects. Currently half of the students who take the American government exam are placing out of one semester.

A number of courses on special topics pertaining to American national, state, and local politics have been designed for these students to enable them to complete the two-semester legislative requirement. It is also possible to receive advanced credit for required physical instruction — a requirement which this September becomes only two semesters rather than the four semesters of the past.

A recommendation recently passed by The University Council and forwarded to the general faculty called for the reduction of English semesters required of students from four to three, reflecting both the ability of many students to place out and the increasing shortage of teaching staff to accommodate those enrolling for the fourth semester.

Last year the Measurement & Evaluation Center processed some 105,000 questionnaires filled out by students anonymously on the effectiveness of their courses and their instructors. Results were returned to the professors who were seeking the data for improving their teaching effectiveness. In the spring of 1972, some 4,000 sections participated in the course evaluation program, and many others were evaluated in fall tests. Kelley correlates the increasing number of teacher evaluations to a "trend toward more concern for evaluation. Teachers are asking how good a job they are doing and what more they can do."

Material in the M & E files is used for institutional research and the Center has recently received permission to connect its information bank with the information in The University Data Processing Division's Student Records section. Kelley points out that what little personal data is stored is there with the consent of the student involved and is used for studies to help The University determine how students are reacting to their college experience. For example, M & E is currently assisting the Bureau of Engineering Teaching in carrying out a series of studies for investigative factors affecting the academic success of engineering students.

Another project in which the Center is employed is in helping the associate investigators devise evaluation procedures for the many projects involved in a study of computer use in teaching in Engineering and in Arts & Sciences. Still another program, supported by the Hogg Foundation for Mental Health and jointly administered by Arts & Sciences and the Counseling-Psychological Services Center, is gathering data on students who drop out during the school year, what they do and why. In cooperation with the Office of the Vice-President for Student Affairs, the Center helped survey graduating seniors on the quality and meaning of their learning experiences while on the Austin campus.

There will be a growing need for Universities to evaluate their offerings as new teaching methods are devised and students and taxpayers demand varied services from institutions of higher learning. Texas may be ahead of the game in reaching out already for careful measurement of both its income and output. ◼

Hank Moore, BJ '69, is a frequent free-lance contributor to the Alcalde.

*Identifying Emerging Issues Before They Hurt Your Company. Professional Review,
Winter 1993-94*

MARKETING AND SALES

The business climate ahead is tough and filled with uncertainty. Those who believe the old ways still work shall fall by the wayside. Innovation and the ability to fill new niches signal the successful businesses of the future.

Take this quick test, as part of your strategic planning for the next two years:

 Does your company have a cohesive business plan, with results-oriented positioning and marketing objectives, updated every year?

What is the nature of your business now, as compared to when you entered it? What has changed, and who are the new entrants?

Which marketplace factors are out of your control? Which do your competitors control? Which are within your company's grasp?

How well does the marketplace understand your profession and its value to the business bottom line? Are there misperceptions that need changing?

Are you active in a professional association or chamber of commerce? Are they meeting your business needs?

How much has your company given back to the communities which support you? Is there an organized plan of reciprocation, with a business development design?

 How well trained are your employees? Do they have the company vision? With some fine-tuning, how much could you multiply the effectiveness of your workforce?

The successful manager identifies and meets emerging issues before they take toll and, with informed outside counsel, charts the company's course in a judicious manner.

In an era of downsizing, cutbacks and a reluctance to expand, the same four principles of market dominance are still applicable:

Sell new customers. Without adding to the base, the business goes flat.

Cross-sell existing customers. They are easier to convince and see great credibility in your company. Most customers do not know all the product-service lines that you offer. It's your obligation to enlighten them, to facilitate their making wise buying choices.

Create and market new products-services. Having that mousetrap does not mean that the public will automatically beat a path to your door.

Identifying Emerging Issues Before They Hurt Your Company

A Planning Blueprint for 1994

By Hank Moore

 Joint-venture to create additional marketplace opportunities. By combining disciplines, you can attract new business and pursue new, creative solutions for clients. We can no longer do business as Lone Rangers.

Based upon our studies of the business climate, counseling with top corporations and insight into business problems and challenges, I have identified the major emerging issues of the next two years.

Firms Sustain Book Value. American City Business Journals, February 1999

Firms sustain book value by taking big picture view

Growth Strategies

Hank Moore

Each year, thousands of companies consider going public for their own financial reasons. Yet, a small percentage get the support of major underwriters. An even smaller amount make it long term.

In assessing potentialities for dozens of companies and collaborating with niche advisers (attorneys and accountants) in helping them go public, I've seen the relativity of a successful offering to a strategic plan that addresses the "big picture," not just the financials.

When companies go public, they must change mindsets and management styles. Evolving from entrepreneur to a New York Stock Enchange-listed company means taking objective stock and re-engineering toward the future.

The investment community looks beyond the desire for entrepreneurs to growth via expansion capital. Underwriting firms and major brokers look at the organizational vision, planning potential, management structure, marketplace savvy and many more variables.

The public company that sustains high book value must demonstrate its ability to focus on depth and substance, not on flash and sizzle. Those who proclaim that hot ideas make great stock tops are dreamers selling flavors of the month, not public companies with staying power.

Taking a company public must be a process of guiding the organization through the levels of accomplishment.

Following are priorities or strategies for new public companies:

• Evolve from entrepreneurial mindset to corporate culture. The investment community requires that valuable traded companies have strategic plans, cohesive training programs, management development and more.

• Establish shareholder value. Stock value is based on perceptions, realities, transactions, image and other sophisticated factors.

• Evaluate and fine-tune all non-financial aspects of the company. Profit motive is not the only measure of a successful company. Get beyond the bean counter mentality and think more globally.

• Management and leadership activities. Most executives tend to micro-manage and retain limited focus. Resources must be put toward developing the company's most valuable asset – its people.

• Corporate communications. Investor relations, public relations, community relations, government relations, stakeholder relations and more must be weaved into a cohesive program, with qualified outside-the-company advisers.

• Create and sustain corporate vision. It's not the whims of a few people. It's not an image campaign. It's something that is developed, fine-tuned, communicated and supported throughout the organization.

• Achieve shareholder longevity, continuing value.

For public companies to succeed longterm, the visioning process begins with forethought, continues with research and culminates in a strategic plan, including mission, core values, goals, objectives (per each key results area), tactics to address and accomplish, timeline and benchmarking criteria.

Corporate visioning goes beyond the strategic plan. It sculpts how the organization will progress, its character and spirit, participation of its people and steps that will carry the organization to the next tiers of desired achievement, involvement and quality.

Both the strategic plan and the visioning process must be followed through. This investment is one-sixth that of later performing band-aid surgery on an ailing organization. ■

Hank Moore is a corporate strategist, futurist and creator of The Business Tree, his trademarked growth strategies approach.

Speaking Internationally. American City Business Journals, January 2006

Week of January 6–12, 2006

American City
Business Journals

Professionals based in Houston found at podiums near and far

BY THORA QADDUMI
HOUSTON BUSINESS JOURNAL

During the past year, Houston-based speakers and consultants on a variety of topics have shared their expertise with organizations that are based locally, throughout the country and even internationally.

LOUISIANA VISIONING

Futurist/corporate strategist Hank Moore, who concentrates on global trends and big picture issues, is working with agencies in Louisiana on visioning strategy and comeback plans. He will serve as the keynote speaker for the Louisiana Travel and Tourism Summit Jan. 20

"Ironically, the week before the hurricane hit, I attended a progress Luncheon at Columbine High School in Littleton, Colo., charting how far the city had come in its growth strategies," he notes. Moore had advised city officials after the tragic shootings that took place there.

This year, he worked with the City of Syracuse, New York, on an in inner-city revitalization strategy. He spoke at conferences sponsored by DestiNY USA, to get buy-in and support from community opinion leaders, business customers and collaborators.

He also was the opening futurist speaker for an outlook conference sponsored by software giant SAS, held in Sao Paulo, Brazil; for the Midwest Food Processors conference in St. Paul, Minn.; the Commonwealth Club, in San Francisco; and the CEO Council of Tampa, Fla.

Among other activities, Moore was speaker at an agricultural industry conference for client Cargill, presented a think tank on management of retail pharmacy practices for Organon Pharmaceutical Co. and keynoted meetings for associations in the areas of banking, finance, agriculture, health care, technology and nonprofit organization management.

He speaks frequently on corporate ethics and responsibility, diversity, quality and crisis management and preparedness and works with company boards and key leadership in crafting Visioning programs and strategic plans.

Moore's latest book, "The Classic Television Reference," has just been published. His next book, "The Future Has Moved ... and Left No Forwarding Address," is due to be published late in 2006.

PHOTO COURTESY OF HANK MOORE

At a conference sponsored by software giant SAS in San Paulo, Brazil, Hank Moore, left, after giving the keynote address, is interviewed by Brazilian journalist Paulo Henrique Amorim.

Small Business Today Magazine, May 2012

ABOUT THE AUTHOR

Hank Moore is an internationally known business advisor, speaker and author. He is a Big Picture strategist, with original, cutting-edge ideas for creating, implementing and sustaining corporate growth throughout every sector of the organization.

He is a Futurist and Corporate Strategist™, with four trademarked concepts of business, heralded for ways to remediate corporate damage, enhance productivity and facilitate better business.

Hank Moore is the highest level of business overview expert and is in that rarified circle of experts such as Peter Drucker, Tom Peters, Steven Covey, Peter Senge and W. Edwards Deming.

Hank Moore has presented Think Tanks for five U.S. Presidents. He has spoken at six Economic Summits. As a Corporate Strategist™, he speaks and advises companies about growth strategies, visioning, planning, executive-leadership development, futurism and the Big Picture issues affecting the business climate. He conducts independent performance reviews and Executive Think Tanks nationally, with the result being the companies' destinies being charted.

The Business Tree™ is his trademarked approach to growing, strengthening and evolving business, while mastering change. Business visionary Peter Drucker termed Hank Moore's Business Tree™ as the most original business model of the past 50 years.

Mr. Moore has provided senior level advising services for more than 5,000 client organizations (including 100 of the Fortune 500), companies in transition (startup, re-engineering, mergers, going public), public sector entities, professional associations and non-profit organizations. He has worked with all major industries over a 40-year career. He advises at the Executive Committee and board levels, providing Big Picture ideas.

He has overseen 400 strategic plans and corporate visioning processes. He has conducted 500+ performance reviews of organizations. He is a mentor to senior management. This scope of wisdom is utilized by CEOs and board members.

Types of speaking engagements which Hank Moore presents include:
- Conference opening Futurism keynote.
- Corporate planning retreats.
- Ethics and Corporate Responsibility speeches.
- University—college Commencement addresses.
- Business Think Tanks.
- International business conferences.
- Non-profit and public sector planning retreats.

In his speeches and in consulting, Hank Moore addresses aspects of business that only one who has overseen them for a living can address:
- Trends, challenges and opportunities for the future of business.
- Big Picture viewpoint.
- Creative idea generation.
- Ethics and corporate responsibility.
- Changing and refining corporate cultures.
- Strategic Planning.
- Marketplace repositioning.
- Community stewardship.
- Visioning.
- Crisis management and preparedness.
- Growth Strategies programs.
- Board of Directors development.
- Stakeholder accountability.
- Executive Think Tanks.
- Performance reviews.
- Non-profit consultation.
- Business trends that will affect the organization.

- Encouraging pockets of support and progress thus far.
- Inspiring attendees as to the importance of their public trust roles.
- Making pertinent recommendations on strategy development.

Hank Moore has authored a series of internationally published books:
- The Big Picture of Business series
  o The Business Tree™ (with multiple international editions)
  o Pop Icons and Business Legends
- Non-Profit Legends
  o The High Cost of Doing Nothing. Why good businesses go bad.
- Houston Legends
  o The Classic Television Reference
  o Power Stars to Light the Flame.
  o The Future Has Moved…and Left No Forwarding Address.
  o The $50,000 Business Makeover.
  o Plus, monograph series for Library of Congress Business Section, Harvard School of Business, Strategy Driven and many publications and websites.

Follow Hank Moore on:
Facebook: www.facebook.com/hank.moore.10
LinkedIn: www.linkedin.com/profile/view?id=43004647&trk=tab_pro
Twitter: twitter.com/hankmoore4218
YouTube: www.youtube.com/watch?v=jFax7XZvz0U
Pin Interest: www.pinterest.com/hankmoore10/
Google+ www.plus.google.com/u/0/112201360763207336890/posts
Atlantic Speakers Bureau: www.atlanticspeakersbureau.com/hank-moore/
Business Speakers Network: www.directory.espeakers.com/buss/viewspeaker16988
Silver Fox Advisors: www.silverfox.org/content.php?page=Hank_Moore
Facebook business page: www.facebook.com/hankmoore.author/?fref=ts
Hank Moore's website: www.hankmoore.com.

CPSIA information can be obtained
at www.ICGtesting.com
Printed in the USA
LVHW090847190420
653674LV00004B/283